A Minstrel
and the Amazon

by

John Harwood

- a musical biologist moves to Manaus -

- a weft of Amazonian information woven into a warp of personal experience -

GRAFISA

Thanks

To Carlos Probst – friend, author and owner of Amazon Clipper Cruises
for inspiration and sponsorship.

To Walter Kershaw – friend and artist
for encouragement and all the illustrations, except figures 8 and 13

To Claudia Roedel – friend, naturalist and artist
for enthusiasm and figures 8 and 13.

To Paul Hardy and Martin Shead, friends and musicians
for letting me reproduce part of their song "Cacau Pirêra King."

To any reader who spots errors in the work and brings them to the attention of
the author, thereby helping to improve future editions.
Contact address: johninmanaus@hotmail.com

COORDENAÇÃO EDITORIAL
John Harwood

PROJETO GRÁFICO E
EDITORAÇÃO ELETRÔNICA
Thiago Barata

CAPA
Thiago Barata

FICHA CATALOGRÁFICA
Grafisa Editora

FICHA CATALOGRÁFICA

B869 Harwood, John
    A Minstrel and the Amazon - Manaus: Ed. Grafisa, 2007.
    282p.; il.

    ISBN - 978-85-99122-03-7

                CDU - 394.2 (811)

GRAFISA
Rua Pará, 630 - N. Srª. das Graças - CEP: 69053-001 - Manaus - Amazonas
Fones: +55 (0xx92) 2101-1200 - FAX: +55 (0xx92) 2101-1213
E-mail: grafisa@vivax.com.br

Contents

Chapter 1

Fig 1. Bar in Compensa   WK

Blondie's Bar

Sleep lasted just until my head hit the keyboard. The thunderous discord of a dozen notes struck simultaneously brought me back to my senses and the upright position. Drowsily I looked at my watch, then at the other musicians. They were still frenetically pounding out a local Brazilian rhythm, despite my problems at the electric piano. It was three-thirty in the morning of the first of January in Compensa, a huge poor district on the west side of Manaus, an area so unglamorous that it took its name from a nearby plywood factory.

Had it not just happened, I would have thought it impossible to fall asleep in such a din. The band's amplifiers were set at maximum and the overloaded loudspeakers produced immense amounts of distorted sound. But fatigue was understandable. We had already been playing for four-and-a-half hours. Nevertheless, the contract required us to keep going until dawn. With the city located only three degrees south of the Equator, this meant playing until 6.00 AM. The end of the gig was still another two-and-a-half hours away.

Deciding to freshen up, I switched the piano off and pushed my way out towards the street through the mass of brown-skinned dancers, mainly girls in their late teens and young men in their early twenties. As if by magic a hand tendering a pint bottle groped through the gyrating couples to offer me a beer. I poured some of the refreshingly cold, almost frozen liquid into an abandoned glass and drank it down in one gulp, handing the half-empty bottle back, with thanks, to an acquaintance, who like myself, like the band and like most of the customers, lived nearby.

As a foreigner, scientist and the only person there with the privilege of higher education, I suddenly wondered how I came to be an exhausted musician in a poor bar, so far from roots and peers. My sleepy brain didn't concentrate for long, but some factors sprang to mind before my thoughts wandered. Firstly, alternative entertainment possibilities in Manaus were not great. Secondly, I enjoyed meeting people born in the Amazon and I often found them in the poorer bars. Middle-class bars attracted mainly people from south Brazil and overseas. Free beer for the musicians was a further attraction, as were the groupies: in spite of the mediocrity of our band, called *Cascavel* (Rattlesnake), there were always some females nearby who enjoyed fooling around.

Certainly I wasn't there for money. Cascavel, an eight-piece band, normally played from 11.00 PM to 3.00 AM for a total of thirty dollars. Even for the seven-hour New Year's Eve gig, the fee was only fifty dollars between us, hardly enough to pay for the instruments, some of which were expensive American and Japanese products purchased in the Zona Franca, Manaus' free-port shopping area designed to attract rich Brazilian tourists from the South.

Refreshed by the movement and the cold beer I reached the street and looked back to enjoy the scene. Because Amazonians are small like their Indian ancestors, it was easy to see over the bubbling black sea of dancing heads and admire it all. At the back, a wooden hut with shutters served as the bar. In the centre, a primitive roof of corrugated iron on wooden poles covered the cement dance floor. On one side, lots of people were drinking beer at cheap metal tables. On the other side, the band played wildly. The establishment had no sign outside, but was known to locals as *o Bar da Loira* (Blondie's Bar), so called because blonde hair was rare enough in Compensa to be the proprietress' most remarkable attribute.

The startling light hair in Blondie's otherwise Indian appearance probably came from a Dutch or French ancestor who had settled the northeast Brazilian coast three or four hundred years ago, before Portugal asserted her sovereignty in that area. North-European features, such as blue or green eyes, are still common in the state of Ceará, birthplace of Blondie's grandfather.

However, Blondie had not simply moved from the coast to Compensa. Her family had taken the tortuous route followed by many of Manaus' forefathers. Attracted by the prospect of making money as a rubber tapper, her grandfather had migrated into the Amazon basin from northeast Brazil at the beginning of the twentieth century. He headed first for the southwestern Amazonian state of Acre, a rich rubber area transferred from Bolivia to Brazil at that time. But his dream of riches never came true. As the British started to produce cheap rubber in Malayan plantations, Brazil's rubber trade crashed catastrophically in 1912. Nevertheless, in spite of poverty and disease, the poor migrant from Ceará raised several progeny, including Blondie's father. The latter, also a tapper, continued to eke oul an existence in Acrc through World War 2, at which time there was a brief economic upsurge, because rubber was a strategic commodity for making military equipment. Japan's control of Malaysian rubber plantations forced the Allies to turn to the Amazon for increased supplies. Nevertheless, at the end of the war the slump in the Amazon's rubber economy resumed, to such an extent that Blondie's father, like many others, abandoned rubber tapping and moved to Manaus, where Blondie was born.

Three generations ago Blondie's family had been poor in Ceará. Subsequently they were poor in Acre, and the situation remained unchanged in Manaus. The bar was little more than a shack containing freezers full of bottled beer and soft drinks, all made by the same company.

Even the lack of choice of brands indicated poverty. Several brands of lager-style beer were available in Manaus. The major ones, Antarctica and Brahma, were brewed locally; Cerpa came from Belém; and others came from the South. However, the credit vital to Blondie's precarious enterprise could only be obtained by working with one of the leading makes in an exclusive deal. In exchange for exclusivity, the brewery guaranteed regular supplies and equipped the establishment with colourful metal tables and chairs painted in the company livery.

Seeing the place packed and lively, it was hard to imagine that most of the time Blondie's Bar was empty and dead. On workdays, rare customers, all male, came to drink *cachaça*, rough sugar-cane liquor about the same price per bottle as beer and nine times as strong. They chose the clear firewater because it was the cheapest drink. Many of them, having no jobs, could not afford anything else.

On Saturday afternoons and Sunday mornings a few men came to the bar to play dominoes. They played the popular Brazilian version of the game, in which a team of two players competes against another team of two players. Points were scored each time the ends of the string of dominoes added up to a multiple of five. The style of play was typical. When it was his turn, each player would noisily slap his domino down on the table and shout out the score or a challenge to the opponents in hearty Portuguese slang. A player waiting to place a particularly important domino would impatiently spin it face down on the table, then raise his body and/or voice triumphantly, as he made thc winning move.

Busy times at Blondie's were when there was dancing; that meant Friday and

Saturday nights and special events like the New Year's Eve party. On those occasions Blondie didn't serve *cachaça*, otherwise someone might get drunk too quickly and start a brawl which would end the party before the bar made any money.

Dance space was made by removing the tables and chairs from in front of the bar and installing them in the driveway of the neighbouring car body repair shop. Fortunately, at night no one needed access to the yard and hut next door, where in the daytime a badly paid young welder in shorts and thong sandals miraculously restored wrecked and rusting cars, using a range of spare parts seldom seen in countries with high labour costs.

Moving the furniture not only made room for dancing, it also gave anyone with an eye for detail an opportunity to observe a curiosity of the bar's construction: the wooden poles supporting the dance floor's zinc roof had natural, long, deep grooves in them. This showed that they were made of *acariquara*, a termite-resistant Amazonian hardwood extensively used for posts in municipal electricity supplies. If sanded and varnished, the wooden columns could have been very attractive, but no frills had gone into Blondie's decor. The timber was painted matt pastel pink, the same colour as the rest of the establishment.

While I stood in the street, reflecting on the bar and its owner and gradually waking up, Cascavel continued playing *forró*, an immensely popular musical style from northeast Brazil. The band specialised in this type of music and so far this evening they had played no other. The lack of musical variation was deliberate: despite New Year's Eve being the start of the carnival season, we did not want to get into carnival mood too soon in our performance. It would be impossible to change back to a less boisterous style afterwards; a reduction in the energy level would kill the atmosphere. We therefore paced ourselves for as long as possible with *forró*. Then we would change to samba. Finally we would play carnival numbers from around 4.00 AM until sunrise.

In keeping with the programme, a few minutes later Cascavel's music changed to samba, a style unsuited to the piano and consequently one in which I habitually took a break. Safe in the knowledge of now being able to relax officially, I looked around for some distraction to pass the time before rejoining the band for the final carnival slot.

My attention turned to the street, a simple strip of asphalt with no sidewalks. Across the street stood a bar architecturally similar to Blondie's, but painted matt pastel blue. This was the *Bico Doce* (Sweet Point), run by Dona Maria, a friendly matron from the upper Amazon. She, like Blondie, traced some of her ancestry to rubber tappers. However, although she didn't call herself Indian, she had the dumpy contours of a Tikuna Indian woman. Obviously part of her family had been at home in the upper Amazon from time immemorial.

The Sweet Point had no band. Instead, a powerful record player provided dance music. Its sound was loud and distorted, just like that at Blondie's. Because of the lack of orchestra, the Sweet Point had fewer clients. Nevertheless it looked full. The two establishments appealed to different sections of the public. Younger people liked Cascavel's live *forró*. Dona Maria's somewhat older customers preferred recorded ballads and foxtrots, to which they swayed ecstatically in quasi-coital embraces.

Next to the Sweet Point one of the area's many all-night car tyre repair services was doing good trade with vehicles going to and from New Year's Eve parties. A yellow Volkswagen Beetle taxi with one wheel removed stood in front of the workshop. The car's radio blared away loudly, the owner quite oblivious to the fact that its discotheque music was acoustically incompatible with Dona Maria's foxtrots next door and Cascavel's sambas across the street.

A black man, one of relatively few in Manaus, worked efficiently with levers and a rubber hammer to extract the damaged inner tube from a tyre. Probably about twenty-two, he had the worn features of someone twice as old. Nevertheless he was remarkably cheerful for one working while others partied. From time to time he exchanged quips with the taxi driver, sticking to the uncontroversial themes of potholes and garbage, which were common in the streets of Compensa. He commiserated with the motorist about these causes of flat tyres, but seemed unaware that if roads were improved, there would be less demand for his puncture repair services.

This was my new neighbourhood, a place where people lived on the street and knew each other. Although I now own a house in a quieter part of town, at that time I could easily walk from Blondie's to the small, zinc-roofed cabin I shared with Nascimento, who during the week was my research technician and at weekends was Cascavel's lead singer . A dirt road, frequently impassable by car, led to our humble home built on stilts on a precipice where land prices were cheap.

It was a very different world from the quiet, orderly, and by Compensa standards, rich central English city of my youth. I liked the difference. My move to Brazil had started as a desire to see something new and the poor districts of Brazilian towns certainly had no English equivalent.

While the idea of difference appealed to me, every individual difference did not. In particular, at that moment I could not stand the three-pronged musical attack on my eardrums at sound levels illegal in English streets. So I moved away from the noisy bars and the taxi to a nearby area where street vendors had set up their stalls. Recognising a significant market in the dancers and in the motorists waiting for tyre repairs, a group of refreshment sellers had installed themselves along the roadside; just far enough away to be quieter and just close enough to be convenient.

There were four stalls, all run by middle-aged mothers with lots of children. The contrast between the married women vendors and the single girls dancing could not have been more striking. The girls combined lascivious sensuality with desperate romance. Brought up in a culture of TV soap operas, an art form in which Brazil excels, the young women of Compensa confidently expected miraculous and dramatic futures. The miracle, in view of the inadequacy of Brazilian state education, was to get into university without having attended a fee-paying school. The dramatic element was to fall in love with and marry a rich boy – a happy-ending that was also illusory. Many well-off young men from Manaus' high society went to Compensa in fancy cars and found easy dates. However, in spite of sowing its wild oats in the poor districts, the upper class married inside its own stratum.

The street vendors, a generation older than the dancing girls, had lost their illusions and reconciled themselves to a life with few financial resources. Yet they were not bitter. Despite their economic straightjackets they showed tremendous spirit and found happiness wherever they could. Selling refreshments not only brought in a little revenue; it was a way to get out and enjoy the excitement of a party at no expense.

The most elaborate of the four roadside stalls was that of *Tia* (Aunt) Bena, who sold *tacacá*, a thin, spicy, shrimp soup from the coastal state of Bahia, home of

Brazil's African culture. Connoisseurs adored all its ingredients, including fermented manioc juice, hot peppers, shrimps and green leaves called *jambú*. However, on aesthetic grounds, neophytes were likely to avoid adding the soup's optional thickener, which was a slimy colourless paste made from manioc starch.

Women selling *tacacá* usually dressed in Afro-Brazilian costume. Accordingly, Tia Bena, despite looking more Indian than African, wore an immense white skirt that spread out over numerous petticoats; a loose, white blouse displayed her shoulders; and she sported a white headscarf tied at the front. Giant imitation-gold earrings, numerous heavy necklaces and large, bright bracelets completed her attire. Ritual dictated that *tacacá* be served in a calabash raised directly to the lips for drinking. Consequently no spoons were supplied; just a toothpick to spear the shrimps and *jambú* leaves.

The other stalls were less exotic. Dona Raimunda, equipped with a small charcoal brazier, offered skewers of barbecued meat, cooked while you waited. An unlimited supply of manioc flour accompanied the purchase. Customers spooned this yellow, dry, gritty carbohydrate from a communal tin on the table. There were no plates.

Dona Ildete, with a similar brazier, sold fried *jaraqui*, a herring-sized fresh-water fish that constituted one of the cheapest and most popular sources of protein in local diet. As with the barbecued meat, copious manioc flour accompanied the main dish. The vendor supplied plates and spoons, but neither knives nor forks, thereby obliging her clientele to eat peasant-style, with spoon and fingers. Before eating, diners crushed pieces of small, hot, green peppers onto the plate, using the back of the spoon. Rubbing each morsel of fish over the peppered area controlled spiciness at will. Local people enjoyed this dish so much that they said visitors who ate *jaraqui* would never leave the Amazon. Perhaps it's true. Originally planning a visit of a couple of years, I'm still here, many *jaraqui* and almost three decades later.

The last and simplest of the roadside stalls belonged to Dona Tereza, who sold coffee and cakes. I made my way towards this stand, intending to fortify myself with plenty of coffee ready for the final music session with the band. I also wanted to meet Dona Tereza's superbly smiling daughter, who had come along partly to dance and partly to help her mother. Earlier in the evening I had seen the young woman dance with several different men. On the dance floor she moved with the sensual security of someone happy to have lost her virginity a long time ago. However, there seemed to be nobody around to whom she wanted to be particularly close. If a man started to get too attentive, she abandoned him and returned to the coffee and cakes to help her mother for a while. Called Terezinha (Little Tereza), she had inherited from her mother not only her name, but also a cheerful good nature and a broad smile.

I ordered a *cafezinho*, Brazil's small, strong, sweet, black coffee, virtually the only style of coffee available after mid-morning. (Large cups of milky coffee usually only accompanied breakfast.) Dona Tereza served me from a thermos flask, the indispensable tool of her trade. Meanwhile Terezinha busied herself arranging cakes on a small table. While waiting for the scalding liquid to cool down enough to drink, I joked and chatted with the two females. The Portuguese endings "-*inha*" and "-*inho*", as in Terezinha and *cafezinho*, imply smallness, so it was easy to make a joke about how the mother should serve large coffees and the daughter should serve small ones.

After a second helping, I asked Terezinha if she would like to dance. Although evidently willing, before replying she shot a quick glance at her mother, more or less asking permission to leave and dance with an older man. With no other customers at the stall, Dona Tereza could hardly claim to be short-staffed. Moreover she was confident in her daughter's experience, recognised me from the band and knew that I would have to return to the piano soon. So she conferred consent with a maternal smile and a shrug of the shoulders that said, "it's up to you".

I paid the bill and led the cheerful girl back past the car tyre repair shop, which the taxi was just leaving. We squeezed onto Blondie's dance floor and shook down into the melee of vibrating bodies. Since samba was normally danced free, it was not really necessary to have a partner. However, people in couples danced for one another. Each partner served as a focus for the other's dance display. Although no great dancer myself, I was happy to be Terezinha's focus.

Not out to impress anyone in particular, my partner wore simple sports clothes: a white singlet and brief, tight, black shorts. The ensemble left her shoulders, arms, youthful legs and a good deal of bosom uncovered. Rubber thong sandals were the only indication that she was in fact dressed for work rather than to play ladies' basketball.

Terezinha's dancing skill lay in getting the part of her body in the singlet to vibrate in counter-rhythm to the part in the shorts. At the same time she radiated immense pleasure in a job well done. Fortunately for me, male *sambistas* were not required to be so elastic.

On first arrival in Brazil, I would not dance samba for fear of making a fool of myself with the syncopated rhythm. Things improved one day, when a musician friend happened to mention that samba is basically a two-step. From that point on I noticed that many men, particularly the older, more portly ones, danced samba almost as a march, the exotic character being conveyed by a swaggering, "look-at-me" stance. So I imitated the men I had observed, while Terezinha gyrated in front of me.

The sensual gyration of the hips, known as *rebolar*, was a dance technique in which Terezinha excelled. From time to time she came very close and teased me to copy her. When I tried, my stiff movements sent her into hoots of laughter and also amused those near to us. Occasionally we linked up with other couples and danced in a circle. When our frolics led us close to Cascavel, I took the opportunity of checking that the musicians were not missing me. The band seemed happy enough. In fact everybody in the bar seemed happy enough.

On seeing so many smiling faces, the reason why I was at Blondie's suddenly became much clearer. It was the delight of being surrounded by carefree people. Brazilians really knew how to enjoy themselves. Their cheerfulness might stem from youthful inexperience, but that did not make it less real. The country's high birth rate had resulted in a population in which there were many more hopeful young people looking forward than nostalgic old ones looking back. The young bias in age-distribution had produced a nation that was optimistic to the point of naïvety and irresponsibility, but always ready for a party.

In fact, if Brazilians did look back, they would see a record that was not good. Three hundred years ago analysts described Brazil as the land of the future, but even these days many inhabitants are still desperately poor. At the same time, old problems like illiteracy, social injustice, corruption and impunity haven't gone away. Nonetheless, the generalised, blind optimism was contagious. Personally, I was already entertaining irrational hopes of winning Terezinha's affection, in spite of knowing I would soon have to rejoin the band.

After about half-an-hour of samba, the music stopped and Nascimento, a natural communicator with the microphone, made an announcement in the frenetic, machine-gun style fashionable among Brazilian football commentators. Besides acknowledging the presence of several well-known figures from the local community, he did a quick commercial for the local beer, wished everyone a Happy New Year, and stated that as soon as the instruments had been rearranged, the band would start its session of carnival music.

During the announcement many couples remained standing around the edge of the dance floor. They didn't have tables to which to return. They had come along and danced practically all the time, spending nothing on refreshment. It was a pleasant aspect of places like Blondie's, run by poor people for poor people, that such non-spenders were not chased away. Everyone in Compensa was acutely aware of and sympathetic to the problem of lack of money. Consequently social life had evolved in such a way that even those who were penniless could participate.

Terezinha and I were standing with the table-less dancers, holding hands. At the mention of carnival we knew our dance session was over; I had to go back to the band. We turned round and walked into the street, where, at a point silently agreed to be mid-way between her mother's stall and the dance area, we parted. I wistfully let go of her hand and returned to the piano.

The rhythm section of the band was making a tremendous racket, shuffling around and beating drums randomly as space was made to install the snare drum, an essential instrument for carnival marches and polkas. I sat down, switched the piano on, tickled a few keys to check the settings and decided I was ready. Unless we had rehearsed otherwise, our method of beginning a number was very basic. The rhythm guitar set up the fundamental harmony and beat; then everyone else joined in as they got the feeling. I looked at the guitarist's fingers to find the musical key, prepared my hands accordingly on the keyboard, and waited.

Suddenly we were away: a song with absolutely no logic about girls liking bald-headed men; without a pause, one about robbing underwear to make dishcloths; followed by one about drinking *cachaça* as if it were water; then one about getting your face burned as you crossed the Sahara desert – and so on – in a two-hour continuous stream of musical nonsense. Hoping to see Terezinha later, I did not fall asleep again before the first sunrise of the New Year.

Chapter 2

Fig 2. Brazilian Début

WK

Brazilian Début

Although I live in the Amazon and have done so for almost thirty years, when I first came here I had absolutely no intention of staying. In keeping with my previous wandering nature, I expected to work for a couple of years, have a look around and then go somewhere else – the East perhaps. As a footloose young Englishman I had lived and worked in Germany (doing botanical research), France (as a passenger-barge captain), Swaziland (as a biology teacher), Burundi (as a science teacher in French language) and the USA (recruiting for an oil company). But I had always moved on. Thirty years ago I certainly wanted to visit South America, but I never imagined that I would become a tropical naturalist, take part in Amazonian river journeys totalling over 100,000 miles, join a Brazilian band, dance with Indians and probably stay in the region for ever.

Before my move to Brazil, the University of London had given me a degree in botany and a doctorate in microbiology. Its folk-music clubs had taught me three chords on the guitar and a song repertoire of little commercial value. While possibly earning drinks and pocket money with music, an academic job would most likely be my prime source of income. I started to look around for openings that would get me to South America.

My two initial attempts to find a job in South America were disastrous. The first involved the University of Maracaibo, Venezuela, where I thought I had good contacts. However, after lengthy correspondence the don I was in touch with unexpectedly left the faculty and no one else at the university was interested in employing me.

In the second of the disasters an international placement agency in Switzerland found me an opening lecturing medical microbiology at the University of Baranquilla, Colombia. The subject was compatible with my qualifications but not my speciality. However, since I particularly wanted to go to South America, I accepted the offer and simultaneously rejected offers elsewhere. Unfortunately in my letter of acceptance I mentioned that I had no experience in medical microbiology. (This should have been clear to anyone reading my *curriculum vitae*.) The university replied, withdrawing the offer of employment.

My situation turned suddenly bleak. I was unemployed, had no prospects in South America and had rejected offers elsewhere. I decided to make one last attempt to get where I wanted. I would pack my bags and look for a job on the spot. A month later I left England.

My plan was to make a four-month trip around South America in search of an interesting position. In preparation I visited relevant embassies in London, trying to obtain work permits before setting out. To my surprise (and that of everyone I spoke to later) Brazil gave me a "Permanent Resident" visa on the strength of my qualifications. No other country did so. It seemed logical therefore to concentrate my job hunt in Brazil, where I now had the right to work. I would also visit Venezuela and Colombia to see if there was anything to salvage from the previous disastrous contacts. The adventure would start in Guyana and finish in Trinidad, because they were stops on the same cheap charter flight from and back to London.

The planned itinerary, executed fairly faithfully, consisted of the following legs:
(1) across Guyana to its border with Brazil
(2) by road and river to Manaus
(3) down the Amazon to Belém
(4) overland down the coast to South Brazil
(5) up the western, inland route back to Manaus
(6) up the Amazon into Colombia
(7) overland through Colombia to Venezuela
(8) fly to Trinidad to pick up the plane back to England, if I was still jobless.

To reduce expenses with food and accommodation, my kit included a tent, paraffin stove and cooking pot; and against tedium, a guitar and a new songbook. To cut down on weight I took few clothes, washing dirty ones immediately for reuse. The most important item in my luggage was a book on the Portuguese language, since I knew not a word in the tongue of the country of which I had just become a legal resident.

Thus equipped, I arrived in Georgetown, Guyana. The Guyanese capital was a terribly run-down, violent little city. I stayed there just the amount of time necessary to get to Brazil. From my short sojourn I recall some handsome old colonial buildings, including the lofty, wooden, Gothic, St. George's Cathedral, centre of local Anglicanism and the colourful, wrought-iron Starbroek market, located by the Demerara River. I remember that the National Museum contained a stuffed Devil Ray 22 ft across and 3,500 lb in weight at capture. Also on display was a table made of the country's 455 different types of timber. Yet these highlights could not compensate for the oppressiveness of the city's ubiquitous violence.

Crime dominated urban life, destroying even simple pleasures like going out for a drink. The pubs I went to looked like jails, with iron bars over the counters to prevent thieves jumping across into the serving area. Small talk at the tables consisted of depressing tales of robberies and assaults. I was not sorry to leave the city.

Though my sampling was short and perhaps not representative, I found people from the Asian communities generally friendlier than the black Guyanese. Asians came to Guyana from India and Pakistan in the days of the British Empire as merchants and sugar plantation foremen. Since then they had become important elements in society, with cultures, religions, traditions and languages different from those of the blacks. On the second day of my stay, Hindu and Moslem men befriended me and introduced me to the joys of "sky juice" (rum and coconut milk) at a wedding party in a wooden shack on the west bank of the Demerara River. The first man to speak to me was Muslim, although the wedding was Hindu, with Hindu music, Hindu food served on pieces of banana leaf, and (regrettably, I thought) the Hindu practice of separating men from women at parties.

In addition to Guyana's problems of crime and lack of ethnic homogeneity, the country's politics were complicated by a long-standing border dispute with its westerly neighbour, Venezuela, which claimed all Guyanese territory west of the Essequibo River. Guyana inherited this on-going squabble from the British colonial administration. The disputed area functioned as part of Guyana, but big companies refrained from investing there, because of the uncertainly involved. This of course meant that there was no economic development in that zone.

Unable to obtain permission for an overland trip, I took the first available plane across the country to Lethem, the Guyanese frontier town opposite Bom Fim in north Brazil. With its diverse freight and passengers, the ancient DC 3 aircraft in which I flew resembled one of the many country buses I had travelled on in Africa. The seats from one side had been removed to make room for cargo, which was held in place by strong nets. My fellow passengers stemmed from various of Guyana's racial groups: lots of black government officials; one or two whites left over from colonial times; a sprinkling of Orientals and Asians, apparently involved in commerce; and a couple of Amerindians. Most of the cargo had to do with gold and diamond mining.

The plane had no pressurisation system, so it flew low and the stewardess served boiled sweets frequently to help reduce pressure effects on people's ears. For me the low flight was a joy: it allowed me to get good views of the vegetation below. The mangroves of the coastal creeks soon gave way to an unbroken canopy of humid forest with no signs of human habitation. Although I knew none of the names of the trees, their myriad textures, colours and forms indicated an awesome diversity of species.

As the aircraft neared the border with Brazil, the view through the window changed to savannah plains with isolated mountains. We were in a drier climatic belt that ran southeastwards from Venezuela. This belt of grasslands and low trees separated the rainforest of Guyana (to the north) from the Amazon rainforest (to the south). The mountains, home to many plants not found elsewhere, were remnants of an ancient layer of quartzite, which long ago covered the area much more extensively. I was looking at the Guiana Shield, some of Earth's oldest rocks. Later, on the south side of the Amazon, I visited an equivalent formation called the Brazilian Shield. Unfortunately for prospective farmers, the soils derived from these ancient shields have been leached by tropical rains for so long that they have little agricultural potential.

The plane landed on a red-earth landing strip in hot sunshine. The other passengers quickly dispersed about their business, leaving me to cross the frontier alone. It was not difficult. The checkpoint out of Guyana was adjacent to the airfield. From there, a short dirt road led down to the river, which constituted the border.

As I walked towards the frontier, I passed an awning, in the shade of which a solitary man lay in a hammock. In front of his shelter stood two bowls of disinfectant. He informed me that he was a government employee involved in controlling foot-and-mouth disease. All visitors from Brazil had to wash their shoes or feet to prevent them from bringing the disease into Guyana. Since I was going in the opposite direction, the control didn't apply to me. Apart from this lone official, there was not a soul on the road or the border.

The road ran straight into the river, with no bridge. I stopped at the water's edge, alone with my thoughts, a mixture of wonder at the pastoral beauty of the scene and perplexity as to how I should get across. The water sparkled in the sunshine. On the Brazilian side a horse was drinking in the shade of low trees. Suddenly, out of nowhere, a little brown-skinned boy appeared in a slender dugout canoe and offered to paddle me across for the equivalent of a few pence. I laid my rucksack and guitar in the bottom of the unstable craft and embarked cautiously. The youngster laughed heartily at my obvious fear of capsizing. As we slid through the water, I suddenly became excited by the thought that the fifth largest country in the world, my new home, lay beyond the far bank, waiting to be explored.

Having paid the young ferrymaster, I walked up the track on the Brazilian side of the river. As I left the watercourse and the shade of the riverside trees, the heat increased and a panorama of savannah plains began to unfold. After some aimless wandering, I spotted the green, yellow, blue and white colours of a Brazilian flag flying at a police post about half-a-mile away. I headed towards the mast and checked into the Promised Land.

The Brazilian frontier town of Bom Fim consisted of a few houses and the border control point. No formal public transport system connected it to the territory's capital, Boa Vista, my destination for the day. However, trucks and army vehicles took passengers on the three-hour trip for a standard fare. I found a jeep and embarked along with two Brazilian passengers.

As we sped along the dirt road, my colleagues began teaching me Portuguese, starting with the words: *quente* (hot) and *chuva* (rain). The choice of vocabulary was hardly surprising, since in the wide-open spaces of the savannah, we could see isolated thunderstorms forming around us in the intense heat. We knew well in advance whether we were going run into a particular downpour or not. Although we twice drove through torrential cloudbursts, we mostly remained in bright sunshine, with spectacular lateral views of thunderheads in the distant mountains.

During the journey we stopped only once to refresh ourselves, taking a break at a small roadside bar with a table set in the shade of a fruiting cashew nut tree. We helped ourselves to the fruit on the tree while waiting for drinks to be served. I had never seen whole cashew nuts before and found their structure intriguing. Each kidney-shaped nut (biologically, the true fruit of the tree) grew beneath a succulent, yellow or red "apple", which was the part we ate. To my surprise the "apple" contained no pips or other reproductive structures. I later learned that botanists call it a pseudofruit, because anatomically it is really a swollen fruit-stalk.

There were other things to learn about cashews, as I found to my cost on trying to crack a nut open with my teeth. The nutshell contained caustic oil, which painfully burned my lips and made them swell. (Apparently, if I had persisted in eating substantial quantities of shell material, I could have died.) Since I discarded the still unopened nut promptly, my suffering was relatively slight, the effect passing after about 20 minutes. The Brazilians, to whom the dangers were well known, found my naïvety hilarious. The barman, who spoke some English, told me that commercial cashew nut growers roasted the caustic oil out of the shells before extracting the kernels, which were a major Brazilian export crop. With only one kernel per fruit, I could see why cashews in shops were expensive.

Once my lips had ceased burning I was able to marvel at the efficient fruit dispersal mechanism evolved by the cashew tree. In nature, spider and capuchin monkeys ate the "apples", carrying them away from the parent tree. However, the monkeys were obliged to jettison the seed intact, because of the caustic oil in the shell. The seed then germinated at some distance from where it was produced.

Suitably humiliated, I resorted to consuming the cashew in the same way as my Brazilian companions: each of us held a cashew apple in one hand and a glass of sugar-cane liquor in the other. The routine consisted of alternating bites of the "apple" with gulps of the liquor. In this way we achieved a primitive *batida* (fruit punch). *Batidas*, drunk throughout Brazil, are somewhat similar to Caribbean punches, except that in a punch one uses mellow, aged, brown rum, whereas in a *batida* the liquor *(cachaça)* is fiery, young and clear. The most common Brazilian *batida* is made with sweet limes and is called *caipirinha*.

It was the first time I had tasted *cachaça* and I found it very rough and burning. My colleagues, gulping it down fast, were amazed that I could stand to sip it. The truth of the matter is that not being familiar with the drink, I feared its potency.

In the late afternoon we arrived in Boa Vista, an evidently booming town. Cattle ranching and gold mining were expanding in the area and a road was under construction southwards to Manaus. The region, then a federal territory, was about to become a fully-fledged state. However, since the road was not yet ready, all surface transport to the rest of Brazil depended on barges on the Rio Branco. Consequently there were few vehicles on the broad streets.

The Jeep's occupants were demonstratively proud of Boa Vista's gold production. As we drove through the downtown area, they excitedly pointed out to me the many gold dealers' shops. I soon noticed that all these shops contained two standard items: firstly a precision balance and secondly a cubicle equipped with a crucible and blowtorch. Logically one needed scales to weigh the gold, but I did not know what the cubicle was for. When I researched the subject, the story turned out to be complex and sinister. The salient details are summarised as follows.

Most gold found in the Amazon occurred along with other sediments as a finely divided, alluvial powder, panned by hand or with motorised mud-pumps. It was separated from the mud around it by amalgamation with mercury (which dissolves gold). The miner then needed to heat the mercury-gold amalgam to drive-off the mercury and recover the gold. This he did in the gold dealer's cubicle, using the blowtorch and crucible.

The evaporated mercury was a potent source of pollution. Inevitably it found its way into the atmosphere and then into biological food chains in the form of intractable, poisonous, organomercury compounds. In practical terms this meant that fish and water birds from gold-mining areas could contain so much mercury that eating them would be dangerous. Stretches of the rivers Madeira, Tapajós, Branco and Negro, and especially some of the smaller tributaries of these rivers have been listed as threatened by mercury pollution from gold mines.

Near Boa Vista, gold was mined both in rivers and on land. River mining was carried out from rafts equipped with a mud pump, a cascade of baffles and a compressor. Alluvial mud from the riverbed was pumped over the baffles, where any gold settled out preferentially. A diver, supplied with air via a tube from a compressor on the raft, held the nozzle of the mud pump in the appropriate area of the riverbed. Conditions were appalling; divers stayed underwater for about four hours, often in strong currents and total darkness. There were few safety precautions and no decompression facilities. Deaths and injuries were common.

Land-based mines were not much better. Concessions were 3m (10ft) square. Every miner dug vertically down at his own speed, so that the original chequer-board gold field soon became a mixture of deep pits and columns, in which fatal landslides were common in the rainy season.

The jeep dropped me near town centre at a simple guesthouse consisting of a bar with a row of wooden bedrooms in its back yard. There was a communal shower and toilet. The establishment was humble, cheap and just what I needed at the beginning of the trip. I did not want to spend much money until I had a better idea of what living expenses would be in the next four months. I checked in.

My room doubled as a depot for beer crates, which occupied all the space not taken by the single bed. In the evening, looking for a place to sit and write letters, I installed myself at a table in the bar. While I was absorbed in my correspondence, a middle-aged man with an accordion entered, installed himself at a table near mine and started to play. The Pied Piper could not have had greater success. Immediately the bar filled with rough, young men, practically all gold miners. I stopped writing and watched the scene.

The musician played a string of lively tunes, while the public started to drink beer copiously. Conversations became loud and animated. I was about to order a drink myself, to get into the party mood, when the bar's owner approached me, explaining in a mixture of Portuguese, Spanish, English and mime, that he had seen me carrying a guitar and wanted me to play. In the same languages, but in different proportions, I replied that indeed I had a guitar, but I was reluctant to play, since I knew no songs in Portuguese and knew nothing from the accordionist's instrumental repertoire. The proprietor, however, was not to be deterred. He told several customers about the guitar and it became obvious from the excitement, that it would be difficult for me to avoid playing. With considerable apprehension I fetched the instrument.

Fortunately the accordion was at concert pitch and I had checked the guitar against the tuning fork only a short while before, so I didn't have to keep the already boisterous public waiting while I tuned up. I announced that I had just arrived in the country and did not speak Portuguese. The latter was quite obvious, since I spoke in Spanish, which, as Boa Vista is near Venezuela, some customers understood and translated. I then launched into *"Guantanamera"*, a Cuban song that had been popular in the English folk clubs of my student days.

The accordionist quickly found the key and embellished the performance, making us an instant success, signalled by applause, shouts of *bis* (more) and the arrival of beer, which I drank heartily. The question now was how to follow this initial hit. My Latin American repertoire at the time amounted to three songs in Spanish and none in Portuguese. The well-known number I chose next, *"Besame mucho"*, was in an awful key for the accordionist, but he coped well and again our duo was warmly appreciated. More beer arrived at the table.

Something told me that my remaining song in Spanish, *"Cielito Lindo"* would not be appropriate, because of its waltz rhythm. This turned out to be correct, since I discovered later that Brazilians sang their version of the song as a samba. Desperately trying to think of something in English that was not an obscure folk-song, my choice settled on the Beatles' number, "Let it be", which the public enjoyed, but which the accordionist did not follow. It seemed an appropriate time to get back to Brazilian music. A young fellow with a straggly beard asked me if he could borrow the guitar and I agreed with relief.

Without further ado, the guitarist started to sing an animated series of songs in *forró* style. The accordionist joined in with gusto, glad to be back in the show. A friend of the musicians disappeared briefly, returning in the middle of the next number with a lightweight conical drum, which was immediately added to the orchestra. The public joined in, singing, beating the tables and clinking beer bottles. As owner of the guitar I received a cut in the beer, which I imbibed happily while I savoured the atmosphere of my first Brazilian party.

As the event proceeded, some studiously sexy, evidently well-known, young ladies entered the bar. They were gold diggers of a different type. With their arrival the men's excitement increased perceptibly. I was suspicious of such blatantly lascivious females. However, I later learned to distinguish between hard-line prostitutes *(putas)* and good-time girls *(garotas de programa)*. Those in our bar fell into the latter category; they were girls who, in a country where well-remunerated jobs for women were few, had decided that the most rewarding pastime was to hang out with men who would foot the bill. The more generous the men were, the more friendly the girls were and *vice versa*.

The *garotas de programa*, five in number, provided company that was largely empty-headed and fawning, but sometimes innocent and genuinely amusing. To one another they were simultaneously best friends and worst rivals. They adored attention and fought to be the centre of it, to which end their clothing was scandalously tailored. The shirt of one was daringly low-cut; of another precariously loose. One's jeans were provocatively tight; another's shorts extraordinarily brief. The girl who sat for a while at my table wore a shocking, leopard-print miniskirt with a matching sleeveless blouse. She had magnificent, black hair, so long she could sit on it. She was festooned in necklaces and bracelets with seashells on them. In a "Me – Tarzan, You – Jane" type of conversation, very appropriate for her jungle attire and my level of Portuguese, I learned that my companion's name was Vânia. She proceeded to drink my beer and chat coquettishly in an animated monologue, most of which I did not understand. While she spoke, I took the opportunity to examine her face in detail, a fascinating occupation, rendered easy by the fact that she held it disturbingly close to mine.

Like the other girls, she had smooth brown skin and dark eyes. However, these basic Indian features had received influences from other continents. Her fleshy lips and the hint of crispiness in her beautifully brushed hair came from Africa, while the pretty freckles, a rare attribute among brown-skinned people, stemmed from Europe. Despite my lack of Portuguese and the difficulty of conversing over the now rambunctious music, I deciphered that Vânia came from the coastal state of Bahia, a story at least compatible with her racial mix and the presence of seashells on her jewellery.

When I did not give Vânia the kind of attention she wanted, she left me and joined higher-spending company. I preferred it that way. It is easy to make a false move in situations involving booze and fast women, especially if one is a complete stranger and can't communicate fluently. However, the evening was not a disappointment. On the contrary, I was elated to have found a country whose inhabitants loved music; a land where one was quickly invited to join in the fun; a nation of spontaneous, young people; an exciting place, where it was difficult to be lonely. I did not regret my decision to abandon the London commuter belt and felt pleased that Bahia lay on my itinerary, with the promise of more people as good-looking as Vânia, and hopefully less interested in gold.

Chapter 3

Fig 3. Pusher-Tug with Barge

WK

Job Hunt with Incidental Music

Having reached Brazil, the next step was to look for a job. I had arrived in Boa Vista, but I had not yet left the northern hemisphere. I still had a long way to go to reach the country's main cultural and economic centres. They lay much further south.

The first institution I planned to visit regarding possible employment was the Amazonas State University in Manaus. I had heard that Manaus was the largest inland city in the Brazilian Amazon and as such constituted an important strategic and commercial centre. It seemed to me that it would be a place with a reasonable infrastructure – meaning a possible job – even though it was more than two thousand kilometres away the country's largest cities, Rio de Janeiro and São Paulo. It lay at the confluence of the Rio Negro and the Amazon River, just inside the southern hemisphere, 800 km south of Boa Vista.

Besides having the university in mind, I also vaguely knew about a research institute in Manaus called the Instituto Nacional de Pesquisas da Amazônia (INPA). But I had no plans to try to work there, because I erroneously thought it specialised in ichthyology, having wrongly guessed that the word *pesquisas* in its name meant "fish". (In fact it is simply the Portuguese word for "research".) Obviously I had a lot to learn. Naïve and optimistic, I set out for Manaus and my first job interview. In any case, from Boa Vista, one had to go through Manaus to reach anywhere else in Brazil.

An asphalt road, built by the Brazilian army through the homelands of the Waimiri-Atróari Indians now links Boa Vista to Manaus. It may be closed occasionally by heavy rain, but for most of the year buses and trucks travel its 800-km length in about 12 hours. However, at the time of my job hunt, the highway was still under construction. Goods and travellers bound from Boa Vista to Manaus first went 80 km south by road (avoiding rapids on the Rio Branco) to the town of Caracaraí. There they boarded riverboats down the Rio Branco and Rio Negro. The journey took about a week.

With a hangover, but still exhilarated by the previous night's party, I took a paying lift on the back of a passenger-carrying truck heading for Caracaraí, a two-hour trip along a dusty, red road. The most remarkable feature of the ride was the sudden change in landscape from savannah to rainforest; the grassland seemed to run straight into a solid wall of forest trees. The abruptness of the switch was probably due to ranchers extending the natural savannah into the forest using slash-and-burn techniques. Dense rainforest did not burn unless it was first felled and allowed to dry out. However, farmers habitually torched grasslands to stimulate the growth of new grass and to eliminate cattle parasites. In the process they also burned slashed areas of forest.

We arrived in Caracaraí without any hitches. It was a quiet little town, shown on over-optimistic maps as located at the intersection of two apparently important highways, one running north-south and the other running east-west. Although the former, which is the BR174 linking Boa Vista to Manaus, is now operational, the latter, known as the Northern Perimeter Road, has never been built. Its would-be builders stopped work after difficult terrain made progress slow and expensive.

The truck dropped its passengers in the waterfront main street, which I quickly scoured for news of boats leaving for Manaus. Since none were sailing that day, I pitched my little tent near the river on the outskirts of town and lived in it until there was a departure.

My camp aroused considerable curiosity among the locals, especially children playing in the area. The guitar was a tremendous icebreaker. Even a person reluctant to struggle with my poor Portuguese would approach, his left arm extended sideways, his right hand strumming his belly, indicating that he wanted me to play a tune. I soon made friends. These included an English-speaking doctor and his colleagues from the government malaria control programme (SUCAM). The medical team had plenty of work in Caracaraí, because the road-building camps and gold mines brought migrant workers together in crowded conditions, ideal for the introduction and propagation of malaria. For the same reason – the doctor said – malaria also occurred where hydroelectric dams were being constructed.

My three-day wait for a boat passed very agreeably. Each morning I strolled around the market, discovering novel foodstuffs and goods. I would practice my

Portuguese by asking what the strange things on sale were. After returning to the camp, a cool swim in the clear waters of the Rio Branco refreshed me from the heat and revived my spirits if I had been frustrated by problems with communication. I tried cooking some of the new foods I found. This turned cooking into an adventure, even when I prepared and ate my meals alone. In the afternoon, after a siesta, I practised the guitar, in preparation for making music at night with my new friends in the bars of the port.

People were friendly. The first morning, a fishmonger wanting to clear his stall gave me enough fish for me to eat regally for the rest of my stay. The owner of a nearby bar generously let me store the fish in his freezer.

The fish I received included four types of piranhas, all with sharp pointed teeth, but clearly differentiated by colour: red-bellied, black, silver and lemon-coloured. I had not previously realised that there were several species of piranhas. However, whatever the variety, their legendary ferocity seems to be an exaggeration. In over a quarter of a century of Amazonian experience I have never had any trouble from fish in the water and only know two people who have been bitten while swimming. Each of them suffered just one bite from an unidentified attacker, possibly piranha or perhaps the vicious little catfish, *candiru*. The idea of piranhas instantly turning swimmers into skeletons is pure fantasy. One must remember that piranhas are most used to eating other fish – there being few mammals in the water. Moreover when skeletons are recovered after boating accidents, piranhas may have eaten the flesh of the corpses, but the victims actually died by drowning. Piranhas rarely attack large living mammals.

Cooked piranhas turned out to be tasty, but bony. Were it not for the latter trait they would be a much more popular food item, but that, I suppose, is why the fishmonger had not managed to sell them. I liked barbecuing piranhas over my campfire. Small piranhas were good roasted until crisp. I ate them whole, "bones and all". On the second day, a young woman, who came to the riverside to wash clothes, showed me how to make piranha soup, which – in addition to the fish – contained potatoes, onions, garlic, a boiled egg, chives, fresh coriander leaves and hot chilli peppers. She claimed the soup was an aphrodisiac, but did not give me chance to test this hypothesis.

One of the fish given to me by the fishmonger was visibly not a piranha. It had a very strange appearance. It resembled a laterally squashed eel with oversized scales. Its large, upwardly directed mouth obviously allowed it to eat floating material and to snap insects from overhanging vegetation. It had a tendril on each side of its chin. The malaria doctor told me it was an arowana, known world-wide in the aquarium-fish trade, but locally considered a bonier, less tasty version of its larger, superbly edible cousin, *pirarucu* which, he said, was the biggest scaly fresh-water fish in the world. He showed me that my fish (like *pirarucu*) had a bony tongue and explained that both species belonged to an ancient fish family called the "bony-tongues". He said that *pirarucu* was so large that people used its scales as nail files and its tongue as a kitchen grater. Although boneless fillets of *pirarucu* often substituted cod in Amazonian versions of Portuguese recipes, I soon discovered that it was very difficult to fillet arowana.

After three days a boat was ready to leave Caracaraí. The vessel was a 16-m wooden riverboat, which had long ago been converted into a pusher-tug by building stout buffers onto its bow. It was going to push two rectangular metal barges laden with empty beer bottles back to a brewery in Manaus. Instead of my camping for the fourth night, the captain invited me to sleep on board, so that we could cast off at first light. There were six other passengers, each of whom – following the custom on Amazonian riverboats – brought along a hammock to sleep in. Because of language problems, I was unaware that I needed a hammock and consequently did not possess one. So I slept on a rolled-up old tarpaulin I found on the front barge.

My lack of understanding about sleeping facilities arose from a Portuguese pronunciation rule that I had not yet discovered: R at the beginning of a Brazilian word sounds like an English H. The boat crew told me I needed to bring something for the trip, using a term that sounded like the English word "hedge". I had no idea what the item was, so I looked in the dictionary for an appropriate word beginning with H, G or J, the letters that represent aspiration in English and in Spanish respectively, but not – I learned later – in Portuguese. I didn't find the word and remained baffled until well after embarking. The word I was looking for was actually written "*rede*" and, of course, meant "hammock".

Still asleep as the convoy set out, I awoke surrounded by the beautiful, tranquil scenery typical of the next seven days. The Rio Branco is one of the most picturesque, yet deserted, areas of the planet. The forest, in a thousand tints of green, came right down to the sparkling river. Banks of pure, white sand marked every meander. Sitting on the front barge, away from the noise of the pusher-boat's engine, one could scarcely believe the serenity of the landscape. From time to time a solitary cocoi heron flew languidly away at our approach. The ringed kingfisher jabbered its rapid, clicking cry, as it darted past. Fresh water dolphins, coming up to breathe, regularly broke the surface of the calmly flowing water.

I soon discovered that there were two species of dolphins in the Rio Branco. The larger one, up to 8 ft long and often pink in colour, was the pink dolphin. Its characteristic features were: (1) a long, slender snout, leading to an abruptly blunt forehead and (2) a back with an angular keel, but no pronounced dorsal fin. The smaller species, up to 4½ ft long and usually grey in colour, was the tucuxi dolphin. It had: (1) a streamlined, conical snout merging smoothly into the head, and (2) a prominent dorsal fin reminiscent of a shark. Colour was not always helpful in distinguishing the species. Pink dolphins could be piebald or grey, while tucuxi dolphins could be pinkish underneath.

Trying to photograph surfacing dolphins proved to be a frustrating business. The animals disappeared before one had time to frame them. Nevertheless, the brief time they spent at the surface sufficed to identify them. The pink one, because of its pronounced forehead and angular back, gave the impression of a double roll, whereas the tucuxi made a single roll, with the dorsal fin clearly visible. If a dolphin snorted audibly while breathing, it was likely to be a pink dolphin. If one jumped clear out of the water, it was always a tucuxi.

Since it was low water season (November), our convoy sometimes had difficulty finding a deep enough channel to navigate. We frequently ran aground. If the front barges got stuck, the motorboat usually pulled the convoy off backwards. But often it was the pusher, with its deeper draught, that grounded after the lightly laden barges had passed over a shallow area. We knew trouble was likely whenever we saw the convoy undulate like a roller coaster, with the two barges rising and falling, one after the other, as they slid over a bar. Everyone would hold his breath, to see what would happen to the pusher. If it stuck, the crew untied the barges and let them drift downstream on a long rope. The motor unit, unimpeded by the convoy, then attempted to free itself. If it could not, sailors and passengers alike jumped into the water and pushed until the craft was clear. By noon of the first day, everybody on board, with the exception of two ladies, had been in the river.

In the water, the only things people obviously feared were stingrays. These were not especially aggressive fish, but unfortunately they occurred in exactly the type of place in which the pusher got stuck: sandy shallows. Since rays lay flat on the bottom, the danger was to tread on one, giving it no option but to react. For this reason, when wading, people shuffled their feet sideways and avoided taking high steps. Usually, one of the crew went first, probing the riverbed with a pole. This helped to drive rays away and also sounded the depth to locate deeper channels.

No one was stung during our voyage, but one sailor had an ugly scar on his ankle from a previous encounter with a ray. In vivid mime, to help my poor Portuguese, he portrayed stingray wounds as excruciatingly painful, slow healing, yet seldom lethal. He also took bawdy delight in describing the folk remedy for such stings, which involved a naked woman sitting astride the affected limb with her vagina in contact with the wound.

There are several species of stingrays in the Amazon. They are exclusively freshwater types and some are known world wide, because young specimens are caught and sold for the aquarium-fish trade. Evolutionary biologists suggest that the ancestors of Amazonian sting rays, as well as the ancestors of pink dolphins, came into the Amazon area from the Pacific before the rising Andes cut Amazonia off from that ocean. They think that the tucuxi dolphin probably evolved more recently from Atlantic stock.

Running aground was normally a pleasant interlude, but one day we stuck so fast, that no amount of manoeuvring freed us. We were obliged to wait several hours, until a powerful convoy coming upstream towed us off.

Whenever the crew had nothing else to do and wanted to party, they and any passengers who cared to join them would go to the front barge. There, away from the noise of the engine, they would sing. Since I slept on the front barge, I was usually with them. Through working together over a long period, the sailors constituted a very confident choir. Hence I was able to accompany them on the guitar, without worrying that any mistakes I made might put them off. They appeared to enjoy the guitar, whether it played the correct harmony or not, as if its physical presence inspired them to sing. As a result, I learned several songs by trial and error.

When tired of singing, the men would teach me to swear in Portuguese. It was an unending source of amusement for them to hear colloquial Portuguese curses pronounced with a strong, English accent. They also derived immense childish pleasure from miming particular oaths to make sure I understood the meaning. By the end of the voyage, I still didn't know the correct English translation of the INPA research institute's name, but I could swear "damned well", or *bem pra caralho*, as they say in Portuguese.

The day's navigation often climaxed in an exciting manoeuvre to tie up for the night. The front barge would be propelled head-on into the riverside bushes, to which, amid a fury of breaking branches, a sailor, fearful of wasps, ants and snakes, would try to tie a rope, before the current swept us away. Sometimes the crew repeated the performance several times, before the rope held. Where the current was weak, we simply rammed the front barge hard onto a sandbank.

As soon as the boat stopped, the crew started fishing, using lines as thick as tennis-racket strings and heavily-weighted, coathanger-sized hooks baited with chunks of meat or fish. They fished on the bottom and tried to catch *piraiba,* a giant catfish up to 3 metres in length and 150 kg in weight. Although never landing a really big one, they caught several substantial young ones (known as *filhotes*) about 1 metre long. The catch was served for meals on board, but not everybody liked it. Some passengers preferred to eat any type of scaly fish rather than eat catfish. They believed that catfish could transmit leprosy. This superstition about catfish and leprosy turned out to be quite widespread in Brazil, but did not occur in Colombia. There was no biological basis for it; it may have arisen because the hide of catfish looks somewhat like leprous skin. *Filhote* tasted fine to me and caused me no problems.

With the boat moored close to the trees and the main engine stopped, we could hear the nocturnal sounds of the forest. These became even more significant after dinner, when the electric generator was also switched off, leaving the boat dark and completely quiet. I would listen excitedly. Above a saw-like drone made by insects, several biological solo artists made themselves heard. Up to about 2.00 AM, frogs were particularly vocal, especially the small tree frog *(Hyla granosa)*, whose high-pitched chirp sounded like a light hammer bouncing off an anvil. The large tree frog *(Hyla boans)* had a deep-throated croak. We could often spot it with a flashlight in bushes overhanging the river. It typically sat about 1 to 2 metres above the water level.

While fishing and listening to the night sounds, the sailors often amused themselves looking for an owl-like bird known in English as the common potoo. They would whistle a descending cadence of five flute-like notes. Any potoo roosting nearby would respond with the same song, enabling us to locate it with a flashlight. Its eyes reflected brightly in the light beam. We normally found the potoos perched on isolated trunks that offered a good view over lower vegetation. They were there in the daytime too, but their dead-branch coloration and posture, a perfect camouflage, made them difficult to spot. About an hour and a half before dawn, howler monkeys, the heaviest Brazilian primates, proclaimed their presence in the forest, with a frightening roar evocative of the big cats of Africa.

The journey on the Rio Branco was not, however, entirely idyllic. Sometimes swarms of minute biting black flies attacked us. The aggressors belonged to a species of tiny simuliid fly known locally as *pium*. They were restricted to certain areas and were only active by day, but when they were around, they made life most uncomfortable. At such times I swathed myself in my mosquito net, but it was impossible to protect oneself completely. At a certain moment, I counted fourteen bites on the back of one hand. Each bite consisted of an itchy bump on the skin, with a characteristic red spot of coagulated blood in the centre. Once bitten, one's best course of action was to try stoically to ignore the irritation. Scratching only increased the damage to one's body and nerves.

During the five days on the Rio Branco, we saw only two villages, São José and Santa Maria. We stopped at both. The inhabitants had few material possessions and their lifestyle visibly depended on the river and the surrounding forest. Their canoes were hewn from single, massive tree trunks. House beams were lashed with vines rather than nailed. Roofs were made of palm thatch rather than of corrugated metal or asbestos. Moreover, despite environmental protection laws, the villagers ate lots of turtles, which they considered a delicacy. They used the large shells for washbasins.

Strange fruit trees, mostly local species with difficult Indian names, grew in the yards of the houses. One fruit in particular was so spectacularly large, that I struggled to find out what it was. It turned out to be jackfruit, a tree now widely cultivated in the Amazon, but not a native species. The Portuguese introduced it from the East, along with its relative, breadfruit, which we found later. Jackfruit and breadfruit both yielded edible seeds and pulp, although the sailors told me that locals usually ate the seeds of breadfruit (discarding the pulp), whereas they ate the pulp of jackfruit (discarding the seeds).

As I stood in the dark shade of the jackfruit tree, looking up at the greenish-yellow fruit, the size of rugby footballs, I realised with awe how different the flora here was from that which I had studied in my botany course in England. It was not just size. Everything seemed strange. For instance the fruits of jackfruit, like those of cacao and many other tropical species, were born directly on the tree's thick trunk and major branches – quite different from an English cherry, which hangs from small twigs. In the light of such obvious differences between the plants here and those in my training, I started to feel I knew very little about Amazonian biology. By extension, I questioned whether I deserved to find an academic job as a biologist in Manaus.

One of the sailors scampered up the tree and brought down a squelchy, ripe jackfruit weighing several pounds. He took care not to let the cut stalk of the fruit touch his skin or clothing, as an unpleasant sticky white latex dripped out of it for some time after harvesting. We smashed the fruit open on the ground and pulled out handfuls of the pulp to eat. It had the texture of stewed rhubarb and a taste reminiscent of bananas.

Before reaching the Rio Negro, we stopped one further time. This happened when we met a pusher convoy from the same navigation company coming in the opposite direction. The barge being pushed upstream, an old, deep-draughted hull from which the motor had been removed, would probably not have passed through the shallow area where we had run aground. So the captains decided to exchange barges: we would take the deep one back to Manaus and our shallow ones would return upstream. This, of course, meant swapping the cargoes, an operation that took a whole day. During this time, I had ample opportunity to reflect on the adventure so far and to speculate about what lay ahead.

One subject on which I ruminated, while waiting, was the need for patience. Navigation schedules in the Amazon were obviously very flexible. They depended on the condition of the river, which was not always favourable. Events such as running aground and swapping barges were part of day-to-day life. Nothing was to be gained by being in a hurry – as was poignantly demonstrated within the next few hours. A couple of our passengers became impatient and decided to transfer from our boat to another one that passed us, going our way. The following morning we had the last laugh; we overtook their new boat while it was tied up at a trading post at which we did not stop.

My second subject for contemplation was how hard the boat crew worked transferring the cargoes. The job involved carrying literally hundreds of crates of empty beer bottles in one direction and full ones in the other. People in the developed world commonly consider Latin Americans to be lazy, but the sailors certainly did not conform to that stereotype. The crew worked like brutes all day in hot sunshine and high humidity, conditions that would have knocked me out in twenty minutes. Furthermore, they used no protective clothing, not even gloves or shoes, and managed to laugh most of the time.

On resuming navigation, we soon left the Rio Branco and sailed out onto the Rio Negro. Just below mouth of the Rio Branco we passed impressive rock formations, some of which bore ancient Indian engravings in a primitive, almost abstract style. Strong eddy currents round the boulders could easily have caused shipwreck if the pilot had not known where he was going. However, after a couple of hours on the Rio Negro, the navigation became very easy and we could motor all day and night in wide, deep channels. The biting black flies disappeared too, making the final two-day run comfortable, but uneventful.

In the early morning of the eighth day after leaving Caracaraí, I awoke to find the boat moored among other vessels on a muddy, litter-strewn riverbank in a large urban area. This, the skipper told me, was São Raimundo beach, the end of the voyage. We were located about 2 km upstream from the centre of Manaus. Some passengers and crew had already left, but the rest of us ate our last ship's breakfast of coffee and cream crackers and said our farewells with mixed feelings – sad that our community was breaking up, but happy to be in charge of our own destinies again.

Without really knowing where I was going, I took my bags and walked away from the riverside towards the buildings situated on higher land. I found some alleyways and stairs between tightly clustered houses and arrived at a street. Still with no specific destination, I caught a bus to town centre and arrived at the main bus station near the cathedral. After a week in the quiet of the forest, it was a shock to find myself in the heart of a bustling city. The streets were decorated for Christmas, an imminent event I had forgotten about during the river trip. Giant luminous snowflakes hung across the main street and an extensive loudspeaker system blared out seasonal music. Bing Crosby crooned "White Christmas"; a sugary American choir sang "*O Tannenbaum*"; and a Paraguayan trio interpreted "Jingle Bells" on the harp, charango and guitar. With no conifers indigenous to the Amazon, there were no real Christmas trees, but fir tree silhouettes were depicted in coloured lights in shop windows and on the sides of high-rise buildings.

The city struck me as a bizarre mixture of New and Third World, a condition Brazilians descriptively called "chewing gum and bananas". Nevertheless, I had much better feelings about Manaus than about the first South American city I visited, Georgetown, Guyana. Manaus seemed happier, friendlier and safer. In an optimistic frame of mind, I settled into a small guesthouse in the centre. Within a few days I had made English-speaking friends and arranged a job interview at the University, where I spoke to the courteous and helpful head of Medical Microbiology, Dr. de Goes.

Since I could not speak Portuguese, the job interview consisted of a long chat in a mixture of English and Spanish. During our talk, Dr. de Goes frankly assured me that I would have better prospects at the INPA research institute. He then picked up the telephone and arranged for me to see its director, Dr. Warwick Kerr.

I was unaware at the time how lucky I was to get a meeting with Dr. Kerr. Most of INPA's administrative decisions were made in Brasília and the director spent much of his time in that city. Later I learned that many frequent visitors to INPA had never met its director.

My luck continued the following morning. While looking for a bus that would take me to INPA, I happened to ask directions from an attractive young woman, who said she was going there by car shortly and offered to take me. I accepted the lift gratefully and on arrival she introduced me to the director's secretary.

After a positive initial interview, I spent a couple of days writing research proposals and filling in forms, with the result that Dr. Kerr tentatively offered me a job, subject to approval in Brasília. While involved in the paperwork and formalities, I got to know a number of young research workers of various nationalities.

Overjoyed at getting a conditional job offer so early in the trip, I naturally invited my new friends at INPA to celebrate with drinks. We met at about 9.30 PM at the *Pinguim* (Penguin), a popular bar in the square at the top end of Manaus' main street. The building in which the Pinguim was located, along with the nearby Opera House, Law Courts and Ideal Club were all fine constructions erected at the end of the nineteenth and beginning of the twentieth centuries, that is, they were built when the export of Amazonian rubber was at its most lucrative. Their grandiose style showed that Manaus was a rich city, fit for important people to be seen in. Even today the Ideal Club is a meeting place for Manaus' high society.

My drinks party broke up at around midnight and I started to walk back to my lodgings situated a few blocks away. Suddenly someone called me as I passed in front of the Ideal Club. Surprised to hear my name late at night in a city where I knew few people, I looked up at the club's well-kept, two-storey, colonial building and had some difficulty recognising the young lady who had given me a lift to INPA. She was now radiant in a strapless long dress and accompanied on a small balcony by a group of young men and women also in gala dress. That year's class of graduating medical students was regally celebrating the successful completion of six years' hard study.

The group on the balcony beckoned me to join them. I looked at their fine suits and dresses, then at my simple travelling clothes and signalled back my inadequate dress. They countered that it didn't matter and that they would send someone down to meet me. I remained hesitant, until noticing that they had a guitar with them. Unable to resist a party with live music, I made my way excitedly to the entrance, over which a stone engraving marked the impressive rubber boom date, 1903.

Some swift talking on the part of my strapless friend, with another charming girl providing moral support, assured my admission. The doorman and maitre d'hotel, all starch and buttons, looked askance at my dishevelled appearance, but evidently weren't going to countermand two imposing young ladies from the influential end of society. The ladies accompanied me up a grand staircase, made of various local hardwoods, through the upstairs salon (with a fine, wooden floor), to join the group on the small balcony.

The organised part of the celebrations had finished. That is, the speeches were over and the dance band had stopped playing. But the young people, laughing, chatting and flirting, were determined not to go home yet. My group had occupied the balcony area, where it was loudly singing sambas to the accompaniment of an acoustic guitar. Immaculate waiters with silver trays were still serving beautifully presented, powerful *batida* cocktails of various flavours. The drinks slid down my throat like fruit juice, but within seconds I could feel their effect: I stopped worrying about looking like a tramp.

Through the INPA grapevine my hostess knew I played the guitar. Consequently, as soon as I sat down, she passed me the instrument. This time I was better prepared to sing than I was at the gold-miners' party in Boa Vista. I had learned a few Brazilian songs on the boat trip down the Rio Branco. So I sang the romantic lament, *"Quem eu quero não me quer"* (The one I love doesn't love me), choosing it because its slow style, *música de seresta* (night music), was easier to interpret than samba, which I still could not master.

The group was delighted and amazed to hear a newly-arrived foreigner sing a Brazilian song. Nevertheless, they asked me to sing something in English, since Anglo-American music was chic among young, upper-class Brazilians. After obliging with a couple of Beatles' songs, I tried to steer the party back to samba, in the hope of learning something of its illusive rhythm. Fortunately, it was easy to direct the high-spirited graduates back to the repertoire of sambas that they knew and sang well. I returned the guitar to its former player and sat back, intoxicated by the music, the liquor and the ladies' perfume.

The end of the evening I neither remember nor find described in my travel notes. I must have been quite drunk. One thing is certain: the events at the Ideal Club convinced me that I would enjoy living in Brazil. To be invited by pretty girls to parties with live music and free drinks seemed a commendable way of life.

Chapter 4

Fig 4. Ver-o-Peso Market, Belém

WK

Festive Travels

When I originally conceived the plan of looking for a job in South America, I imagined a long trip. Yet I had apparently succeeded in finding employment in the first city in which I looked; I had reached Manaus, where the INPA research institute was willing to hire me, subject to approval by authorities in Brasília. That was fine. However, I had seen very little of Brazil. What should I do? Should I continue sightseeing? Or should I stay in Manaus and wait for the contract to mature, taking advantage of being on the spot to push the business on?

I decided to continue the job hunt as if nothing had happened. In any case, federal approval of my INPA contract would be handled in Brasília, not in Manaus, so that staying in Manaus might not help me much. Furthermore, there could possibly be better jobs elsewhere in Brazil and there could be hitches in the INPA deal. Perhaps most importantly, looking for a job provided an excuse for travelling and an excellent framework for meeting people.

Having made up my mind to continue exploring Brazil, I set off towards more developed parts of the country. That means I headed first for the coast and then the south. In terms of job interviews, my next goal was the prestigious Goeldi Museum in Belém, the large city at the mouth of the Amazon. To get there I decided to go to the town of Santarém, situated 36 hours by riverboat downstream from Manaus, almost halfway to the Atlantic Ocean. From Santarém I would reach the Transamazônica Highway and travel along it eastwards until it linked with other roads leading to Belém. Learning from the voyage on the Rio Branco, I bought myself a hammock in which to sleep on the boat journey down the Amazon.

Saying goodbye to my new friends in Manaus, I embarked in a large double-decker riverboat packed with people travelling to Santarém for Christmas. There were so many people on board that it was difficult to move around the decks. Most passengers spent practically the whole voyage, two nights and a day, in their hammocks, a comfortable pastime, but one with limited sightseeing possibilities. However, most of the time the boat sailed down the middle of the river in order to obtain maximum speed from the current. So we were usually too far away from the banks for even those standing at the rails to see much detail. What was visible indicated that the banks of the lower Amazon were much more populated than those of the Rio Branco and Rio Negro. We saw many big ranches on the broad Amazon floodplain. They contained large herds of zebu cattle and water buffalo, the latter evidently an increasingly popular farm animal in the region.

The boat called at several small towns on its way down the river. On-going passengers who ventured ashore during such stops normally had just enough time to walk up the main street and back, or drink a cold beer in a waterfront bar, before the boat sailed again. One of the places we pulled into was Parintins, the city famous for staging a huge ox-dance festival (*boi bumbá*) every year at the end of June. Another was the city of Óbidos, one of the few places along the Amazon where it is was possible to observe the full width of the river with no islands. This special feature made Óbidos a point of military and hydrographical significance and meant that the city contained an old colonial fort and a river gauging station.

Later I became good friends with an American hydrologist, Dr. Bob Meade, who had worked in the lower Amazon. With his contagious enthusiasm for the academic study of rivers, Bob made me feel proud to have been to Óbidos, even though at the time of my visit I didn't attach any special significance to the pretty little riverside town and its hill-top fortress. He considered the measurements done at Óbidos to be fundamental data for understanding the Amazon's tides and seasonal variations of water level. He told me that, although the river gauge at Óbidos was situated 584 miles inland from Belém, during the dry season it showed a small, twice-daily oscillation in water level. The fluctuation amounted to about an inch and constituted the most upstream measurement of tide on the Amazon. He also said that at Santarém the tidal variation was somewhat more pronounced, amounting to a few inches in the dry season. Thereafter, as one travelled downstream, the tide became progressively more important and seasonal (rainfall) effects on water level diminished.

Bob drew my attention to several other simple facts about the tidal zone of the Amazon. One is that when the tide rose in the ocean, the main stem of the Amazon did not reverse its flow. Rising ocean tide at the estuary reduced the river's slope, causing the river to slow down and swell. And in a similar way, falling tide in the ocean increased the slope of the river, causing the current to speed up. But the river always flowed towards the ocean. Logically, he pointed out, cul-de-sac side arms, with little or no net current, did reverse flow, alternately filling (with river water) and draining as the main stem rose and fell.

Finally, Bob, who had a lot of energy for talking about hydrology, told me that not only did Óbidos mark the upstream limit of detectable tide on the Amazon, it also represented the most downstream point at which the Amazon's volumetric flow was routinely monitored. The gauge at Óbidos measured a flow equivalent to ten times that of the Mississippi. This figure was even more impressive when one considered that major rivers such as the Tapajós, Xingu and Tocantins met the Amazon further downstream. In this context it surprised me to learn that many geologists think that, 50 to 100 million years ago, before the formation of the Andes, water in the region may have flowed from east to west, with headwaters situated near Óbidos.

At sunrise on the second morning, the riverboat tied up in Santarém, a sizeable, relatively quiet city, located where the transparent, greenish waters of the Tapajós ran into the muddy waters of the Amazon. Santarém's long waterfront street, bordered by boats on one side and buildings on the other, looked picturesque in the early morning light. The low, red sun brought out warm, bright colours on shopfronts, warehouses and restaurants. Leaving my rucksack and guitar at an open-air snack bar, I took an unencumbered stroll to look around before breakfast.

With around 500,000 inhabitants, Santarém was in many ways what Manaus would have been like without the tax incentives of the Zona Franca de Manaus. Santarém had two major functions; it was an administrative centre and a trading post. Its commerce consisted of collecting rural products and distributing manufactured goods. Merchants in Santarém purchased rubber, jute, Brazil nuts, timber, fish, beef, buffalo cheese and a host of fruits, resins, fibres and essences from local sources. In return they sold all sorts of industrialised products: machines, spare parts, fuel, tinned milk (for the numerous babies), batteries, machetes, ammunition, fishing equipment, tools, clothes, sugarcane liquor, soap, pans, medicine and occasional luxury items. Santarém's trading area stretched over the valleys of the Rio Trombetas, Rio Tapajós and the central section of the lower Amazon.

In addition to river transport, Santarém had a modern airport and a road link to the Transamazônica Highway. It thus enjoyed a good infrastructure for commerce. However, the city's prosperity was particularly related to gold mines located at Itaituba, a town on the Rio Tapajós about 250 km to the south. Santarém supplied mining equipment to Itaituba and attracted some of the considerable wealth the mines generated. Many gold dealers lived in Santarém. Shops of all sorts were well stocked. In particular, in keeping with the time of year of my visit, lots of plastic Christmas trees with fake snow were on sale.

(At the time of writing this book, the waterfront of Santarém looks much like it did then, thirty years ago. However, one particularly important change has taken place: Santarém now has a special port facility for handling soybeans. This crop, which is spreading into the southern Amazon region, is transported to Santarém by truck from the Transamazônica Highway. In Santarém the beans are loaded into ocean-going, bulk-carrier ships.)

As I sauntered along the waterfront, I noticed that the covered market was preparing for the day's trade. I went in to examine the strange wares displayed in the narrow alleys. Because of the early hour there were as yet few customers in the market, so the stallholders had plenty of time to explain to me what they were selling. They were also exceedingly patient with my poor knowledge of Portuguese. Unable to conceive that I was seeing many of their goods for the first time, they were amazed at my ignorance and amused by my curiosity. Among the items that caught my attention were the canes and iron tips used for making arrows for shooting fish and turtles. Then there were rolled up vines for lashing house beams together, basket presses for squeezing manioc flour, conical metal bowls for panning gold, black magic supplies, herbal remedies and powdered fish meal made from sucker-mouthed catfish.

Although most of the market was still quiet, the fish section, needing to complete its activities before the heat of the day, was in full swing. I had to jostle with shoppers to see things. However, it was worth the effort, even if the crowded conditions didn't allow me to glean much more than the names of the various types on sale. All the fish came from fresh water. Some were very large and the number of species was astounding. Just on a basis of appearance I picked out over twenty species, empirically classifying them as follows:

(1) armoured fish *(bodó, tamuatã)*

(2) large catfish *(caparari, surubim, dourado, piraiba, pirarara)*

3) scaly fish weighing less than 2 lb. *(pacu, aracu, piranha, matrinxã, jaraqui, curimatã, sardinha, carã)*

(4) scaly fish weighing more than 2 lb. *(pirapitinga, aruanã* [arowana], *pescada, tambaqui, tucunaré, pirarucu)*

Fish obviously constituted an important component of local diet. In general it was cheaper than meat. The first two sorts on the list were the cheapest fish in the market. The last three were the most expensive.

Returning to the snack bar where I had left my luggage, I sat down and ordered milky coffee and a bread roll for breakfast. As I ate, a shapely girl in school uniform came and sat down beside me. Could I do quadratic equations, she asked earnestly. Her educated Portuguese was much easier to understand than that of the stallholders in the market. Amused at the novel subject with which she chose to open a conversation with a total stranger, I replied affirmatively. At this she heaved a sigh of relief, smiled and opened a voluminous file of school notes. Finding a sheet of paper for me to use, she gave me ten problems to solve and explained that they were homework, which she had to complete before school started.

While I performed the simple algebra, she announced that she was a beauty queen and, without pausing for my reaction, produced from the same academic file a series of press cuttings and colour photographs showing her parading in a minuscule bikini with a bevy of similarly clad young women at a carnival party in Santarém. Everyone in the pictures seemed very jovial, causing me to marvel at Brazilians' uncomplicated enjoyment of the female form. Young women were proud to be pretty and the public, of both sexes, happy to see them. My amazement also extended to the girl's typically Brazilian lack of inhibition about wearing such a brief bikini and about accosting a stranger with quadratic equations during breakfast.

I finished the mathematics successfully, even though my mind, inspired by the pictures, started wandering from my figures to hers. However, the interview was almost at an end. Taking the answer paper, she thanked me profusely and packed everything back into the file. Then, with great aplomb, she struck a sexy, pouting pose for me to photograph her, kissed me modestly on the cheek and continued her way to school, leaving me to muse how quickly children grow up in Brazil.

Refreshed by the brief, light-hearted, female company, it seemed a good moment to start organising my trip along the Transamazônica Highway. The snack bar owner had been amusedly watching my encounter with the schoolgirl. I ordered another coffee and asked him about road transport. Within seconds he had drawn several customers and passers-by into an animated discussion about bridges, ferries and potholes along my proposed route. The collective opinion was finally encouraging: I could go south about 200 km to Ruropolis, the junction with the Transamazônica, from where it would be possible to go east through Altamira, Marabá, Imperatriz and finally to Belém. A man in the discussion offered me a lift to a spot on the edge of town, where I could either hitch a ride or, if necessary, later in the afternoon catch the bus to Ruropolis. I accepted the lift gratefully and we left the café a few minutes later.

Hitchhiking proved impossible. There was very little traffic and the few vehicles that passed me were full. As the day became hotter, red dust from the dirt road began to form a disagreeable paste on my perspiring, burning body. My suffering must have shown, because at midday a man of scarce resources, living in a nearby shack, took pity on me, inviting me into the shade of his rustic home to share a simple lunch of manioc flour and fried fish. The afternoon vigil by the roadside was no more successful than the morning one, with the result that when the bus for Ruropolis appeared at around 5.00 PM, I boarded it thankfully. I was glad to be on the move again.

The roadside farms near Santarém looked quite prosperous. The forest had been cleared for a few hundred yards on each side of the road. Some isolated ancient trees still stood in the fields, but massive, felled trunks lying haphazardly on the ground testified to the forest's former presence. The bus sped like a dusty, red comet through mature plantations of citrus, black peppers, papayas and coconuts, as well as ranches with zebu cattle. The latter, however, were noticeably leaner than the cattle on the pastures of the Amazon floodplain. Further along the route, the farms were newer and more rustic. Further still, after dark, we passed areas of active deforestation, with fires of recently cut forest burning close to the road.

Driving through burning forest scared me. The flames were often close to the bus and one could feel the intense radiant heat through the windows. I feared the bus would catch fire. The fuel in particular worried me, since Brazilian diesel, unlike that in most parts of the world, was readily flammable. (Refineries in Brazil mixed naphtha into the diesel in order to make as much heavy-transport fuel as possible from each barrel of crude oil.) I was also frightened that our bus might drive off the road or collide with another vehicle, as we hurtled with unabated velocity through dense clouds of smoke.

Fires in the distance were a safer spectacle and, though I hate to say it, I found some of them quite pretty, in the way that a Christmas tree with candles is attractive. Such fires frequently outlined ridges and valleys in a landscape that would otherwise have been invisible in the dark night. In places where flames had passed recently, glowing embers on smouldering trunks and branches formed eerie silhouettes like a red neon picture of a forest.

By the time the bus reached Ruropolis, most of the town's inhabitants had gone to bed. So I did too, laying my sleeping bag alongside my rucksack and guitar in a corner of the dimly lit, wooden barn that served as bar, restaurant and bus station. In the contentment of having reached the Transamazônica Highway, sleep came quickly, despite my sunburned arms and red dust everywhere.

The Transamazônica Highway runs roughly east-west across Brazil, several degrees south of the equator, more or less at the latitude where the country bulges furthest out into the Atlantic Ocean. It is for the most part a dirt road. Its inland end connects with the Porto Velho/ Manaus road (BR 319) at the town of Humaitá on the Rio Madeira, about 3,000 km from the coast. Some maps erroneously show the Highway continuing inland to Lábrea or even beyond, but that section has never been built. At the time of writing, both the Manaus/ Porto Velho road and the western part of the Transamazônica are impassable, although it is still possible to travel on the eastern part described below.

The government's aim in constructing the Transamazônica Highway was to link the sparsely populated Amazon to the densely populated, poor regions of northeast Brazil. Politicians hoped that destitute people from the northeast would migrate along this corridor into the Amazon and make good by turning forest into farmland. Towns and villages were planned at regular intervals along the new highway, with all sorts of services for those moving into the area. In reality, virtually none of the projected infrastructure was installed. As a result, many of the original settlers gave up and sold their plots to those remaining. Hence, the number of people living along the Transamazônica is far less than planned; and as a method of relieving population pressure in the Northeast, the highway has had only symbolic value.

The following morning, after washing the red dust off my body in the bus station's primitive shower, I set out to experience the Transamazônica for myself. There was no rush. Ruropolis was hardly any livelier by day than at night. Not much to investigate: a sleepy filling station and a sleepy main street with sleepy stores and bars. A few pick-up trucks circulated locally. I watched them carefully for a lift, finally observing them all day. Not a single vehicle set off down the Transamazônica Highway from dawn to dusk.

At least this time I didn't stand in the hot sun. I remained in a roadside bar, where there was shade, company and cold beer. During the vain wait, I talked to some of the people who were trying to set up farms in the area. In conversations strained by my inability to concentrate on Portuguese and watch for lifts at the same time, men described their lives as poor settlers with no capital. That meant no tractors, no machines, no fertilisers and no insecticides. Most were trying to tame the forest, armed only with an axe and a box of matches. Infertile soils were a great problem. After cutting and burning the forest, good harvests could be produced for only two years, three at the most. Highland rice was a favourite crop, along with low-density cattle ranching.

Towards evening, tired of a day of physical inactivity, I walked out of town along the Highway. Rustic homes, often little more than a thatched roof and a collection of cooking pots, stood in 125 hectare lots, some of which were more extensively deforested than others. Away from streams, the cleared land was dry, with red dust everywhere. Nevertheless, there were signs that rainfall was sometimes intense; deep gullies had eroded into any incline with no tree-cover. Specifically, some of the road embankments and cuttings looked dangerously unstable. However, in spite of the hazardous state of the road, I had no hesitation in boarding the overnight bus, when it finally came, two hours late.

The bus was heading for Altamira, an old town that already stood on the banks of the beautiful Xingu River long before the Transamazônica was conceived. Altamira was older than Ruropolis. It was also larger and was growing rapidly. With the arrival of the Transamazônica, the town had become a focus for opening up new land away from the river. Cowboy hats and red dust had proliferated to such an extent that there was no longer any standing forest for several miles around the urban area.

Brazilians freely admitted that the western end of the Transamazônica Highway linked "nowhere" to "nowhere else". There wasn't much going on in the west. But around Altamira, where I now was, there was certainly enough commercial activity to justify the road's existence. For instance, some of the biggest cattle ranches on Earth were situated near Altamira, while the planet's largest iron-ore deposit, Carajás, was located close to the next town, Marabá. Also nearby were the much-photographed gold mine, Serra Pelada, and the world's fourth most powerful hydroelectric dam, Tucurui. These immense projects had stimulated the growth of Altamira and Marabá. They could not have been implanted without the presence of a highway.

I noticed the increase in traffic as I moved east. Several heavily laden trucks passed me on the outskirts of Altamira heading in the direction I wanted to go. However, no lifts were forthcoming. Once more, I found myself on an overnight bus, this time to Marabá. There, I decided to abandon hitchhiking and catch the next bus to Belém, where I could visit the Goeldi Museum and relax after what was becoming a tiring journey.

Speeding along the asphalt road to Belém, I realised I was leaving the forest and approaching a large city which was much more integrated into mainstream Brazilian culture than Manaus was. Belém had played an important role in Brazil's history since the seventeenth century and the asphalt road was a modern reinforcement of the historic links. For most Brazilians Belém was the gateway to the Amazon, but for me it was the exit.

Yet although my first foray into the Amazon basin was coming to an end, the parties along my journey continued. There had been parties in Boa Vista and in Manaus; and as I travelled round the rest of Brazil, there were lots more – I loved them. The next one took place at the Goeldi Museum in Belém.

After arriving in Belém I made contact with the curator of the Goeldi Museum, who kindly allowed me to stay in the establishment's guesthouse while we discussed employment possibilities. The lodgings, set in the zoo/botanical gardens, were a wonderful place to take things easy after the rigours of the Transamazônica Highway. Surrounded by one of the world's best collections of Amazonian animals and plants, I learned a lot about the area I had just traversed. I particularly remember the immense buttress roots of the giant Kapok tree, the black electric eel that could swim backwards, the gigantic leaves of the *Victoria amazonica* water lily and the concentrated power of the caged jaguars.

In the same lodgings as me there was a group of male students who had not yet gone home for Christmas. On the second night of my stay they invited me to an impromptu Christmas party, to which, contrary to a strict ban on unofficial visitors, they had smuggled some good-time girls from the Bar do Parque, a notorious pick-up joint near Belém's main theatre. It was a great party, but I was uneasy in case the administration found out about it. Nothing was mentioned about it during my interview, but ominously no job offer materialised.

My next job-hunting stop was at CEPLAC, the government's cacao research station in the state of Bahia. Here I again received accommodation from my prospective employer and an invitation to a party. I arrived at the establishment only two days before Christmas, after a 36-hour bus trip from Belém. Since it was the festive season, the director, Dr. Paulo Alvim, generously allowed me to stay on campus through the holiday period. A guitarist himself, he not only interviewed me for a job, but also entertained me regally, teaching me several Brazilian songs that are now in my repertoire.

Dr. Alvim's fine hospitality reached its zenith on December 24, when he invited me to accompany him to a Christmas party given by a rich cacao exporter. It was a smart event requiring men to wear jackets. Since I had none, he lent me one, doing so with a natural grace that spared me embarrassment in our employer/ interviewee relationship. He drove me 25 km to the party, which took place on the outskirts of Ilheus, Brazil's major cacao-exporting port. Ilheus was for many years the home of the now-deceased, best-selling Brazilian author, Jorge Amado.

The party's host, one of Brazil's wealthiest international traders, staged the elegant Christmas festivities at his home, an enormous split-level colonial-style house set in landscaped gardens overlooking the ocean. In spite of the large number of guests, he found a moment to greet us personally and to make us welcome. He certainly knew how to entertain. On a romantically lit patio situated between palm trees and the swimming pool, a discreet orchestra played bossa novas just loud enough to dance to, without disturbing the conversation at the tables. A bevy of lovely girls, obviously chosen for their looks, undulated in blue satin jump suits, serving imported whisky and beautifully prepared Christmas food. The Scotch was a particular demonstration of the host's wealth, since although Brazilian beer and sugarcane liquor were cheap, imported alcoholic drinks were extremely expensive on account of high import duties.

Dr Alvim, whose research station was financed by a levy on cacao exports, knew most of the people in this well-to-do world and introduced me to many of them. Although unaware at the time, I probably met some of the most influential figures in Bahian society. As the Scotch took effect, my impression of Brazil changed. I had expected poverty and found opulence. Even when dealing with royalty in the Third World (teaching at the King's School in Swaziland), I never saw wealth like that demonstrated by the cacao exporter in Bahia.

After Christmas I left CEPLAC and headed south. By the end of December I had reached the city of São Paulo, where, while job-hunting at the university, it was time for a New Year's Eve party.

With over 17 million inhabitants, São Paulo was by far the largest conurbation in South America. As such, it was big enough to support distinct immigrant cultures. For instance, its Liberdade district was Japanese, while Brás district was Italian. I stayed in Santo Amaro district, which was Germanic. My hosts were well-to-do, middle-aged Austrians, who had originally moved to Brazil as young, penniless, post-war immigrants. They were aunt and uncle of one of the new friends I had made in Manaus.

Having spent several weeks in the hot tropics, interacting in Portuguese with brown people in the Amazon and black people in Bahia, I found it strange to be in São Paulo's cooler climate, surrounded by white people who spoke German. To complete my sense of having been transported back to Europe, shops near my host's house sold *Sauerkraut*, *Wurst*, rye bread, *Schnapps* and *Malzbier*. Moreover, a little further away, marches, polkas and waltzes resounded in a Bavarian beerhall, where blonde girls in Tyrolean costume served beer in tankards. Even the beer had a German heritage. It was called *chopp* in Portuguese, from the German word *Schoppen* (half-a-pint).

My hosts, who kept a Viennese pastry shop, planned to celebrate New Year's Eve at a party given by the German community. The venue for the event was a large, Black Forest-style chalet set in hills north of the city. They invited me to join them, on condition that I took the guitar. Happy to see another facet of life in Brazil, I accepted the offer.

When we set out from São Paulo for the party, it was already dark. So it was hard for me to know where I was heading. However, I would have sworn on arrival that I was in Germany or Austria. People were dancing in a massive wooden chalet to the oom-pah sound of a Tyrolean polka band. The musicians, all men, sported alpine hats and *Lederhosen* and played clarinet, flute, accordion, drums and the obligatory tuba. Those not dancing or playing music drank beer from huge, porcelain or pewter tankards. The men generally conversed with each other in German. If they spoke Portuguese, they did so with strong German accents. The women and the few children present provided the clues to the party's true location: many of the ladies had distinctly tropical complexions, and their offspring spoke perfect Portuguese.

At midnight the guests hugged, kissed and made toasts to celebrate the arrival of the New Year. Then, tired of dancing, a substantial number of them retired to the cellar to sing. I was expected to lead this activity, in spite of the fact that my German song repertoire, even worse than my Spanish repertoire at Boa Vista, amounted to only two numbers. These were the rather hackneyed "*Muss i denn*" (the song Elvis Presley made famous in an English version called "Wooden Heart") and the sea shanty, "*Wir lagen vor Madagaskar*". With spirits high from copious drinking, the two songs were good enough to get people singing heartily.

Led by a few especially good singers, the group launched into a medley of rowdy folksongs, of which I occasionally recognised snippets. In any case, many of the numbers were so well sung that I could accompany them instinctively. Finally, everybody became so excited singing, that they didn't need the guitar at all.

I was pleased with the performance, because I had been apprehensive about trying to get Germans to sing. Many Germans I had met on other occasions would not sing their country's many folksongs, because the Nazi party had exploited them for political ends during World War 2. To my great delight, Brazil's Germans were happy to sing anything and everything.

At about 5.30 AM, exhausted, I retired to my hammock slung between pine trees in the dewy garden. Waiting for sleep, which came slowly in the chilly, dawn air, I reflected on São Paulo's Germans. Such a large manifestation of Germanic culture outside Europe was impressive. Yet although sheer numbers made integration a slow process, Brazil's melting pot was gradually absorbing the immigrants. The next generation would not have exclusively Aryan features and most would only be able to speak Portuguese.

The longest party of my trip around Brazil lasted five days and occurred while I was ostensibly looking for employment at the University of Cuiabá in Mato Grosso. I travelled to Cuiabá by long distance bus from southern Brazil. On the way I happened to meet a young singer/ guitarist, named Renato. He had seen me board the bus with my guitar and, because of his interest in music, he decided to sit next to me, so that we could talk. During the conversation I learned that Renato came from Salvador da Bahia (a city with a fine musical tradition) and that he was going to Cuiabá to attend his girlfriend's sister's wedding. He told me he planned to stay in a cheap hotel, since his girlfriend's home would be full of relatives congregating for the marriage. If I wanted, he said, we could room together and I could join in the fun. I accepted his offer and on arrival Renato and I moved into a dive near the bus station.

In the next few days we met lots of young people gathering for the wedding. We all had little to do in the evenings, so we partied every night for the four nights before the reception. The first two nights, armed with the guitar and a supply of beer, we gathered on the veranda of the family home and sang. Renato, a competent performer, provided most of the entertainment, with me helping out occasionally. On the third night the young men brought along drums, a shaker, cowbells and a tambourine to play sambas, to which the girls danced sensually. This, I learned subsequently, was a common formula at impromptu samba parties: women most often danced alone and rarely played percussion instruments; men made the music, but danced only occasionally.

On the fourth night we went out to *fazer uma serenata* (literally "to do a serenade"). This traditional pastime meant we sang in the street under a girl's bedroom window, until she woke up and came out to join us. The residents of the street tolerated the late-night noise remarkably well. Apparently they considered *serenatas* something "romantic" that "nice" young people did. As one might expect, our *serenata* was prompted by an amorous link between one of our troubadours and the girl, but its message was really directed to her parents and said, "Look, your daughter's friends are out in the street. Please let her come and join us. With safety in numbers, no harm will come to her." We succeeded in dragging a sleepy, smiling girl out of her house after midnight, to spend another two hours partying in the street.

Finally the wedding took place, a grand ceremony in the second largest church in Cuiabá, a lofty building with a 1950's feel about it. Inside the church huge ceiling fans churned the hot, humid air in a vain attempt to prevent the overdressed congregation from perspiring. Lots of white gladioli decorated the aisle and altar. The bride looked gorgeous, in a white lace dress with a veil and a long train. The bridegroom looked handsome, in a suit he would probably never wear again in the hot climate.

Notwithstanding the beauty of the occasion, bats were the most memorable feature of the wedding service. The creatures nested in the roof of the church and came into the nave in large numbers through holes where ceiling panels were missing. They constituted a problem, not because of their simple presence, which most people could stand, but because as they flew around they were unable to detect the rotating fan blades. Sometimes they hit the fans. This meant that dead, injured or stunned bats would fall out of the sky, causing considerable consternation.

Despite the biological fall-out, the priest concluded the service satisfactorily, after which the guests returned eagerly to the bride's parents' house for the reception. The bride's father, a hard-working, small-scale rancher, had slaughtered a cow and provided a copious, unsophisticated spread of meat and beer. Entertainment consisted of dancing to recorded *forró* music, interspersed with song sessions by Renato and myself. The festivities continued until sunrise. As soon as they were over, with job interviews already concluded days ago, I boarded another long distance bus and was already sleeping soundly before the vehicle left the suburbs of Cuiabá.

One musical encounter on the trip was different from all the others, because it concerned classical music. It took place in the city of São João del Rei in the state of Minas Gerais. There, two church orchestras had a remarkable uninterrupted musical tradition spanning back over two centuries. I had the unexpected privilege of attending a performance of one of the orchestras. It happened quite by chance, when I temporarily suspended the job hunt so as to visit the only people in Brazil whose address I had before leaving England. The couple I visited were "friends of friends" and I had not met them before. My stay with them was purely social and I didn't look for a job in the area. The experience was like stepping into a history book.

The name of the state my contacts lived in, Minas Gerais, means "General Mines". It referred originally to a large area inland from Rio de Janeiro and São

Paulo, where many important mineral deposits were found during the colonial period. In particular, goldmining in the 18th century produced enormous wealth. The gold rush fomented a huge artistic proliferation centred on church life. During the boom period, known as the Minas Gerais Baroque, artists in towns such as Ouro Preto, Diamantina, São João del Rei and Tiradentes produced innumerable masterpieces of architecture, sculpture, painting and music. These glories can still be appreciated today. For example, UNESCO has recommended that much of Ouro Preto's colonial architecture be preserved as part of the World Cultural Heritage Programme.

Though I did not know it before I met them, the couple I was visiting, John Parsons, an English gentleman, and Ana Maria, his dynamic Brazilian wife, owned a beautiful hotel in the centre of the former gold mining town of Tiradentes. Their hotel occupied a stone colonial building called *Solar da Ponte* (literally "Mansion by the Bridge."). Nearby were smaller buildings also in colonial style. Not far away on a hillside stood a marvellous baroque church ornamented with carvings made by the renowned crippled sculptor, Aleijadinho. Off to the side, crystal clear drinking water flowed into the ornately sculpted basin of St. Joseph's Spring. The whole place emanated the spirit of an ancient community in harmony with the majestic hills around it. To complete the old-world feeling, a narrow-gauge steam locomotive hauled the train from São João del Rei twice a day to a station just down the street from the hotel.

When I arrived in Tiradentes, Ana Maria, with her habitual energy for cultural activities, had just finished helping to organise the two-hundredth anniversary celebrations of the Lira Sanjoanense Orchestra belonging to the church of Nossa Senhora das Mêrces in São João del Rei. She enjoyed giving a hand, although she herself was part of the same city's marginally younger Ribeiro Bastos Orchestra belonging to the Church of St. Francis.

My hostess explained to me that the tradition of church music in Minas Gerais was as old as the churches themselves. At first, musicians were paid, but when gold ran out, the church orchestras continued on an amateur basis. Each church had its own composers, who wrote new works every year for all the feasts in the ecclesiastical calendar. Production of music was consequently prolific and the orchestras' archives were full of musical treasures, most of which were unknown to the general public. Few of the works had ever been recorded, and then only in rare special editions.

Enthusiastic and indefatigable, Ana Maria took me to São João del Rei to hear the Ribeiro Bastos Orchestra play for Sunday mass in St. Francis' Church. The setting was awe-inspiring. The gold-covered sanctuary was a superb example of baroque art, although gold had run out before the statues in the nave could be plated. I sat with the orchestra at the back of the church in the lofty balcony, which had a magnificent view of the altar.

Meeting the orchestra was a lesson in humility. In a country where many people were illiterate, here was a group of people who could read and write music. They had quietly passed on their musical skills from father to son, without seeking fame or commercial success. The musicians were ordinary provincial folk, going about their lives in obscurity. Their professions included nurse, tailor, truck driver and schoolteacher. They numbered eighty persons: forty instrumentalists and forty choir members.

As may be expected from a group of amateur musicians, the musical quality was not of virtuoso standard. However, the zest of the performance was contagious. Adoring all forms of homemade music, I was exhilarated. The work, "Mass for Five Voices," by the local composer, Antônio dos Santos Cunha was written around the year 1800. It compared favourably with European compositions of the same period. On hearing it I immediately revised my impression that Brazilian music lacked depth. I found it a powerful, inspired creation.

I travelled around Brazil for a total of three months, ostensibly looking for a job, but in fact getting to know the people, their culture and their history. A huge overland loop took me north through Porto Velho to reach Manaus again, where I checked on the INPA job offer. My contract was still awaiting approval in Brasíia, so I decided to return to the UK to wait for it to mature. Thus I headed up the Amazon by riverboat and visited Colombia and Venezuela for a month, before flying over to Trinidad to use my return air ticket to London.

It was carnival weekend when I left Brazil. To leave the country I went over the land border between the upper Amazon town of Tabatinga (Brazil) and the adjacent town of Letícia (Colombia). The Colombians were working normally, but the Brazilians had closed their control point so that the guards could celebrate carnival. Since friends I had met on the boat were staying in a hotel in Letícia, I went with them into Colombia for the night and crossed back the following day to pick up my Brazilian exit stamp. For three months I had had the feeling that Brazil was a land to which I would return. But I never imagined that I would first go back just so that I could leave officially.

Chapter 5

Fig 5. Making Manioc Flour

WK

Indian Dancing

After three months in Brazil and a month in Colombia and Venezuela, I returned to England to wait for an employment contract to mature from the contacts I had made. Half a year later, the only news I had received from South America was a letter from the cacao research centre in Bahia, asking me to send a copy of my research proposals, as they had lost the originals.

Nine months after my return to the UK, still with no news, it seemed that once again I had failed to find work in South America, so I started to organise myself for long-term residence in Europe. Suddenly, in the same week, unheralded by intermediate correspondence, two job offers arrived, one from the University of the Andes in Trujillo, Venezuela, the other from the INPA research institute in Manaus. Knowing that the Venezuelan university was suffering from a lot of political unrest, I accepted the INPA position: full-time research worker studying the production of methane fuel from rotting forest vegetation.

INPA wanted me immediately, but when the offer arrived, I had just arranged an engagement as a singer-guitarist in the French ski resort of Les Arcs, an opportunity I did not want to miss. Since the Brazilians had made me wait nine months before sending me a contract, I felt that I could make them wait a few months before accepting it. Heading for France, I told INPA I would be available after the ski season. It was a wise decision. The time in the French Alps proved most enjoyable. Singing in the evenings, I had plenty of time to ski during the day. Furthermore, it was the only place in this chapter where I met any girls.

As snow melted in the Alps, I packed my bags and flew to Brazil, this time taking much more luggage than on the job hunt. The Brazilian government paid the bill. Three years had passed since my first attempts to find work in South America.

However, not everything turned out as fine as I expected. On arrival, INPA had nothing ready for me. Now, in retrospect, the lack of preparation seems quite normal, but then it came as a severe shock: I had no laboratory equipment and no budget with which to buy any. Fortunately, there were no problems concerning my salary, which was not only generous, but also periodically corrected to withstand Brazil's soaring inflation. The first month's pay-cheque, supplemented by a handsome settling-in allowance, covered all the expenses I had incurred on the job-hunting trip.

As first step towards securing research funds, I named my department "Alternative Energy Supplies" and gave it a brief to look at all types of renewable energy sources, not just the methane project specified in my contract. This strategy enabled me to cast the fund-raising net wide, increasing the chances of finding money quickly.

In the meantime I had to work in such a way that any costs I incurred could be born by existing activities at the institute. As a result, for my first research project I hitched a ride on an INPA agrobotanical expedition setting off up the Rio Negro. I planned to make a survey of local people's use of energy. The journey would give me an insight into rural Amazonian life and form a background against which I could orient relevant research for the future. On the way, but not part of the plan, the expedition happened to have a hilarious musical experience with Tukano Indians.

The two scientists responsible for the expedition I joined were Charles Clement, an American still working in INPA's Tropical Fruit Department, and Wanders Chaves, a visiting fruit researcher from Peru, now at INPA too. They aimed to collect all sorts of edible tropical fruits for further study. In particular Charles had a long-term goal to breed better agricultural varieties of the peach palm, a traditional Amazonian food crop. To do this he needed a large number of genes for recombination experiments. Hence he wanted samples of all sorts of peach palms different from those already in his collection (shorter, less spines, more fruit, bigger fruit, etc.). The expedition planned to stop at *caboclo* and Indian houses along the river to barter for specimens, which would be taken back to Manaus for analysis, description and experimentation.

Onto the above objective I attached my project, which investigated such things as: (1) what fuel people used for cooking, what amount, where from and at what price, (2) what machines were used in the work environment (outboard motors, generators, manioc flour mills, chain-saws etc.) and how much fuel they consumed, (3) other fuel uses (e.g. kilns, refrigerators). The survey was not an activity in which my personal flair was best used, but it cost nothing and required no equipment. The institute's riverboat was making the trip in any case and the expedition's budget could easily absorb my food bill.

We set out up the Rio Negro in November, low water season. Our riverboat was the Pyatã, a single-decked, covered, sleek, wooden vessel about 18m long. Powered by a 45 HP diesel engine, she made about 8 knots. At the front and back were cabins housing the wheelhouse and service areas respectively, but for most of the length, the sides of the vessel were open except for handrails. The deck was built high above the water level, making the hold and engine room comfortably spacious for storing specimens. We slept in hammocks and when insects were bad, used special banana-shaped mosquito nets. Six people were on board: three foreign scientists (Charles, Wanders and myself) and three Brazilian crew (pilot, deckhand and cook).

About four hours upstream from Manaus, we reached the beautiful Anavilhanas Archipelago, a region in which the river divided into a maze of narrow channels around uninhabited, forested islands. Our maps indicated that the distance from the true bank on one side of the watercourse to the true bank on the other was 15 to 20 km, although with so many islands in between, it was impossible to tell from the boat. I later learned that the islands were an inland delta of sediments deposited when a post-Ice-Age rise in sea level caused the Negro to slow down and swell.

Some people said that the Anavilhanas group contained over three hundred islands in its more than 100 km extension, thus constituting the world's largest river archipelago. However it was difficult to interpret any attempt to count the islands: a single island at low water might be cut into a chain of progressively more numerous, smaller islands as water rose. Finally at high water, in June, all the land of the archipelago was submerged and there were arguably no islands at all – just trees growing out of the water.

The Anavilhanas Archipelago was a biological reserve and no one had the right to live on or cultivate the islands. The area would have been, in any case, difficult to inhabit, since it consisted entirely of seasonally flooded forest growing on acid, infertile soil. The protected status of the area was not surprising: many of the world's biological reserves are in areas with little or no commercial potential.

Because cultivation was prohibited, the archipelago, in spite of its beauty, was of no interest to Charles and Wanders. They wanted fruit from peoples' gardens and farms. The same kind of consideration held for my project; there was no activity on the islands and consequently no energy use. So Charles, who controlled the purse strings, decided we should skirt the islands and navigate along the river's north bank, where a few people lived and could be visited.

Up to about five hours' journey from Manaus, more or less as far as the mouth of the Rio Cuieiras, most of the properties we visited belonged to absentee landlords and the people we met were live-in caretakers *(caseiros)*. Each *caseiro* was supported in some way by his landowner, often in a rather feudal relationship. In addition to living on the property, most *caseiros* received a small salary and produced fruit and manioc. Few sustained themselves exclusively by agricultural activity.

The large number of absentee landlords reflected the high status value of land ownership in Brazilian society. In addition, buying land constituted an important hedge against rampant inflation. Speculation was a factor too, since many owners expected land prices to rise as the area became more developed.

Close to Manaus, most of the landowners we met had valid title deeds to their property. However, as we travelled further upstream, the number of *posseiros* (homesteaders without documents) increased enormously. Many of these homesteaders ought to have received title deeds to the land they occupied, but the documents had never been issued because government bureaucracy moved desperately slowly. Some of the victims of the snail-pace administration admitted, in fairness to the government, that checking land claims was an expensive business, involving topographical surveys and legal investigation of counter-claims. They were aware that in many rural areas neither government nor the homesteaders had enough money to cover such expenses. Through lack of funds many *posseiros* never bothered registering land claims at all. Unfortunately for conservationists, the law encouraged homesteaders to cut down their forested areas and replace them with pasture or crops in order to show "useful occupation" of the land they claimed.

As one who had only recently arrived from a country where every square inch of land had a clearly defined owner, I found it hard to imagine how *posseiros* could survive without documents to their land. However, I gradually learned that they recognised each other's land "ownership" on a basis of usage. They bought and sold plots amongst themselves, issuing simple receipts, without any formal register. This anarchy functioned adequately most of the time, but disputes frequently arose about who-owned-what, when an "owner" died or divorced. A major economic problem was that *posseiros* could not use their untitled land as collateral for bank loans. Consequently, their farms were always undercapitalised. Shortage of capital forced the farmer to plant short-cycle crops, such as manioc and pineapples, with immediate returns; whereas the land might have been more suited to longer-cycle crops, such as fruit trees, which protected the soil better.

Whether we visited *caseiros*, *posseiros*, or fully titled landowners, the properties looked remarkably similar. A few *caseiros* near Manaus had water pumps and electric generators. Apart from them, everyone else lived in simple poverty, with practically no machines. One or two people owned 3-HP petrol engines, intermittently used to power manioc mills or straight-drive outboard motors. My energy survey started to become ludicrous. Almost no-one living more than 100 miles from Manaus owned a motor at all. Nevertheless, I was surprised to note that most people cooked on wood fires; for some reason I had expected them to use charcoal. Astonishingly, I found bottled-gas cooking stoves in the more well-to-do homes. If people produced charcoal, they sold it in Manaus or used it only in special circumstances, such as in charcoal-burning clothes irons, or in portable charcoal-burning stoves found on some boats.

Our visits ashore generally went well, although the riverside people were frequently uncommunicative at the moment of our arrival, taking time to warm to strangers. We usually encountered women first, because they spent a lot of time washing clothes at the water's edge. Nevertheless, we always asked to speak to the men, because the rural society was male-dominated.

Once the ice had been broken, we spent a long time chatting to the people we met. This was the required social protocol for establishing good trading relations. However, our conversations were not idle etiquette. We genuinely did find the life of the riverside people interesting. After all, our research projects at the institute were basically aimed at trying to improve that life. For instance one good little research project that came out of the trip concerned people's domestic water supply. On the riverbank I learned that it was the women who habitually fetched water from the river. At the same time I knew that the

Rockerfeller Foundation had money available for research designed to reduce the workload of women in the Third World. Back in Manaus I was able to obtain funding from the Rockerfeller Foundation to design, build and publicise an inexpensive, river-powered pump, which could supply water to riverside houses.

The expedition's visits ashore culminated in obtaining fruit samples, for which we swapped medical supplies brought along especially for trading purposes. The exchange was not really commercial, more a matter of courtesy. The medicines, reflecting common health problems, included:

(1) Aspirin. Helpful in relieving symptoms of colds and minor insect-transmitted fevers.

(2) Analgesics. Helpful in relieving arthritic pains in old people who had spent their lives facing the sun and rain with little protection.

(3) Vitamins. Probably more popular than their true medical worth, although children might benefit from them.

(4) Worm cures. Since outhouses were rare, it was easy for the riverside people to become infected by parasites. Children playing in faecally contaminated areas close to houses were particularly at risk.

(5) Antibiotics. When clearing forest to make plantations, workers frequently injured themselves with thorns, splinters, or machetes. Puncture wounds and deep cuts were common and appropriate antibiotics could be very effective in preventing the development of infection.

(6) Antiseptics. Helpful in preventing superficial wounds from becoming infected.

(7) Stomach and liver medicines. Since the riverside people's food supply was erratic, with no refrigeration to preserve surpluses, spoiled food might be eaten, giving rise to digestive problems. Medicines for diarrhoea, stomach cramps and biliousness were always in demand. Furthermore, although the main stream of the Rio Negro was fit to drink, the widespread practice of drinking unboiled water collected near habitation was dangerous. Many people filtered their drinking water through inexpensive ceramic filters, but these were far from totally effective.

Notwithstanding our use of medicines for bartering, I later found out that other good trade items were: clothes (including used ones), shoes, machetes, knives, coffee, sugar, tinned milk for babies and, in the rare cases when people had machines, fuel.

One fruit-collecting visit impressed me particularly because the soil in which the fruit trees were growing looked unusually fertile. The earth was black rather than red. When I asked Charles about it, he said that I was looking at *terra preta do índio* (literally "Indian black soil"). He agreed that the soil was indeed fertile and told me that it meant that Indians had lived in the area in the past. By bringing food into their settlement over long periods, the Indians had produced enough waste to gradually make the area around their houses more fertile. He said that we would probably find ceramic shards in the soil – remnants of pottery utensils that the Indians had used. Sure enough, when we mentioned this possibility to the landowner, he showed us a number of pottery fragments he had found in the soil while planting his fruit trees. The shards were mainly parts of pots with red geometric designs, but some small knobbly pieces, possibly handles, had gargoyle-like faces.

For the most part, our trip up the Rio Negro was quiet and beautiful. With water level low, we normally moored for the night on white sand beaches, good places to wash, swim and freshen-up. Sometimes we fished. However, the day I caught a *candiru* (literally "devil of the water") enthusiasm for bathing diminished greatly. *Candiru* was a small catfish, which had the reputation of swimming into and getting irreversibly stuck in a man's urethra. The slimy fish I caught looked more capable of vaginal penetration, being reminiscent of a penis in size and shape – it seemed much too large to penetrate the male urethra. It had minute eyes and a vicious round mouth armed with a circle of sharp teeth. The scaleless, cylindrical body carried only diminutive fins.

Because of the excitement that catching a *candiru* produced in the Brazilian crew, the fish's reputation started to intrigue me, particularly as I could not imagine what biological adaptation might drive a fish to become lodged inside a human being – the fish would certainly die, even if the person did not. So, on returning to Manaus, I discussed the question with fish experts and doctors.

Back at INPA, a colleague in the ichthyology department informed me that there were at least five species of *candiru*, all in the catfish family. The one I caught was *candiru açu*, the largest type. It was a free-swimming fish that fed on carrion, which is why I had caught it on a hook baited with meat. He also said that because *candiru açu* ate dead meat, it justified its gruesome reputation of devouring the corpses of people who had drowned. He then showed me preserved specimens of the other, smaller species of *candiru*, which were normally parasites and therefore less often caught with bait. The parasitic *candirus* (sometimes called toothpick fish on account of their size and shape) looked like miniature versions of the fish I caught, but were only around two to four inches long. They had sharp spines on their lateral fins, with which they held themselves in place after burrowing into the flesh of their host. They normally parasitised the gills of big fish, but sometimes attacked urinating human beings by mistake. My colleague explained that they found their prey by seeking the source of nitrogen compounds they scented in the water. Since fish gills and human kidneys produced such compounds, parasitic *candirus* sometimes erroneously homed in on a human urethra instead of on the gill of a host fish.

None of the doctors with whom I spoke had seen a case of urethral penetration by *candiru*. So it was obviously rare. However, while writing this book, a well-documented case occurred in a lake in the Lower Amazon, near Itacoatiara, 210 km downstream from Manaus. The fish penetrated the urethra of a naked, bathing man who was urinating. The man realised immediately what had happened, but was not quick enough to prevent it. He felt pain principally at the moment of entry, less so afterwards. He went to a clinic, where by means of ultrasound scanning a doctor was able to ascertain the exact position of the fish inside the penis. Using special, long, thin scissors the doctor was able to cut the spines off the fish. He then extracted the fish and finally the spines, without the need for complicated surgery.

Although on the banks of the Rio Negro I did not yet know these details of the biology of *candiru*, the fish I caught looked sufficiently awful to make skinny dipping less attractive. From that point on in the expedition, when we went swimming, we were sure to have our swimsuits on.

In the town of Barcelos, 240 miles upstream from Manaus, we stopped to pick up a river pilot to help us navigate the shallower upper reaches of the river. The pilot did not know we were coming, so it took him some time to pack and make arrangements to leave his family. In this interval, while the crew relaxed in the town's bars, drinking and playing billiards, I took the opportunity to check out urban uses of energy. As I walked round the town, little more than a few streets parallel to the river, it was hard to imagine that this former Indian village had once played an important role in the colonial administration of the Amazon. Three centuries ago the Portuguese gave it a Portuguese name and turned it into the capital of their Western Amazon Province. At that time, Barcelos was more important than Manaus.

My investigation of energy use started with a visit to the municipal electricity generating station, a small hangar housing three 75-KW diesel generators; one supplied the town's base load, the second supplied the peak load, and the third was a spare.

The machines did not function 24 hours a day; they produced electricity during the day and evening, but not throughout the whole night. The power was used in houses, streetlights, the school and a sawmill. The hospital was closed and consequently didn't use any electricity. Diesel to power the generators arrived by barge from the refinery in Manaus, there being no road links between Barcelos and other localities.

To my immense surprise, I also found in the powerhouse two large, functional, Brazilian-made, Mernak wood-fired steam engines, abandoned in favour of the diesel units. Ironically the government employed me to research alternative energy supplies, while at the same time it was phasing out proven machines that used renewable, local fuel. The steam engines gave me my first insight into the fact that Brazil's development problems were not simply technical, but depended on other factors too, such as coordination, political will and fashion.

Next I visited the electrically powered sawmill. Again contradictions in government energy planning became apparent, this time in relation to pricing. I was astonished to find that the price that the sawmill paid for the expensive-to-produce thermoelectricity in Barcelos was the same as that which other consumers paid for cheap-to-produce hydroelectricity in south Brazil. In other words, electricity in Barcelos was being subsidised. It would be difficult for any unsubsidised alternative energy source I researched to be competitive with subsidised conventional power. I began to feel that the right hand of the Brazilian government did not know what the left hand was doing.

The lumberyard's saw was a museum piece – an ancient, reciprocating machine, affectionately known as "the woodpecker". It was slow, but reliable and inexpensive. The proprietor showed me the different types of logs waiting to be sawn. They had been towed to the sawmill as rafts. For the handyman who wanted wood that was easy to cut and nail, he recommended *jacareuba*, *louro* and *cedro* (in order of increasing quality and price). For fine-grained planks, heavy, hard, difficult to nail, but good for cabinet making, he had *sucupira* and *cumaru*. He also showed me some attractively coloured timbers including *violeta* (violet-coloured) and *amarelinho* (yellow). *Saboarana* and *angelim rajado* were particularly decorative, because they had streaks of light and dark.

Two industries in Barcelos used firewood as fuel. One was the baker, who made delicious French bread in a wood-fired oven. The other was the hearts-of-palm cannery, which used firewood to raise steam for sterilising its product. I had seen wood-fired bakeries in Manaus, so I chose to visit the cannery, an industry new to me. Charles came with me, because the peach palm he studied also was a possible commercial source of hearts-of-palm.

On the way to the factory Charles told me a lot about hearts-of-palm. He said that one could obtain edible palm hearts in some quantity from most species of palm. He suggested that if one had to survive in the forest, palm hearts would be one of the recommended sources of food, because palms were so easy to recognise. Unfortunately, he said, one had to sacrifice the palm to obtain the heart, which consisted of the soft internal growing tissue, situated where the leaves sprouted from the trunk. He informed me that the cannery on the Rio Negro worked with the *jauari* palm, cut from wild stands along the riverbanks. Near Belém they used the *açaí* palm; and in Brazil's dry northeast region they used the *babaçu* palm. Charles favoured using the peach palm, which had the advantage of regrowing from suckers when the main trunk was decapitated.

The palm-hearts factory was quiet when we arrived, because it was not harvest season. As a result the manager had ample time to show us around. In fact he seemed glad of the distraction. He explained that since hearts-of-palm could be eaten raw, the canned material was not cooked, just autoclaved for sterility and sealed to prevent infection and oxidative discoloration. A wood-burning boiler provided the necessary steam. Low-paid women workers sealed the cans, using hand-operated machines. According to the product's fibre content, cans were labelled "export quality" (soft) or "standard" (more woody). Naturally, the former sold for the higher price. Despite the small size of his cannery, the manager proudly told us that Brazil was the world's largest producer of hearts-of-palm.

On my return from the factory to the waterfront, I found that our crew was still in town. To continue killing time usefully, I decided to interview the skippers of the nearby riverboats, to see what they carried and where they went.

Several boats were setting out to cut and collect *piaçava*, the palm fibre used for making broom bristles, an export product of considerable value. Harvesters made long voyages into small rivers and creeks in the upper Rio Negro area, where the appropriate palm (also called *piaçava*) grew abundantly on the riverbanks. They cut the fibres from the leaf-bases of the wild palms, tying them into lightweight conical bundles, which they stacked on the boat's roof when the hold was full. For this reason from a distance one could easily recognise craft loaded with *piaçava*.

Two boats I visited contained lots of rectangular, shallow, white, plastic tanks like seedboxes. I was naturally curious to know what they were. The skippers told me that such boats specialised in catching aquarium fish. Fishermen caught the minute fish with fine nets in small watercourses. They sorted them in the plastic trays, then transported them by boat to Manaus and subsequently sent them by airfreight to distributors in Miami and São Paulo. Barcelos airport (then under construction; now functional) promised to speed up transport, which was the critical part of the aquarium fish trade. Catching ornamental fish was a lucrative business, because a small specimen weighing a few grams sold for the price of a kilogram of edible fish. The fishermen said that I should come back to Barcelos in January for the annual aquarium-fish trade fair, a huge party with visitors from all over the world, including hobbyists, breeders and dealers.

Although the aquarium fish industry brought a lot of money into Barcelos, many of the riverine people didn't like it. They complained that the spry of commercial food species were exported as ornamentals, to the detriment of traditional fishing interests. The sucker-mouthed catfish, *bodó*, eaten directly or as fishmeal, was a species that had become rarer because of the aquarium fish trade. Arowana, another edible fish, was also a victim. In the breeding season, hundreds of minute, young arowanas were shaken out of the mouths of adult male fish, where they normally sheltered, and sold to the pet trade.

Fishermen told me that they considered the Rio Negro biologically poorer than the mainstream Amazon, in the sense that twenty times more weight of fish reached Manaus market from "white water" (muddy, like the Amazon) than from "black water" (tannin-rich, like the Negro). Nevertheless, they said, in spite of its low fish density, the Negro contained more species, and many of the extra ones, such as discus and tetras, were well-known ornamentals.

I had not finished probing around the port area, when our crew came back with the pilot. We embarked without further delay and continued our journey upstream. The voyage proceeded in much the same way as before: tranquil cruising punctuated by visits to local inhabitants. The difference was that now the river was shallower and more difficult to navigate. From time to time the pilot would direct us specifically towards one bank or the other, or make us traverse at a particular angle.

With the riverside vegetation apparently devoid of distinctive features, it astonished me that the pilot always knew where he was and where the channels were. Sometimes, after making an alteration in course, we were able to spot the shallows or rocks he had avoided. Not once in the whole trip did he look at a map or compass. Yet we never ran aground, in spite of the low water level.

Several years later, after driving my own riverboat regularly around local rivers, I was able to develop the pilot's skill of recognising reference points. Landmarks were subtle: a tree, or a particular group of trees, the shape of the forest's silhouette, the degree of curvature of a bend, plus the memory of what one had already passed and how long ago. With practice I could subsequently even navigate at night with no lights. However, as a newcomer, I was impressed.

After passing the village of Tapuruquara (also known as Santa Isabel, 330 miles from Manaus), the pilot announced we were entering Indian territory. This came as a surprise, since Charles' map showed no Indian reservations here, only further upstream. Nevertheless, on our next visit ashore we met people who didn't speak Portuguese. The pilot was correct; we were among Tukano Indians.

Without the clue of language, we would not have immediately realised we were visiting Indians. Most riverside dwellers were black-haired and brown-skinned, whether they called themselves Indians or not. In both Indian and non-Indian communities the women wore shift dresses, the men wore football shorts and the agriculture consisted of manioc plantations with haphazard fruit trees.

There was a difference, by no means absolute, in housing. The Tukanos favoured adobe houses with earth floors, whereas non-Indian riverside dwellers usually had wooden houses with platform floors. However, Salesian missionaries, the major Christian sect in the area, had already changed Tukano architecture. Originally Tukanos built very large communal houses, in which many families lived together.

Our visits to Indians followed the pattern of our previous stops at *caboclo* houses. Inability to speak Tukano never totally impeded our activities. Normally at least one person in the community, often a young male, could translate for us. Charles and Wanders continued to collect fruit, while I persisted in my quest for motors and machines. Not surprisingly, Tukano life turned out to be almost totally unmechanised. I found one 15 HP outboard motor with no fuel, and a few other machines scrapped because of lack of maintenance and/or spare parts.

On this stretch of the Rio Negro we saw several isolated mountains like those I had seen near the Guyana border on my job-hunting trip. From certain angles, some of the peaks looked remarkably like man-made pyramids. This resemblance has caused some flying saucer enthusiasts, both Brazilian and foreign, to postulate that ancient civilisations of extraterrestrial origin built pyramids in the area. I'm sceptical, but it has to be admitted that away from navigable rivers, this part of Brazil is virtually unexplored.

Nearly two weeks and 450 miles after setting out from Manaus, we reached the town of São Gabriel da Cachoeira, the normal navigational limit for boats like ours. The word *Cachoeira* (waterfall) in the town's name refers to rock-strewn rapids that divide the Rio Negro into two distinct navigable sections. The lower section leads down past Manaus to the Amazon, while the upper section leads into Colombia and Venezuela and even onto the Orinoco River.

São Gabriel's downstream port was situated 23 km from town centre. People and goods heading upstream beyond São Gabriel into frontier areas went around the rapids by truck, embarking in other boats on the upper section of the river. We planned to do something similar. Charles wanted to hire a boat above the rapids to continue collecting fruit on the upper Rio Negro and its tributary, the Uaupés. He was particularly interested in the area above the rapids, because he believed it to be the region in which Indians first domesticated many of the Amazonian fruit trees now in cultivation. Moreover, he considered the Uaupés basin to be the centre of biological diversity of his beloved peach palm.

Charles, Wanders and I left the boat in the care of its Brazilian crew and took a truck ride into town, where, as foreigners in a frontier area, we had to register with the military authorities, for whom we had INPA credentials. The army was particularly active in the town because an engineering battalion was building the northern perimeter road to Caracaraí, a project subsequently abandoned after quicksands en route reduced the construction rate to 20 km per year. In spite of not completing the road, the army improved São Gabriel's transport links by making a runway for large jets.

After registration with the military authorities, our next task was to find an available boat on the upstream section of the river. During the search we got to know São Gabriel quite well, noting a substantial Indian presence. Drunken Indians sometimes roamed the streets at night, shouting to each other in their language, Nheengatu. Furthermore some food stores illegally sold smoked caimans (an Indian delicacy), which they hung up for display like salami or smoked ham. Later, friends in Manaus confirmed that eating caimans was typically an Indian habit and said that the only non-Indians who ate caimans were people from the State of Pará. However, further travels revealed that in fact many non-Indians in the State of Amazonas did eat caimans; they simply didn't talk about it.

Charles succeeded in renting a boat, but at the time of closing the deal, the craft in question was located in the downstream port, practically alongside our vessel. This meant that the owner was going to haul the 14-m, 7-ton, wooden riverboat up the waterfall especially for our use. Traversing the rapids seemed an exciting project, so I asked if I could be on board. My wish was granted.

When it was time to move the boat onto the upper river, there were only two other people on board besides me: one was the boat's regular skipper, the other was a local expert who made his living transferring boats up and down the waterfall. They tackled the problem in two stages, with a short break in between. First came the 23-km stretch of rocky river and then the main waterfall. Both parts of the adventure were exciting.

The exploit started with the expert guiding the boat slowly out of the port. We headed upstream though an area peppered with huge boulders, some sticking out of the water, spectacular but harmless, others dangerously hidden beneath the black water. The swift current around the rocks created powerful whirlpools that made steering difficult. In certain places full throttle only produced inch-by-inch progress. Nevertheless we eventually reached the bottom of the main waterfall and pulled into the bank where a pool of deep, calm water turned in a slow gyre. I was detailed to jump onto the nearest boulder, scramble over the rocks with a mooring line, secure the boat to a tree and make contact with the land party.

On the beach above the waterfall I found a team of eighteen men standing near a brand-new, thick, nylon towrope, 50 metres long. They detailed me to drag one end of the rope to the boat. They were going to haul us up the waterfall. The expert checked the line for possible snags, made it fast on the central bollard of the foredeck and went ashore himself to give last-minute instructions. It was impossible for him to shout orders from the boat; the noise of the cataracts in front of us was deafening.

The plan was gloriously simple. We, the boat crew, would motor from our backwater with the line slack. As soon as we reached the current, the land party would take the strain to stop the bow from swinging downstream. We would then motor upstream full ahead. The land party would heave with all their might and hopefully we would have enough control to point the bow into appropriate gaps between the rocks. In no event must the land party allow us to slip backwards, otherwise we would smash the rudder and propeller, with disastrous consequences.

Even though things went more of less according to plan, my adrenaline level was high from the moment we left the backwater. The 40 HP diesel motor, capable of delivering 45 HP for short periods, (i.e., until overheating) was put on the maximum setting, producing a tremendous racket and clouds of black smoke. Despite the increased engine noise, the main sound in the wheelhouse came from the waterfall. Huge jets of water cascaded directly onto the front deck. Fortunately the latter was fully sealed, so there was no danger of swamping, even though the visual effect was exciting.

The expert didn't mind the boat touching the rocks. His job was to avoid hitting them at speed. Since progress amounted to only a few feet per minute, the danger arose not from the forward velocity, but from the possibility of an eddy-current sweeping us suddenly sideways.

The most difficult passage involved the last boulder before the open water upstream. The angle of the towrope and current pressed the boat's forward quarter sideways against the rock, stopping progress. Attempts to steer the bow out only pushed the stern in, further increasing friction. The land team cursed, sang, joked and made bets to produce extra force, but to no avail. On board we vainly tried rocking the boat by two of us running back and forth across the roof in time to alternating rudder settings. Finally, five men climbed onto the boulder, braced their backs against the hull, feet against the rock, pushed outwards, and the vessel slid forwards again.

We accelerated into the calm water at the top of the fall amid loud cheers from the muscle men. The helmsman decreased the engine speed, the expert released the hauling line and we manoeuvred serenely to a quiet berth on an upstream beach. By the time we had moored the boat, the land crew were already drinking sugarcane liquor in a waterfront bar to celebrate the successful completion of their task.

I saved my personal celebration for the return trip. Since I now knew which channel permitted boats to pass, on completion of our excursion on the upper Rio Negro I was given the job of driving our aluminium outboard motorboat back down the rapids. (It had been taken up by truck.)To my relief, I shot the falls successfully, an exhilarating experience terminating in great relief at not adding to the impressive list of wrecks the *cachoeira* has claimed.

Above São Gabriel the Rio Negro became more mysterious. The Casiquiare Canal, a remarkable – but little known – natural link between the Orinoco and Negro rivers lay ahead of us beyond the border. The very existence of such a link was hotly disputed in Europe until the beginning of the nineteenth century when Alexander von Humboldt put it unequivocally on the map. I could feel it beckoning me. I wanted to see it for myself. Fortunately, I was able to visit it at a later date.

The frontier area was not only geographically interesting, it also attracted an exotic human fauna, such as Sabá, an immense, black trader who made it his business to know everybody on the river. We spent a night as guests on his boat, drinking and listening to his stories. With a perpetual smile, an ego proportional to his physical size, and an apparently inexhaustible supply of (and tolerance to) sugarcane liquor, he constituted for Indians a worldly counterbalance to the holiness of the Salesian missionaries.

Another personality up there on the border was a young Swiss engineer named Jean-Pierre Willomenet, who lived with his American wife and two children in a neat 15-m riverboat called "Xavante". In the boat's hold were an immense lathe, a groove-cutting machine and other precision engineering tools. Jean-Pierre travelled around, making spare parts for machines and motors. The army road builders were particularly good customers, as were traders and missionaries. Although Jean-Pierre operated mainly in Brazil, his children went to school in Colombia in order to learn Spanish.

Our expedition, too, was exotic in its own way. It may have contributed to local folklore through a bizarre musical event, stamped indelibly on my memory and possibly on Indian culture. The happening took place during what began as a routine fruit-collecting stop.

Going ashore in our usual manner, we were greeted by a Tukano Indian whose name was Pedro. He was at first very ill at ease, but when it became evident that we had nothing to do with the Salesian mission, he brightened up miraculously. He explained that his initial reticence was due to the fact that he and his Tukano friends were having a party, an activity frowned on by the missionaries. He had supposed, on seeing bearded white men, that we were from the mission and would disapprove of the festivities. Now that he knew who we were, he invited us to join in.

We accompanied Pedro into a thatched adobe hut with a beaten earth floor and sat on low, carved, wooden stools in the company of a dozen Tukano adults and their children. Our host announced that the men were going to dance. After instructions in Tukano, five men in football shorts formed a group of three and a group of two, and stomped around the room, each playing the pipes of pan. Seedpod rattles tied around the dancers' ankles provided the rhythm. What a tremendous idea this percussion system was, I thought to myself. It guaranteed that the dance steps were always in time with the musical beat.

The dance continued pleasantly, although without noticeable artistry, for several minutes. It was followed by an apparently similar dance performed by the women, dressed in shapeless old shifts. Now, Pedro declared, it was our turn to dance. We foreigners looked at each other in horror, explaining that respectable, sober, white men do not dance together – and certainly not in threes.

The Indian men performed another dance, then repeated their request that we dance. I had an idea. My guitar was in the boat. We would sing a call-and-response sea shanty with such a simple refrain that everyone could join in, even without knowing English. I fetched the instrument and invited the Brazilian crew – who up to this time were still in the vessel – to come along as vocal support. They came willing enough. They were used to my singing.

I chose the capstan song, "Haul 'em away", the chorus of which contains only four syllables and one note. Explaining the form of the song to those who understood Portuguese, I found the key on the guitar and rehearsed the refrain a few times. When all seemed as ready as possible, we launched forth:

(self)	(Tukanos, researchers and crew)
Little Lucy Locket	Haul 'em a-way
She's got an empty pocket	Haul 'em a-way
She'll keep an eye open for you	Haul 'em a-way
To me haul 'em high-o	Haul 'em a-way
To me heave away-o	Haul 'em a-way
Little Sally Skinner	Haul 'em a-way
She says she's a beginner	Haul 'em a-way
But she prefers it to her dinner	Haul 'em a-way
To me haul 'em high-o …	

…and so on, for about a hundred phrases, including repeats and ad-libs whenever my memory failed.

The hypnotic monotony of the song appealed to the Tukanos, who gave every indication of being ready for the next hundred verses. The women danced again. "Now you dance," said Pedro. Evidently, this time it would be less easy to deflect his demand.

One must remember that the Tukano request was difficult to meet, not only because of our inhibitions as men dancing together, but also because we would have to make our own music. We had no pipes of pan or rattles. We needed a non-partner dance that we could sing.

It was time for the Hokey-Cokey (also known as Hokey-Pokey), the dance, apparently from World War 2, in which, standing in a circle, "You put your right arm in/ Your right arm out/ In, out, in, out/ You shake it all about..." simply performing the actions indicated in the lyrics. Then comes a simple chorus, followed by verses with left arm, right leg, left leg, right side, left side and finally whole self. I had learned the simple routine at parties as a youngster and still don't know if the dance is English, Irish, American or Australian. Every English speaking country seems to think it is their song.

The other two scientists spoke English, so they would be able to dance if I sang and led. With three people dancing, the rest could easily follow. Everybody in the hut formed a big circle, holding hands. A touching sight: three continents – North America, Europe, and South America – united in a childish dance.

So we put our arms and legs in and out, shaking them all about, as the words dictated. Perhaps the dance is more philosophical than I realised as a child. Maybe (to quote the refrain) "that's what it's all about".

I like to think that someday an anthropologist will visit the Tukano Indians and find them still performing a version of the circular dance that our expedition taught them. His explanation of the strange steps might well run along the following lines:

"The dance apparently symbolises the ambiguous love-hate relationship between the Tukanos and Roque-Coque, the spirit of the peach palm, a tree with desirable fruit and dangerous spines. Various parts of the dancer's body are alternately attracted to and repelled by the spirit, who is so terrifying that performers shake visibly."

After dancing with the Tukanos, the return trip to Manaus was figuratively and literally downhill all the way.

Chapter 6

Fig 6. Preto Velho   WK

Settling in

Having moved to Brazil, besides finding my feet at work, I had to settle into Manaus socially. The first and most important step was to learn the Portuguese language, key to everything from banal necessities like shopping and house rental to finer points of culture and etiquette. Fortunately, in spite of its daunting appearance, Portuguese is not difficult. It is written largely as spoken, with few ambiguities, making it easy to spell words one hears and to pronounce words one reads. Once one gets started and learns the basic pronunciation rules (like what to do with the wiggly accent called tilde), one makes progress quickly.

To improve my vocabulary, I bought a guidebook of Brazil and struggled with the aid of a dictionary through all the novels mentioned in its literary section. Gradually my knowledge of the nation's authors ranged from romantic José de Alencar, one of the country's first novelists, to regional bards, such as the South's Erico Veríssimo and the Northeast's Guimarães Rosa. More recent writers included TV comedian Chico Anísio and the best-selling Brazilian author, Jorge Amado. Among my favourite books were some biting satires of Amazonian politics and history written by the local writer Márcio Souza, some of whose work, for instance "Mad Maria" and "Galvez, Emperor of Acre," is available in English.

After language, my social priorities were to learn more Brazilian music and to meet some girls. Hoping that the former might provide a framework for the latter, I looked for a music class.

One of the major cultural centres in Manaus was the French Institute, *Aliança Francesa*. (The British Council had nothing comparable.) In addition to teaching French language and culture, it sponsored shows of French artists at the Manaus Opera House and promoted French technical journals in academic institutions such as INPA. It also rented-out part of its premises to a small music school named after the Brazilian classical composer, Heitor Villa-Lobos. I enrolled in this music school for evening classes in popular guitar.

My musical ability at the time consisted principally of square and triangular

European rhythms and open harmonies. Now that I lived in Brazil, I wanted to learn the syncopated rhythms and dissonant harmonies of my new home. I soon observed that whereas many Anglo-American hits were difficult to interpret without a studio, Brazilian commercial music contained lots of unengineered arrangements suitable for casual musicians like myself.

The classes taught me that although samba was rhythmically complicated, its harmony was simple. Many sambas could be played with only three chords (often A major, B minor and E seventh); few required more than five positions. Bossa nova, in contrast, was harmonically more complicated, but rhythmically easier because it was slower. Simpler rhythm proved to be the decisive factor for me: I got to grips much more easily with bossa nova than with samba. Furthermore, as many bossa novas had English versions, I could avoid the problem of my foreign accent in Portuguese, by singing in English.

"*Garota de Ipanema*" ("Girl from Ipanema"), "*Corcovado*" ("Quiet Nights") and "*Desafinado*" ("Off Key"), all world-renowned bossa novas with well-known English versions, soon became standards in my repertoire. I particularly liked the last mentioned. It was a superb dissonant study written by Tom Jobim to vindicate chords so strange that many traditionalists considered them out-of-tune. The harmony wandered around mysteriously without resolution, never once allowing the singer the comforting support of a simple major triad.

Attending the Villa-Lobos school two evenings a week gave me an education far broader than just learning dissonant harmony. I discovered, for instance, that evening classes were often simply an excuse for girls to get out of the house. Faced with a male-dominated society, in which fathers jealously guarded their daughters, many girls enrolled in schools to have an excuse to go courting. Hence academic interest in some courses was practically non-existent.

While waiting for classes, the music students hung around in the street along with pupils from the French Institute and those of a nearby crammer college called "Einstein". The area outside the school was always full of adolescents sitting on the bonnets and bumpers of convenient cars, irrespective of ownership, discussing politics and topical themes, or simply flirting.

Through the music school's staff and students I met virtually all the professional and amateur musicians in Manaus. One person especially helpful in introducing me to other musicians was a pretty young lady named Alice. She taught piano and was fourteen years old.

Alice's precocious musical ability stemmed from a rare combination of aptitude and opportunity. Intelligence and musicality ran in her family. Her mother, soon to become a judge, had been a record-breaking, top-of-the-class law student, while her father was a professional trombone player. The teacher who had moulded Alice's musical gift was the elderly Hungarian master pianist, George Gestzi, a former student and colleague of Bela Bartok and Zoltan Kodaly. After leaving Budapest during the 1956 Hungarian uprising and working for many years in Rio de Janeiro, Gestzi had moved to Manaus late in life, when he felt a desire to use his musical skills in a culturally deprived environment. He taught at the precariously structured Manaus Conservatory, which Alice attended.

The presence of an illustrious, foreign figure like Gestzi was strangely typical of Manaus. A century ago, despite the city being situated a thousand miles up the world's mightiest jungle river, a Portuguese architect, a French theatrical designer and an Italian mural painter had built an opera house. To find a Hungarian maestro in the Conservatory seemed quite in keeping.

By the time she was fifteen, Alice and I had fallen in love and she came to live with me, creating a situation which was technically illegal, because she was so young. Mercifully, Brazilians were more concerned about happiness than with the letter of the law. Since we were happy, Alice's status as a minor was completely ignored, except by cinema proprietors, who occasionally barred her entry to adult movies. Importantly, our relationship was blessed with the goodwill of Alice's mother, who, as a professional lawyer, was well equipped to protect her daughter from unwelcome advances.

Living with Alice gave me deeper insight into my new homeland. She was constantly at hand to explain things that seemed so foreign, such as the religion sometimes referred to in English as voodoo, but more accurately described as spiritism. The cult is found throughout Brazil under several names. In Bahia, where there is an overwhelming black presence, it appears mainly as *candomblé*. In Manaus, where Indian culture is more expressive, it is usually referred to as *umbanda*. The term *macumba*, corresponding more or less to "black magic", "witchcraft" or "sorcery", is usually pejorative.

Alice told me that there were many varieties of Brazilian spiritism. They differed in detail, but common features included: (1) belief in spirits who affected daily life, (2) use of offerings to obtain favours from the spirits, (3) communication with spirits through mediums, and (4) use of white or red clothing at ceremonies. She knew a lot about the subject because her mother, despite being a lawyer, was a medium for a spirit called *Preto Velho* (the Old Black Man).

One day Alice asked me if I would mind her mother coming to our house to incorporate *Preto Velho*. Although not a religious person myself, I made no objections; the idea aroused my curiosity. In any case, I was in love, so my tolerance towards Alice and her mother was boundless. Alice explained that we must first cleanse the house spiritually, using a special torch of smoking herbs. We would also need a pipe, tobacco, sugarcane liquor and candles.

We went to one of downtown Manaus' several spiritist supply shops to obtain the necessary religious materials, my first visit to such an establishment. The shop, reeking of incense, was full of statues, potions, herbs, candles and ornaments used in rituals. A religious chant in Yoruba with an eerie drum accompaniment emanated from a vinyl record player near the cash desk.

Statues were the most eye-catching merchandise. Some of them were life size. In brightly painted alabaster they portrayed over a dozen deities. The racial diversity of the figures left no doubt about the plural origins of *umbanda*. African roots were exemplified by a statue of *Preto Velho*, a benign, wizened, white-haired black man, who sat smoking a pipe. *Ubirajara*, a red-skinned, muscular warrior, indicated Amerindian influences, while Catholicism was represented by a gory figure of Saint Sebastian, bristling with the arrows that caused his martyrdom. There was even a statue of Buddha, who reputedly helped the faithful in their business transactions.

Alice and I were looking for *vela indiana* (literally "Indian candle"), an incense made out of lavender, candle-wick and a combustible, camphorous resin from wild *breu* trees (related to frankincense). We found the material amidst packets of strange potions designed to achieve particular ends. I read some of the labels of the potions at random. One concoction protected you from envy. Another attracted money. A further one stopped your spouse from being distracted by other loves. Most common domestic problems, such as health, wealth and relationships were catered for by this eminently practical religion. However, not everything in the shop was benevolent. Candles depicting skulls and devils in red or black had a distinctly evil aspect.

As evening came, Alice and I prepared the house. We lit the *vela indiana*, blew out the flame and carried the sweet-smelling, smoking wick sequentially into each corner of every room. Then we put the pipe, tobacco, matches, open bottle of sugarcane liquor and a glass on the living-room table, which had a white tablecloth and was illuminated by two plain white candles. There was not much else in the room. We possessed very little furniture in our simple, two-bedroomed, breezeblock bungalow.

After nightfall, Alice's mother arrived, overweight, excitable and kindly. We exchanged greetings in the kitchen, so as not to enter the living room yet. She asked if the house had been spiritually cleansed and if the table had been prepared. Following affirmative answers, she suggested that we start without delay. Leaving her bags in the kitchen, she proceeded alone into the living room. I heard her light the pipe and pour a glass of liquor. Within a few minutes a man's voice, speaking antiquated Portuguese with a singsong Bahian accent, beckoned first Alice and then me.

It was striking to see the lady lawyer transformed into *Preto Velho*. Her face was screwed up into the wrinkles of an old man and she smoked the pipe and drank the strong liquor in a very natural manner. (Normally she was abstemious.) Her deep, male voice intrigued me, since the laws of physics told me that producing the low tone must have required lengthening, slackening, or increasing the density of her vocal chords. I knew of no physiological mechanism to accomplish the necessary change at will. Discounting the untransformed female body and dress – and looking only at the face and gestures – I would have believed I was talking to the Old Black Man whose statue I had seen earlier in the spiritist shop.

Preto Velho was a benign entity and what he had to say to me through Alice's mother was principally well-wishing. He told me that Alice was a very special person and that I should take good care of her. He expressed satisfaction that he was visiting a peaceful household where good tobacco and sugarcane liquor were to be found. He also said that he and I had much in common, because his ancestors, like me, had left their home country to travel across the ocean to live in Brazil. He wished me well in my new house and in my new country.

Alice and I left the room and soon after her mother came out too, looking once more like the professional woman-about-town who had arrived at the kitchen door half-an-hour earlier. The medium showed no signs of inebriation. We chatted for a while in the kitchen. Then the visit came to an end. Alice blew out the candles and we drove her mother home. No one seeing us in the car would have imagined that we were coming from a rendezvous with the spirit world. Some important aspects of Brazilian culture are simply not obvious to the casual observer.

Life with Alice was full of memorable experiences. One of the most delightful was dropping her at convent school every morning. There was something deliciously subversive about delivering one's lover into the hands of a set of nuns, who, for all their knowledge of the three R's, knew less about men than did the girls they taught. Dressed in her prim school uniform and carrying her books, she would get out of the car looking as if butter wouldn't melt in her mouth. She adored being more worldly wise than her schoolteachers. She drew strength from this superiority whenever she was having academic problems.

Through Alice I met a lot of dedicated young musicians. Because she was not interested in pop music, our circle included mainly classical and ethnic musicians. The latter, whom I liked the best, were artists trying to find or create music expressing Amazonian culture. They most often performed at government-sponsored festivals at the Opera House. Since I too was investigating the music of my new surroundings, I felt a lot in common with them. Out of solidarity, Alice and I went to virtually all concerts by groups involved in the cultural quest. Most of the ensembles had Indian names. One called Tariri was particularly successful.

Searching for cultural roots was a novelty to me. Coming from a society with a well-documented past, I never imagined one could have no roots, or not be able to find them. Amazonia's late entry into world affairs made the search for ancient music difficult. Music was already preserved in print in Europe at a time when the Amazon was still in the Stone Age. For instance, the melody "Greensleaves" was published in William Ballet's Lute Book in 1580. At that time no Europeans had yet travelled up the Amazon and only two expeditions (Orellana, 1541 and Lope de Aguirre, 1559) had come downstream. I quickly realized that most of the Amazon's music was not much more than a century old, coinciding with the rubber boom influx of northeasterners and their coastal *forró* rhythms.

Yet groups like Tariri were looking for something other than *forró*. Their problem was that when they eliminated the northeastern component from Amazonian music, there was precious little material from Indian sources to fill the gap. Amazonian Indians had undifferentiated societies, in which virtually all individuals of a particular age and sex performed exactly the same tasks. With the exception of medicine men, no specialised professional groups evolved – specifically, there were no full-time musicians. This factor, combined with a lack of written tradition and the absence of recording techniques, made the Indian musical heritage poor.

Yet, despite the shaky ethnomusicological base, groups like Tariri always produced an emotive sound. Expressive percussion creating forest noises compensated for the lack of Indian tunes. The long, woven, Indian rattle, *pau de chuva* (literally "rain pole"), imparted a humid, rainy feel. The wobble-board imitated whooping tree frogs. The musical rasp evoked croaking toads. Ocarina whistles, made by Indians from various hollow nuts, reproduced the reedy calls of ibises and anis. The amplified sound of water poured rhythmically from one glass to another duplicated the noise of canoe paddles, while a synthesiser, hardly a folk instrument, buzzed away discreetly, portraying insects.

The songs, composed by the musicians themselves, were usually sad. They typically lamented forest destruction and the dangers and poverty of life in rural Amazonia. The melancholic tunes were frequently in the Dorian mode or in minor keys and often had a 6/8 time signature. They were impossible to dance to, which gave them a certain erudite quality. I longed for happier, faster numbers, but the composers found themselves in a dilemma: if they wrote a lively song, it always spilled over into the popular *forró* idiom they were trying to avoid.

Whether to see ethnic musicians, like Tariri, or to see classical artists, I always enjoyed accompanying Alice to the theatre (the Manaus Opera House). It satisfied me immensely just to sit in the red velvet seats and look at the stage's front curtain, on which was a huge bucolic painting depicted a stylised meeting of the waters: on the left, the Rio Solimões; on the right, the Rio Negro. These two rivers met in the centre of the curtain, forming the Amazon, ready, as it were, to flow out into the orchestra stalls. Iara, a water goddess portrayed with distinctly European features, reclined lasciviously at the confluence, surrounded by aquatic satyrs, in a landscape considerably more rococo than tropical. Since performances always started late, I had plenty of time to admire the picture before the curtain went up. That's why I know it so well.

Another pastime, while waiting for the show to begin, was to put my head back and look at the large, central, glass chandelier from Europe and, beyond it, the scene painted on the inside of the roof-dome. This picture's perspective, inspired by the base of the Eiffel Tower, portrayed four columns converging in a baroque blue heaven. Three of the views between the columns represented respectively music, dance and tragedy. The fourth – and easiest to see because it was closest to the stage – was an homage to Carlos Gomes, Brazil's first symphonic composer. Like murals in other parts of the theatre, the work on the inside of the dome was by the Italian painter, Domenico de Angelis.

Powerful central air-conditioning increased the joy of simply sitting and looking around the theatre. Although not present in the original project, air-conditioning made the Opera House one of the few closed environments in Manaus with a comfortably cool temperature. The compact nature of the auditorium, around 600 places, contributed to the cooling plant's effectiveness. Chilled air also increased the public's comfort indirectly, in that it had allowed the original, cane-bottomed chairs, which were airy but hard, to be replaced by softer seats upholstered in red velvet. Performers too benefited from the reduced temperature; ballet must have been particularly strenuous to perform without air-conditioning.

It surprised me that in many European languages, including English, French and German the building was referred to as an "Opera House", whereas its Brazilian name, *Teatro Amazonas* clearly meant "Amazonas-State Theatre". Theatre was almost certainly the more accurate description for several reasons. Firstly, the list of companies performing in the period 1886 -1937 contained as many drama groups as opera companies. Secondly, of these opera companies many performed operettas rather than grand opera. Thirdly, the Greek masks that ornamented the pillars inside the theatre bore the names of more playwrights and poets than of composers. In all probability the enormous travelling time and considerable health risk discouraged many famous opera companies from making tours up the Amazon at the time of the rubber boom; a troupe in 1900 lost nine dead, six through yellow fever. In spite of what locals said, Caruso never sang in Manaus.

Besides supporting our musical friends, Alice and I patronised most artistic expression centred on the theatre, including performances by the two local ballet schools, one classical and the other modern. Both catered for the daughters and occasionally sons of well-to-do families. They put on excellent shows, sometimes with invited professionals from the South. Although not a connoisseur of dance, I enjoyed seeing girls from the high society in the romantic setting of the Opera House. We also attended regular painting and wood-sculpture exhibitions held in the foyer by local artists.

With music, dance, painting and carving there was a lot of artistic activity in Manaus. The problem was always to find out about it. Even the in-crowd were often ill-informed. Many people – visitors and residents alike – missed events because they did not know about them. This situation continues to some extent today, but at least the newly recruited Amazonas Philharmonic Orchestra has an electronic mailing list that efficiently announces its forthcoming activities.

In comparison to the erudition of Alice's contacts in the Teatro Amazonas, my own artistic endeavours as a singer-guitarist, were plebeian. Nevertheless, determined to make progress, I took a weekend job making background music in the restaurant of the then recently-opened Novotel, situated on the edge of the industrial district of Manaus. The contract called for music three hours per night on Fridays and Saturdays. For the first time in my life I bought an amplifier and a microphone. Previously, in France and in folk clubs, I had performed without amplification.

My performances at the Novotel consisted of a curious pot-pourri of what I could play, rather than what the public wanted. The bulk of my repertoire was still non-Brazilian, so I put together a show with songs in various languages, exploiting the high status value Brazilians attribute to international travel. The first night, I sang in English, French, German, Spanish and Portuguese. At the end of the session a trim young woman dining alone asked me if I could sing something in Italian. Unfortunately I had to disappoint her. However, I have to thank her in retrospect, because the memory of her good looks later inspired me to learn enough Italian to add a couple of songs in that language to my repertoire.

At the Novotel, the mood on Fridays differed from that on Saturdays. Friday was livelier, with more diverse customers, including groups of friends, work colleagues and men with girls who were not their wives. In contrast, Saturday's customers consisted mainly of families or steady couples. Some groups were very large, particularly when celebrating birthdays or other special occasions. The number of diners varied cyclically. At the end of each month, just after salaried workers had been paid, the restaurant was full. The following week there would be fewer customers. Thereafter, customers would be successively less numerous as family finances dwindled until the next payday – when the pattern repeated itself.

Most Friday evenings I invited a couple of Brazilian musicians to join me. This meant sharing my remuneration with them, but was more fun and gave me the opportunity of learning Brazilian music during the gig. Particularly, I could observe which numbers were popular with the public, something impossible to pick up by just listening to records.

Playing at the Novotel introduced me to a lot of the poorer districts of Manaus. If I didn't use my car, I rode the workers' bus home, along with waiters, dishwashers, receptionists, porters and others. The homeward odyssey started shortly after midnight, as soon as staff had clocked off. The bus travelled for two hours through practically all of Manaus' urban sprawl, dropping one person here, another person there. Always the penultimate passenger to alight, I had plenty of opportunity to appreciate the huge extent of the suburbs, most of which I would never have visited otherwise.

Irrespective of which poor suburb we were in, the view illuminated by the headlights of the bus was remarkably uniform: wooden or raw brick houses with corrugated zinc roofs, the shutters already closed for the night; badly drained ground with lots of surface water, both clean and foul; dangerous potholes in the thoroughfare; precarious street lighting supplemented by a few naked bulbs shining outside individual homes; isolated trees, such as mangoes, Indian almonds and hibiscus, growing valiantly in the beaten earth between houses; garbage strewn along the wayside; small bars with snooker tables and loud music; young lovers cuddling in shadows, stretching out time before confronting parental wrath.

Manaus' poor districts were, however, much less desperate than the shantytowns of Rio de Janeiro and São Paulo. In south Brazil I had seen shacks made of plastic sheets or cardboard, whereas in Manaus most people managed to make a house with wooden boards. In the Amazon rough-sawn timber was cheap and abundant. In addition, Manaus had plenty of land stretching to the north and east, so that the city was expanding horizontally, relieving the pressure that would otherwise have pushed land prices beyond the reach of the poor.

After five months as a restaurant troubadour, travel commitments in my research job forced me to terminate the Novotel contract. The hotel naturally engaged another musician, with the result that when I was free to resume playing, no vacancy existed. Musically it was time to move on. Despite knowing a lot of songs in Portuguese, I was still concerned about my English accent, a problem that could be solved if I played in a band in which a local person sang. I decided to try this solution.

The first musical ensemble I joined was called *Os Apóstolos do Som* (the Apostles of Music). As the name implies, the group belonged to a local Catholic church. The Apostles were one of the city's best-equipped bands. They owned excellent instruments, purchased with money donated by Canadian missionaries. However, the generous external finance had created problems. With such marvellous equipment, the musicians wanted to become a major commercial pop group, whereas the church wanted to limit the band's activities to religious music and social programmes within the community.

My first appearance with the Apostles turned out to be their last show. They split up soon afterwards and I moved on to a more modestly equipped group called *Caferana* (literally, "False Coffee"). The new band's intriguing name referred to a forest bush with flexible branches used to make strong fishing rods. Like the Apostles, Caferana had church origins. However, although Caferana occasionally played for church events, it was staunchly independent. It had already survived several difficult periods. Hence the name: like a fishing rod made from the *caferana* bush, the band had been put under pressure, but had not split.

When I met Caferana, it consisted of five members: Frank (vocals), Vítor (guitar), Carvalho (conical drum), Pedro (shaker) and Zé (bass drum). It was the most basic of all line-ups, consisting of voice, harmony, rhythm and no frills. Discouragingly, it already contained my instrument, the guitar. So I wondered what I could contribute. Fortunately, I had two attributes the group wanted. One was a car to transport the musicians and instruments. The other was a good-quality vocal amplifier. Since Caferana's preferred musical style was *forró*, which required a triangle, it was agreed that I would join the group as triangle player, at least while I learned the repertoire. Frank had previously played the instrument while singing. With my arrival, he had his hands free to put more corporal expression into the vocals, or to play the tambourine.

We set out, not exactly looking for fame and fortune, but at least for fun, booze and pocket money. On these terms there was plenty of work. Suddenly we became very busy, with engagements at parties, bars and clubs. The last-mentioned, which are nothing like English clubs, require some explanation, in view of the fact that they provided the gigs we liked best.

Mainstream Brazilian leisure revolved around sport and the beach. In Manaus, which had only a couple of seasonal river beaches, swimming pools had to make up for the lack of coastline. Many clubs, consisting essentially of a swimming pool, sports grounds, bar and restaurant, had sprung up to cater for the recreational needs of middle-class families and their friends. The clubs were particularly active on Sundays, especially from early morning to mid-afternoon: kids played in the swimming pool, girls sunbathed, young men played ball games, and sooner or later everyone ate, drank and danced in the restaurant, the latter usually a thatched shelter open to the four winds.

Of the many clubs in Manaus, some were independent; others belonged to factories or workers' associations. They were busiest in the dry season, when there was plenty of sunshine. In this period they hired bands for background music and dancing. Playing at clubs was, as far as Caferana was concerned, an attractive, relatively undemanding job. No late nights were involved, so it was not as tiring as playing in bars. The members of the band could go swimming when not playing, and at the end of the gig a good meal appeared from the restaurant.

I was glad of the demands made on my time by Caferana, since Alice had recently left me to continue her musical studies at the University of Brasília. My involvement in the band helped fill the enormous gap left by her departure.

Alice was not the only talented young musician to leave Manaus. Our friends, Pedro Sampaio (keyboard), Nilton Amaral (violin), Adriano Giffoni (bass guitar), Elson Johnson (bassoon) and Francisco Ferreira (French Horn) moved almost simultaneously to various southern cities to continue their musical studies at higher level. The situation reminded me of the way a generation ago Australian musicians, as soon as they began to be successful, moved to Europe, leaving their domestic cultural scene impoverished.

After becoming a virtuoso triangle player, I looked for new horizons and, inspired by the memory of Alice at the keyboard, bought an electric piano. Caferana expanded, accommodating not only the piano, but also a dynamic lady singer, Cristina. We were now a lively, happy, seven-piece band. However, most nights we played with considerably more than seven musicians, since the percussion section absorbed numerous unremunerated friends playing for fun and beer. Cowbells, temple blocks, rasp, tambourine, *repinique* (very small drum), congas, frying pan and maracas were instruments added from time to time.

For nearly two years we played one, two or three engagements each weekend, usually Friday night, Saturday night and Sunday morning. They were happy times, from which some burning memories remain. Principal among these is the recollection of how exciting our good performances were; the public incapable of resisting our invitation to dance; the noise deafening; Frank and Cristina jigging and gyrating as they intoned the joys and sorrows of life and love; Carvalho creating wild rhythms on the conical drum, his fingers covered with Band-Aids to prevent blistering; Zé, the oldest member of the group, solid, macho, beating out an unshakable foundation rhythm on the bass-drum; myself on keyboard, following Vítor's guitar harmony; and Pedro, getting pleasantly drunk, but indefatigable on the shaker, which he would play from the dance-floor if he found a pretty girl to partner.

Also unforgettable was the wind-down at the end of late-night sessions. First we would sit around a table with a round of drinks and divide the pay between the band members. Then most of us would go and blow our income at *Tia* (Aunt) Dica's soup kitchen on Constantino Nery Avenue. There, in the company of all-night taxi drivers and other night people, we ate greasy marrowbone soup with bread rolls, and chatted until dawn.

One thing I learned with Caferana, besides *forró* music, was the difficulty of organising half-a-dozen Brazilians to be on time. The two hours immediately before a gig were normally a chaotic mixture of running around after stray equipment and long waits for unready musicians. We were habitually late for engagements. However, after a while I discovered that Brazilians had evolved ways of dealing with the delays inherent in their system; organisers who expected an event to start around 11.00 PM simply announced it for 9.00.

Caferana's good times had to peak sometime. Yet, true to the resilience implied in its name, the group didn't splinter irreparably. Even today we occasionally meet for the joy of playing together. The decline came quickly. Unavoidable travels with INPA kept me away from the group for a couple of months. At the same time Cristina left to get married, while Carvalho and Frank both moved to more remote parts of the city. When I returned, Caferana was too spread out to play on a regular basis.

I had given up my rented house while I was travelling and on return I had nowhere to live. So I went to lodge with my research technician, Nascimento. He lived in the Compensa district of town and was the lead singer in a band called Cascavel, which played at weekends in a bar near his home. He invited me to join his band and I accepted.

Joining Cascavel was different from joining Caferana. Cascavel didn't need my amplifier or my car. I didn't have to start on the triangle. When I sat down at the piano on my first night with them, I already knew the repertoire. My apprenticeship was over.

Chapter 7

Fig 7. Andanças de Ciganos' Carnival Parade
WK

Carnival

Carnival is as symbolic of Brazil as are nuts and coffee. Although it is celebrated in many other lands – particularly those with strong Catholic and black heritages – nowhere else does it reach the importance it has in Brazil. It involves people from all walks of life, in all parts of the country. Every New Year, not much work gets done in Brazil until carnival is over.

On a sombre note the Brazilian government often announced unpleasant economic measures at carnival time. Despite the festivities, or perhaps because of them, one could expect news of wage freezes, price and tax increases, devaluation and so on, as the regime hoped the bitter pill of austerity passed unnoticed in the candy-floss of merry-making.

For musicians carnival was an opportunity to make money. It was the main date in a dance band's calendar; any musical group could find work. Every neighbourhood, social club and workers' organisation held a carnival party. Add to that: commercial bars, hotels, restaurants and private parties; and the demand for live music was enormous. The better bands were booked up months in advance.

I was playing with Cascavel, a band that was far from being the best in town. Nevertheless, in spite of our limited musical prowess, shortly after New Year we started to receive invitations to play for carnival parties. At first we were non-committal in our replies, knowing that our musicians were not unanimous in what they wanted to do. However, we finally had to make some concrete plans. To discuss the matter, we sat around a table full of beer at the end of a gig. This was our usual decision-making procedure.

The first task was to find carnival's date, which varied from year to year and could fall in February or March. We finally found a calendar – a much easier option than trying to find the Sunday after the first vernal full moon and then counting back forty days. Each member of the band argued in favour of whatever plan was most convenient for him personally. As the discussion proceeded, emotions ran high, with fatigue and drink making some of us aggressive, intolerant and loud.

Joaquim, the rhythm guitarist, having no income except what he earned as a musician, favoured playing anywhere and everywhere. Besides money he stressed benefits such as fun, excitement, girls, drink and prestige.

Evaldo, the conga-drum percussionist, came from the interior and wanted to visit his family during the holiday. Consequently he emphasised carnival's disadvantages: gigs were long and tiring, possibly involving playing until dawn five nights in succession. Even if we finished earlier on some nights, the last party would certainly continue until daybreak on Ash Wednesday.

Since I had independent plans for carnival, I supported the arguments against playing. I mentioned further problems: mixing scantily clad women with drunken macho men was a sure recipe for trouble; crowded dance floors meant that jostling was inevitable, easily leading to violence. Scuffles could develop into raging battles. Although we were experienced enough to habitually protect ourselves by positioning the band far from the exit (so that in the event of a fight dancers fleeing in panic did not stampede through the musical instruments), the perils of disorderliness could not be totally eliminated.

A couple of our musicians with a strong preference for *forró* rhythm stated categorically that although they were happy to play a mixed programme, they did not want to perform gigs consisting entirely of carnival marches and polkas. They also pointed out (rightly) that carnival music sounded best with brass instruments, which our band lacked. We did, however, discuss the possibility of contracting a trumpet player.

Eventually, with no way of preventing those who wanted to go their own way from doing so, and with the remaining core not big enough play alone, we decided that Cascavel would not play as a group for carnival and that each musician would be free to pursue his own plans. The outcome suited me well in two ways. Firstly, there was not only a seasonal demand for music, but also a seasonal demand for musical equipment; I earned more by hiring out my vocal amplifier to a well-known band, than I would have done using it with Cascavel in a poor bar. Secondly, I had been invited to participate in a carnival parade and could now do so.

My daytime job in Manaus was researching renewable energy sources at the National Institute for Amazonian Research (INPA). Just before carnival the prototype of a small, floating river-turbine I had designed was successfully tested in the Amazon. The invention looked like a multi-bladed windmill, which, instead of being installed on a tower facing the wind, was hung in the water beneath floats facing the river flow. The blades turned in the current, just like a windmill turned in the breeze, driving a generator. I hoped that such a machine would one day enable isolated inhabitants of the banks of the Amazon to make their own electricity. During tests the prototype produced the target power (1 KW) at standard Brazilian voltage and frequency (110 V, 60 Hz), being in all probability the first hydroelectricity to be generated by the Amazon. I was overjoyed at the results. Consequently, when my workmate, Ruth, invited me to join her in a carnival parade, I gladly accepted, welcoming the chance to express my elation.

Ruth came from a neighbourhood on the east side of Manaus called Cachoeirinha. Its name meant "Little Waterfall" and referred to a cascading stream now culverted under urban sprawl. Cachoeirinha was a spacious area with a bohemian atmosphere. It was well endowed with bars and dance halls and was home to one of the city's best carnival parade groups, Andanças de Ciganos. Ruth belonged this group and wanted me to join it too.

The Manaus carnival parade, modelled on that of Rio de Janeiro, was a competition between well-organised teams, called samba schools, which competed against each other within groups of approximately the same standard. Group 1 contained the best schools; group 2 the not so good. However, if a collection of people wanted to parade at a less sophisticated level, they could form a simpler unit called a block. Blocks competed against each other in a division separate from schools.

Andanças de Ciganos, now a fully-fledged samba school, was at that time still a block. Intrigued to know what I was getting involved in, I went one night with Ruth to one of its practice sessions. Everything was remarkably well organised. Some participants had been preparing all though the year since the end of last year's carnival. They had been busy fund-raising, choosing a theme for the parade and writing an appropriate samba. Most people, however, had been active only since New Year.

The most important tasks in the warm-up to carnival were: (1) to get as many people as possible into the parade, (2) to practice the theme-samba, so that everyone could sing it with gusto, (3) to perfect the precision of the drum band, (4) to publicise details of the uniform, so that members could find materials and make their costumes, (5) to build the carnival floats and other artefacts which would decorate the procession.

Meetings were held on Saturdays at lunchtime, on Sundays at 4.30 PM, on Thursdays at 8.30 PM, and on other nights as carnival approached. The venue was the block's own large cement-surfaced plot of land in the otherwise built-up neighbourhood. The sale of drinks from freezers in a small hut enlivened the activities and boosted funds.

Further money-raising took place at the Saturday lunchtime meetings, the principal activity of which was the sale and consumption of home-made *feijoada*, Brazil's famous pork and black-bean casserole. Ruth explained to me that *feijoada* originally came from the states of Minas Gerais and Rio de Janeiro, but was now popular all over Brazil. In the same way that in France snails had evolved from a dish for peasants into a delicacy for the rich, so *feijoada*, once a food for slaves, was now found in fancy restaurants. It contained the parts of a pig that in former times the Brazilian nobility discarded and gave to their slaves, notably the snout, ears, tail and feet. Throughout Brazil, Saturday lunchtime was the traditionally time to eat it.

The beans for the Cachoeirinha concoction were soaked all Friday night, then boiled slowly with the pork for several hours on Saturday morning. The result was deliciously soft and creamy. Rice, manioc flour, kale, barbecued spare-ribs and fresh oranges accompanied the pork-and-beans. Habitués planned no activity after eating, as the meal lay notoriously heavy on the stomach in the typical afternoon temperature of 35C (95F). The effect was doubly soporific if one had a few drinks.

The late afternoon sessions on Sundays attracted people coming back from daytime leisure activities at clubs, weekend houses, river beaches and local urban venues. Many participants arrived more or less inebriated. Nevertheless, they still had plenty of energy to sing the theme-samba and dance. The drum band formed the centre of the action. Around it swarmed the dancers, some in shorts, T-shirts and sandals, some still in bathing costumes and barefoot. On the perimeter of the group, young men and women indulged in light-hearted courting, known as *paquera*, roughly translated in English as "chatting up". However, whereas in England men traditionally "chat up" women, in Brazil both sexes are equally active in *paquera*, which is a very popular pastime.

At one of the sessions, a girl in high carnival spirits showed me the basic techniques of *paquera*. She didn't worry about the truth, just told me what I wanted to hear. First she declared how handsome I was. Then she said how much she had been looking forward to meeting me; how much she was going to miss me; that next time there was a party, boat trip or barbecue, she would invite me; that she recently dreamed about me, and so on. When she ran out of phrases, she started again and repeated the whole rigmarole. She brushed imaginary hair out of my eyes and held the tips of my fingers lightly, swaying my arms gently. Reflecting Brazilians' love of perfume, she took a deep breath near my neck, like mothers do with babies, and told me how beautiful I smelled. She laughed and smiled a lot during the performance. It was great fun and quite uncompromising.

The Thursday night meeting consisted mainly of a practice session for the drum band, an ensemble of about eighty percussionists, all male, with instruments ranging in size from giant, deeply cylindrical bass drums *(surdos)*, through various sizes of side drums, to six-inch-diameter, one-skinned, treble drums *(repiniques)* used for counter-rhythm. Each drum had a particular function, but basically, if one imagines Terezinha and me dancing samba at Blondie's Bar, I swaggered to the beat of the *surdo*, whereas she vibrated to the *repinique*.

Besides drums, the band played two other types of Brazilian percussion instruments. One of these was the shaker, a metal cylinder containing loose lead shot, often improvised at parties by putting grains of rice in a used beer can. The other was the rasp, in its quiet form a ridged bamboo cylinder stroked with a stick, but in this case a spring scraped with a metal rod to produce a loud noise through a horn.

One instrument typical of carnival in Rio, but absent from Andanças' band, was the *cuíca*, an ingenious device looking like a small drum with a rod attached to the centre of the skin. I tried to play one later in South Brazil: sliding the rod through my fingers produced a loud, laughing, tuneable grunt. For some reason *cuícas* were not common in Manaus.

The drum band took its role very seriously, since in the parade points were awarded for its performance. The percussionists practised regularly and intently. They had special licks for opening and closing their show, as well as for the theme-samba and for instrumental solos. By the time carnival arrived, they were the eighty best-disciplined Brazilians I ever met. The power and precision of their rhythm could turn even newcomers like me into inspired *sambistas*.

When I joined Andanças de Ciganos, carnival was not far away, leaving me little time to make a costume. However, several other would-be revellers were in the same situation, so we worked communally to locate and buy cheap supplies of blue satin, gold Lurex and other exotic requirements. We looked for seamstresses who could work at short notice. Little old ladies with ancient treadle sewing machines were discovered in muddy back streets and hastily contracted. They worked very fast. Used to the job, they saved time by sartorial short cuts, such as making trousers pyjama-style (to eliminate zips and buttons) and waistcoats without backs (because they were covered by the jackets). They charged next to nothing for their services, taking obvious pleasure in helping younger people to have fun. A wonderful spirit of pulling-together pervaded Cachoeirinha, with everyone cooperating to make sure that the block put on a good show.

While revellers busied themselves making costumes, the Manaus municipal authorities prepared the parade area in Avenida Djalma Batista, the main avenue leading out of town on the north side. They closed the road to traffic, decorated it with large, coloured lanterns and built admission-free terraced benches along it on both sides. They installed powerful floodlights, the effectiveness of which was increased by painting the surface of the road white. Getting as much light as possible at ground level was important for TV crews filming the event.

In addition to the official installations, an army of street vendors erected temporary villages of refreshment stalls around all access points to the carnival parade area. In one such conglomeration was the stall of my good friend, Sandoval. He and practically all his relatives lived near the starting point of the parade in a crowded string of houses built in his father's back yard in Avenida Djalma Batista.

As they did every year, Sandoval's family constructed a simple bar in front of their home to sell refreshments to the carnival public. The men sold beer and sugarcane liquor, the women skewers of barbecued meat. The stall functioned non-stop throughout carnival weekend until daybreak on Ash Wednesday. Most of the profits were drunk instantly by the clan, whose principal aim was not to make money, but to have a good time watching the parades and meeting passers-by. There were probably fifty similar makeshift bars along the block, not to mention other temporary booths selling popcorn, candy and carnival knick-knacks.

Andanças de Ciganos' procession was scheduled for 8.00 PM on carnival Saturday, part of a long programme which included the parades of many other groups. We planned a last, brief rehearsal in Cachoeirinha at around 4.00 PM and would then proceed to the competition area as night fell.

At about 2.30 PM I went to Ruth's house in Cachoeirinha to get ready. Her family, like that of Sandoval (and for the same economic reasons), lived in a row of houses built in an ancestor's long back yard perpendicular to the road. When I arrived, the dependencies were full of young men and women in various stages of dress, with seamstresses making last minute adjustments to costumes.

Since *Andanças de Ciganos* means "Gypsy Wanderings", our costumes were inspired by gypsy attire. However, real-life gypsy men were never so dashing, nor gypsy women so scantily clad as those in Cachoeirinha. Tip-to-toe the men's costume comprised: white straw hat with a red organdie band; blue satin jacket with red organdie sleeves and gold trimmings; red neckerchief; gold Lurex waistcoat; blue satin bolero trousers with gold Lurex trims; white leather shoes. The women wore: a gypsy headscarf fringed with gold charms; gold Lurex bikini top; thigh-revealing, see-through skirt of variously coloured nylon scarves hanging from a belt; lots of beads and bangles; sparkling gold ballet shoes. Make-up for both sexes was exaggeratedly heavy, with glitter on the face, as well as on women's shoulders, arms, backs, cleavage, midriff and legs.

By the time we were ready to leave for the 4.00 PM last rehearsal, I looked like a gold-sprayed Morris dancer, but Ruth, whom I had never seen out of working clothes before, was stunning; the glitter on extensive areas of newly-revealed, smooth, mid-brown skin clamoured for attention, which I would have given undividedly, if it weren't for the fact that she had many nubile sisters, cousins and girl-friends, equally bent on showing themselves off to best advantage. From that day on, Ruth never looked quite the same in a lab-coat.

From Ruth's house it was only a short distance to the block's practice ground.

A gang of us walked there together, receiving shouts of approval and encouragement from passers-by. When we arrived, the scene was a shimmering rainbow of red, blue and gold. Almost four hundred fairy-tale gypsies were dancing, talking and drinking. However, in general people were trying not to get too excited. The idea was to warm up slowly, without becoming tired or drunk too soon. A long night lay ahead of us.

It was the first time that we had assembled all the ingredients of our parade simultaneously. Not only were all the dancers and percussionists present, but previously unseen carnival floats and other effects made their appearance. We lined the whole assembly up in the appropriate order and noted our relative positions.

A carnival parade had to have a theme. That year the theme of Andanças de Ciganos' parade was homage to the recently-deceased Brazilian poet and singer, Vinícius de Moraes. He was the internationally famous author of the poem "Girl from Ipanema", which, accompanied by beautiful dissonant music by Tom Jobim, became probably the most famous song of the bossa nova era. As a life-long Bohemian, much of whose work extolled the beauty of Brazilian women and the necessity to live passionately, Vinícius was an ideal theme for a carnival parade.

To illustrate aspects of Vinícius' life, a carnival float about 20-ft square had been constructed. On it stood a giant, glittering guitar surrounded by a bevy of shapely, bikini-clad young ladies, representing the girls on Ipanema beach. The float was mounted on castors and pushed by hand. (The regulations prohibited motorisation.) Further symbols related to the theme were displayed on allegoric staffs used by the dancers. Every participant, including me, received a pole topped by a colourful giant polystyrene representation of a musical note, treble clef or guitar. During the parade, as we danced, we each waved our pole, so as to produce the maximum amount of colourful movement for spectators.

A second float, basically a high, mobile dance platform, transported our nominal leader, the Queen-of-the-Block, a girl chosen for her beauty and skill at dancing samba. Following the tradition copied from Rio de Janeiro, Andanças de Ciganos looked for a *mulata* (dark girl with African and European blood) to be Queen-of-the Block. They considered that *mulatas* best performed the sensual gyrations that samba required.

To the chagrin of local carnival organisers, *mulatas* were rare in Manaus. The main component of the city's genetic mix was Indian; white and black traits occurred in much smaller measure. Despite the scarcity of *mulatas*, Andanças de Ciganos managed to find a startlingly attractive girl with shining, flawless, dark-brown skin, wavy black hair and the vibrant bottom desired in lady *sambistas*. Named Rosineide, she worked in a local bank. Dancing on top of the float, twelve feet off the ground, dressed only in a diamond tiara, silver-sequinned bikini and high-heeled, crystal shoes, she looked tempting enough to lead an army of saints to damnation. The fact that the carnival judges awarded her points for her allure indicated that south of the equator sensuality was relished, not avoided. There are few Brazilian saints.

The group of dancers to which I was assigned occupied a position behind Rosineide and in front of the drum band, a location that allowed me to enjoy both at close quarters. However, the rehearsal was short and subdued, with organisers principally checking the block's overall appearance and reminding us of the basic rules: stay in formation; keep smiling, singing and dancing; don't bunch up or spread out; and don't get tired before the start. We sang the theme-samba a couple of times, then relaxed, saving our energy for the competition. The crews pushing the floats set off for the parade's starting point, while the rest of us waited for transport.

At 5.30 PM. two buses arrived for the dancers and a truck came for the drum band. A quick mental calculation showed me that everyone could be transported only if there were over a hundred and thirty people per vehicle. Something approaching this loading density was achieved, but when it became physically impossible to fit anyone else in, those remaining simply set off walking. Packing the revellers into vehicles increased their excitement, producing much ribald male shouting and girlish laughter. The drum band played loudly as its truck pulled away, while in the buses raucous singing of the theme-samba was accompanied by beating out its rhythm on the seats, roof, windows, handrails and anything else that would make a racket.

When we approached the parade area, traffic was already jammed. Parked cars lined both sides of the main road and side streets, but arriving motorists were still vainly trying to find spaces close to the action. A dense, happy crowd of spectators, revellers and street vendors flowed slowly around the immobile vehicles. After our bus had remained stationary for a few minutes, we realised that it would not advance again in the near future. So we alighted and continued on foot in the milling throng. I headed for Sandoval's bar, where I knew I could count on convivial company and cost price liquor while waiting to parade.

Making for the bar turned out to be a wise decision, since news soon came through that the programme was running two hours late, due to accumulated delays. Although points were awarded for punctuality, everyone, including the spectators, regarded bad timekeeping as inevitable. In fact the impossibility of keeping to schedules seemed to make people more carefree; they seemed to rejoice in knowing that they were not constrained by time. The public waited patiently for each procession and enjoyed it whenever it arrived.

There was, in any case, plenty in the passing scene to occupy one's attention. Those revellers whose processions had already finished mingled with those getting ready, in a strange mixture of gladiators, pirates, Incas, Tarzans, Indians, gypsies, sheikhs and other stereotypes. Drunks danced in extrovert euphoria, while hairy-legged men with balloon breasts paraded in ill-fitting frocks and glamour-girl wigs. Make-believe cameramen and monsters perambulated through the crowd and, of course, there were the friends and pretty girls that make any public occasion agreeable.

Finally, just after 10.00 PM, instead of the scheduled 8.00, our moment came. Last gulps were drunk from bottles of whisky, beer and sugarcane liquor. Some participants sniffed handkerchiefs soaked in the illegal but widespread ether-containing spray, *lança-perfume*, the carnival dancer's quick fix. We formed our ranks and awaited the band's introductory rap. After a powerful crescendo the drums reached the *fortissimo* first beat of our song, on which note the revellers started dancing like demons, waving their poles wildly and singing at the tops of their voices.

A thunderous salvo of firecrackers resounded as Andanças de Ciganos' joyful procession burst into the competition zone. The explosions and the din of the drum band deafened us, while the glare of floodlights on white asphalt dazzled us. Smoke drifting across from the fireworks added to the sensory assault, briefly enveloping the parade in a glowing white fog so bright and dense that I could only see the dancers near me. With no reference points, I felt we were in the sky, dancing on the clouds.

My floating-on-air feeling may have been an illusion caused by the noise, light and smoke. It could also have been the result of a few drinks and presence of *lança-perfume* in the air. I don't know. But when, through the thinning haze, Rosineide's solid curves reappeared gyrating sensually above us, she too was a mixture of fact and fantasy. The magic of carnival had started: dreams and reality were becoming indistinguishable.

Chapter 8

Fig 8. Giant Amazon Water Lilies

CR

Party in the Interior

The period following carnival was quiet, as befitted Lent, and for a few weekends the Cascavel Band, including me, remained inactive. However, after Easter the demand for live music increased and we started playing again. One of the new requests for making music came from the hamlet of Manaquiri, situated several hours boat ride up the Amazon from Manaus. Organisers of amateur football in that remote community wanted a band to perform at a party to celebrate the end of their league championship. Their cup-final match was to take place on a Saturday in late April and they planned to hold their party immediately afterwards. It sounded like an interesting gig.

Many minute towns like Manaquiri were scattered with different degrees of isolation along the Amazon and its tributaries. Together with the land around them they formed a social unit called *o interior* (the interior), a somewhat pejorative term for any inland place that was not a major city. The prospect of playing in the interior appealed to most of Cascavel's musicians, some of whom were born there; it evoked travel and excitement. The only members of the band who owned cars were Nascimento and myself. The others usually led their lives within walking or bus distance of their homes in the Compensa district of Manaus. For them, going to another town represented a welcome increase in the size of their social circle.

Furthermore, the band's members foresaw the chance of new amorous adventures. Playing in the interior meant meeting new girls, to whom the musicians would appear as sophisticated artists from the state capital, while girlfriends back in Manaus would be far enough away to avoid problems of jealousy. Nevertheless, any member who preferred to take his girlfriend with him had the delightful prospect of a watertight excuse to ask her parents if she could sleep away from home.

There were yet other advantages: organisers of events in the interior were often prepared to pay a premium fee for the band; and the preferred musical style was usually *forró* (Cascavel's favourite). The Manaquiri event was particularly attractive because it had to do with football – Brazil's passion.

Despite its exotic lure, playing in the interior had several drawbacks. The first was the large amount of time consumed in travelling. Typically one spent most of Saturday getting to a gig in the interior and most of Sunday coming back from it. Unfortunately some of our musicians had jobs that required them to work on Saturdays, so it was hard for them to get away. There was also the danger of damage to our musical equipment during the long journeys; vibration on trucks and boats and inadequate protection against rain were common hazards. Finally, many places in the interior had no mains electricity and the unstable power supply from portable generators could easily wreck our sensitive and expensive amplifiers. An equipment failure was a double problem: repairs required money, but without music the party would not make any.

However, when we looked more closely at the football party offer, it turned out to be not as straightforward as we imagined. Another band, friends of ours, had already got the contract for the gig but felt they didn't have enough musicians and equipment to do it well. What was actually being proposed was that we should fuse our bands for the event, so as to put on a really good show. In the end we agreed, although not all Cascavel's musicians could make themselves available for the date in question. I was among those who were able to go. I felt it would be an interesting experience and started preparing for it by borrowing a voltage stabiliser to protect my amplifier.

When I asked one of the members of the band exactly where Manaquiri was, he replied that we would travel by boat up the Rio Solimões (i.e. West from Manaus) for about 6 hours and then turn left (i.e. South) down a relatively narrow channel into Lake Manaquiri, on the shores of which the town stood. I was momentarily perplexed until I realised that he meant we would basically travel up the Amazon: Brazilians use the special term Rio Solimões for the Amazon above Manaus – and the term Rio Amazonas only for the Amazon below Manaus.

The river's nomenclature is even more complicated further upstream. Peru has several special names for various sections of its Amazon. The longest stem starts in the Andes as the Apurimac, becoming successively the Ene, Tambo, Ucayali and Amazonas before entering Brazil. The linguistic confusion arose because many different Indian languages were spoken along the river's more than 4,000-mile length. No single *lingua franca* covered the whole area. Among non-Brazilians the term Solimões is little known and hard to pronounce, so I (like many others) generally avoid it in English and use the term Upper Amazon when referring to the main river upstream from Manaus.

Exactly how long the trip from Manaus to Manaquiri took depended on the time of year, or more precisely, on the water level, which followed a seasonal cycle. The port of Manaus lay just off the Amazon, about 9 miles up the Rio Negro. Logically then, to reach Manaquiri from Manaus, one had to travel down the Negro to the confluence, known in tourist circles as "the Meeting of the Waters", then go up the Upper Amazon. This was the route when the rivers were low. However, the rise in level between November's low water and June's high water was typically 9 m (30 ft) and could be as much as 15 m (50 ft). When water was high, the peninsula between the Negro and the Upper Amazon flooded, connecting the two rivers by natural navigable channels that eliminated the need to go via the confluence. The most commonly taken short cut was a channel named after a tree called *Paracuuba* (literally "bow wood"). It reduced the travel time of trips from Manaus to the Upper Amazon by about 2 hours. By the date of the Manaquiri party, river level was already above mid-point and the Paracuuba channel was open.

On the Saturday morning of the gig, the band managed to meet at dawn, despite having played late on Friday night. We gathered where we had been performing a few hours earlier – the *Senadinho* (Little Senate) bar, situated in Compensa, not far from Blondie's. The instruments were still on the veranda where we had left them, guarded by two of our musicians dozing in hammocks they had slung under the roof after the show.

At about 6.15 AM, a pick-up truck arrived to transport the sleepy group and its equipment to the port, where a boat was waiting. Trundling through the quiet streets towards the centre of Manaus, we were lucky it did not rain, since our open vehicle offered the amplifiers and instruments no protection against bad weather. We parked on the waterfront near the beautiful wrought iron market hall built by the British at the beginning of the twentieth century. (The British were very influential in Manaus during the rubber boom. In addition to the market hall, they built the old custom's house, which they transported stone by stone from Liverpool, and the floating docks, which are still in use today.) Notwithstanding the early hour, the market was bustling and boats were arriving all the time with produce for it.

Although ocean-going ships and some riverboats berthed at the floating docks, most small boats, including the one which was going to transport the band, used no proper port facilities; they simply tied-up as best they could on the beach in front of the market.

Men were loading and unloading boats by hand, there being a complete absence of mechanised handling systems. The movement of goods and people was intense, a situation exacerbated by April's rising water level, which reduced the shore area to a thin strip. Vessels lay side by side all along the strand line and in places were lined two or three deep, so that workers had to scramble over one boat to load or unload the next. People with bundles of belongings and merchandise were coming and going in a continuous stream, the poor carrying their own goods, the rich supervising groups of hired porters.

A scout was sent to locate our boat, called the "Three Brothers". Having found it, we moved the vehicle as close as possible, picked up our instruments and joined the throng of carriers plying across the beach. The path to the vessel led us via precarious stepping-stones and planks over open drains, mud and debris. In narrow places we sometimes had to wait with our heavy gear delicately balanced, while people passed in the opposite direction. Rotting scraps of fruit and fish produced a horrendous smell and attracted flocks of black vultures, which squabbled over the offal. Yet in spite of the odour and filth, this beach was the gateway to rural Amazonia. It reflected life in the Amazon much more than the duty-free shops of Manaus ever would.

Professional porters carried huge bunches of bananas and 50-kg sacks of manioc flour. Through constant practice they planted their bare feet solidly in strategic footholds on the path without looking. Our band's musicians were less footsure, but we managed to load the musical equipment on to the vessel without mishap.

With a length of 18 m and one single deck, the wooden, diesel-powered "Three Brothers" was not one of the largest riverboats. It had the typical lines of a local boat built in the central Amazon. With its gently rockered superstructure, it looked quite different from the high, dumpy estuary boats made downstream at Belém, or the low, straight boats made upstream in Peru. It had a projecting, high, pointed bow and a low, round stern. Zinc sheeting covered the long, oval roof, on which stood a large searchlight and a rudimentary mast in the form of a wooden cross. The pilot steered from the front, where he had a good view of obstacles in the water. Neither engineering calculations nor plans had been used to build the vessel, just a good eye and some rules-of-thumb: a length about four times the width, and a shallow U-shaped cross-section, giving lots of stability for the draught.

The wood used in the boat's construction was *itauba* (literally "stone wood"), a species of laurel. It was particularly appropriate for making carvel-built boats, since it was heat pliable; planks needing a special twist or curve were heated and shaped in front of a fire before being fixed in place. No other central Amazonian timber could be used so conveniently.

The "Three Brothers" was licensed to carry 30 passengers. With over 40 on board, including the band, the captain was anxious to set off before the port authorities could check us. Overloading, a perennial problem on Amazon riverboats, was currently a hot issue, since not long previously a lot of people had drowned when an excessively laden vessel went down in a stormy crosswind. In that disaster, the weight of passengers all moving to one side to keep out of the rain, combined with the force of the wind on the superstructure, caused severe listing, followed rapidly by slipping cargo, capsize and sinking. More fearful of the hassle with the authorities than of the dangers of shipwreck, we pulled away from the beach at 7.00 AM and were not challenged by the river police.

Most of our fellow passengers were young or middle-aged people born in Manaquiri and now living in Manaus. They were visiting their birthplace solely for Saturday night's festivities and would all (like us) return to Manaus on Sunday. Coming from large, poor families typical of the interior, they had moved to the state capital in search of a better life, including, they hoped, educational opportunities, health care, employment, modern electrodomestic comfort and legal title to the land they lived on. The rural exodus of which they were part had almost doubled the population of Manaus in the last ten years.

The suburbs of Manaus contained many pockets of such migrants – one neighbourhood housed people mainly from Labrea; another housed people mainly from Coari; yet another housed people mainly from Eurunepé and so on. When, once a year, an interior town held a party in honour of its patron saint, boat loads of its former citizens travelled from Manaus to take part in the merry-making. The football championship, although not a saint's day celebration, had the same effect. Lot's of Manaquiri's transplanted sons and daughters wanted to go to their birthplace for the weekend – so many in fact, that extra boats had to be laid on to supplement the normal ferryboat service. The "Three Brothers" was one of these additional boats.

As our vessel moved away from the shore, a panorama opened up, revealing the main economic activities of the Amazon. Closest to us was the riverboat "port" we had just left. From it you could travel virtually anywhere in the Amazon basin, along rivers longer than any in Europe, with names practically unknown outside Brazil. All you needed was a hammock to sleep in, a lot of time, and the ability to digest endless beans, rice, spaghetti and manioc flour. Fares were about US$ 18.00 per day's travel, including food.

Upstream from the mass of riverboats, containers being unloaded from a cargo ship at the floating docks indicated the arrival of components for Manaus' assembly industries. The city had a huge park of factories that put together electronic goods, motorcycles, watches, and other items. The companies mostly had Japanese and European names, such as Toshiba, Sharp, Honda, Sanyo, Philips and Telefunken. They benefited from tax incentives and special facilities to import components. The assembled goods, stamped "Made in Brazil", were sold in the south of the country or exported. The abundant, docile and cheap labour force resulting from the Amazon's rural exodus was a further attraction for such companies. Some of the passengers on board the "Three Brothers" undoubtedly had jobs in Manaus' industrial district.

The presence of assembly factories in Manaus stemmed from the "Industrial Free Zone" policy implemented in 1966. The military dictatorship in power at that time was anxious to develop the Amazon and to integrate it into the life of the rest of the country, but had no money to invest. It therefore decided to attract industry into the area by giving tax incentives and facilitating the importation of components. A more visible but financially less important facet of the same policy was the "Retail Free Zone", in which local shops were allowed to sell imported consumer goods tax-free. (At that time imports were heavily taxed in the rest of Brazil.) Both the industrial and retail aspects of the Free Zone policy have been relatively successful. Movement of goods assembled in Manaus to their markets in South Brazil has improved cargo transport. At the same time, the flow of South-Brazilians coming to shop has stimulated passenger transport. In the process, Manaus has grown into a strong economic centre.

Looking at the number of containers in the floating port, I was struck by the obvious vitality of the economy of Manaus. Nevertheless, I couldn't help worrying that the city's well-being (and therefore mine too) was very precarious: it depended on rules rather than resources. For instance, one of the most important products of Manaus was television sets; yet there was nothing from the forest inside a TV. If the rules were changed and incentives removed, one would expect assembly industry to leave Manaus and move closer to its suppliers or to its markets. On the retail side, changes have already taken place. Brazil has recently opened its markets countrywide to imported goods. This has had a negative effect on retail import shops in Manaus.

Our craft gathered speed down the Rio Negro as the pilot manoeuvred around floating filling stations, floating warehouses, moored vessels and general river traffic. Since riverboats were the main means of transport in the Amazon, it was not surprising that the waterborne activity was intense, even at 7.00 AM. We were, after all, at the Central Amazon's major port.

We passed a floating ice factory with several commercial fishing boats moored around it. They were loading ice in preparation for trips lasting up to a couple of weeks. Each vessel had a huge icebox occupying most of its hull. Rolled-up nets on the roof, many canoes (to deploy nets) and the fishing-class registration E-2-M painted on the bow were other distinctive features of these boats. Ice was vital to their industry and its availability determined the fleet's range of action.

Behind the ice factory an old suburb, Educandos, home of many riverboat captains and sailors, was waking up. Ramshackle wooden stilt-houses covered the waterfront. The floorboards of the lowest ones formed a horizontal line just above the high water mark. The beach was occupied by boatyards, most of which, as we passed, were doing their last jobs for the season. Soon the rising river would flood their slipways. Thereafter, for a couple of months, until water receded again, there would be no way of hoisting boats out for repair.

Large sawmills stood a little farther downstream. The cliffs beneath them were covered in sawdust and wood waste, dumped because nobody made secondary products such as hardboard, particleboard and chipboard. Under pressure from the port authorities, some mills had stopped dumping wood waste in the river and installed incinerators. The latter, looking like metal wigwams, made smoke plumes in the early morning breeze. In reality they simply polluted the air instead of the water.

In front of one of the sawmills, two powerful tugboats were manoeuvring a long, narrowly triangular raft of tree trunks. It was the mill's raw material arriving from logging operations on the Upper Amazon. At intervals along the raft's length, kerosene flares serving as navigation lights were still burning from the previous night's slow voyage. Such timber convoys were so heavy that on the swift-flowing Amazon they could only travel downstream. However, they could be successfully towed against the weak current of the lower Rio Negro. Despite slow speed, transporting logs by flotation was more common than using trucks. It was cheaper. Waterways were abundant and large, whereas roads were few and precarious.

Before the "Three Brothers" pulled away from the Educandos shore, two further buildings indicating the diversity of Manaus' trade caught my eye. The first was a military-looking concrete bunker set into the red laterite cliff. I would have sworn it was some kind of defensive installation, if I had not asked. It turned out to be the wheat terminal, an important facility because Brazil adopted the Portuguese habit of eating bread, despite the climate being too hot to grow the necessary cereal. Wheat had to be imported on a large scale. In the case of Manaus, it came straight up the Amazon in bulk transport ships and was stored in the huge bunker in Educandos before being distributed to the city's mills.

The other building was a warehouse for jute, the coarse plant fibre used to make burlap bags. Once I had noticed one warehouse, I recognised several more with give-away names like Brasiljuta and Jutal. The size and number of the warehouses showed that jute (along with a similar fibre called malva) was an important local industry. Some years ago these fibres constituted the most important agricultural export of the State of Amazonas. Introduced by Japanese immigrant farmers in the 1930's, they were cultivated only on the fertile, muddy Amazon floodplain (not on poor laterite soils of higher land). We saw people harvesting jute later in the day.

When our boat moved into the open water in the middle of the river, the view became less detailed. Behind us the high-rise buildings of central Manaus were receding into the distance, but downstream we could still recognise several major elements of the industrial landscape: the refinery; the oil-fired power station; the largely unused steelworks (a government-financed white elephant); various private roll on/ roll off ports for pusher-barge truck-carrying services to Belém and Porto Velho; and lastly the terminal of a ferryboat that crossed the Amazon to link with a road nominally leading to South Brazil. Whimsically I remembered that I had travelled along that road during my job-hunting trip. Currently the road was impassable through lack of maintenance.

The urban landscape of Manaus terminated shortly beyond the mouth of the Rio Negro. Further downstream, low forest punctuated by small farms formed the eastern horizon. As the scenery became less absorbing, my attention turned to life on board. Passengers who had not yet slung their hammocks did so now. They economised space by rigging one hammock high, the next one low. In this way everyone found a place despite the boat's overloaded condition. The ship's cook served the typical poor man's breakfast of coffee, cream crackers and margarine, after which, with nothing to watch outside, most people retired to their newly slung berths.

When we neared the Paracuuba short cut to the Upper Amazon, the colour of the river water suddenly changed in appearance from the Negro's transparent black to the Amazon's opaque, milky-coffee brown (called "white" locally). The dark colour of the Negro, caused by dissolved humic, folic and tannic acids from decomposing leaves, indicated an acid, mineral-deficient river flowing off poor soils. In contrast, the muddy turbidity of the Amazon, caused by suspended particles eroded from the Andes, reflected an alluvial river of neutral pH, flowing through a fertile floodplain.

Although the "Three Brothers" did not pass there on account of the short cut, the difference between the Negro and Amazon water types was most evident at the "Meeting of the Waters", where the Negro ran into the Amazon. From that point it took somewhere between six and over twenty miles for the rivers to mix completely, depending on flow, water level and wind. The Amazon colour predominated after mixing.

In the Paracuuba channel we were enticed out of our hammocks again by scenery close by on both sides. With the water level almost up to the height of the fields, the views over the floodplain were delightful. Moreover, the navigation was exciting. The swift current in the narrow waterway formed high stationary waves. Eddies buffeted the boat continually and the helmsman, who didn't have power-assisted steering, had an energetic time keeping us on course.

The area we were passing through had been formerly covered with *várzea* forest, a type of vegetation resistant to periodic flooding. However, in view of the floodplain's fertility, much of the forest had been cleared to make way for cattle ranches and farms. Ranching had the advantage that, after clearing, little labour was required to look after relatively large holdings, an important consideration for homesteaders trying to secure title deeds to as much land as possible: growing agricultural crops required more manpower and investment. Nevertheless, not everyone raised cattle. We saw plantations of maize, beans, lettuce, passion fruit, watermelon, papaya, bananas, chive onions, coriander and cucumbers.

There was a special kind of agriculture on the floodplain: crops were planted as riverbanks became exposed in the dry season and reaped before the water came back up. The lower the position on the beach, the shorter the crop's growth cycle had to be. Consequently a favourite species for cultivation near the low-water mark was "forty-day beans", a quick-growing legume harvestable within six weeks of sowing. Sometimes predictions went wrong and plantations were lost to early floods – the river was already getting dangerously close to some of the maize fields on the port side. Similarly the cattle owner to starboard must have been anxiously watching to see if he could leave his animals on the pasture, or if he would have to hire a boat to transport them to higher land. Alternatively he might consider building a raised wooden platform, called a *maromba*, on which to keep the herd for the duration of the flood.

We passed the entrance to a lake where giant Amazonian water lilies were blooming. The many-petaled, fist-sized, white flowers on the surface of the water and the 5-ft diameter circular floating leaves made a truly exotic scene. However, the plants were only attractive from above; an overturned leaf revealed that all the underwater parts of the plant were spiny. Although the lake dried out seasonally, forcing the lilies to grow new each year, it suited them for two reasons. Firstly, in the lake's still water, the lily leaves suffered no damage from strong currents. Secondly, the fertile mud of the lake's bed provided plenty of minerals for growth. The lilies could not survive in poorer environments. For instance, they were not found in the main part of the Rio Negro.

We were lucky to see plenty of white, newly-opened water lily flowers, because they were so much prettier than the violet-coloured second-day blooms, which had a very dilapidated appearance. Workers at INPA had recently published an article about the pollination mechanism of water lilies and I could remember enough details to understand what I was looking at. When a water-lily flower first opens, which happens after sunset, it is hot, scented, white and functionally female. The hot scent attracts scarab beetles, some of which have pollen on their bodies from other flowers they have visited. This allows pollination to take place. Before daybreak, the flower closes, trapping the beetles for the whole next day. While imprisoned, the beetles eat many unessential parts of the flower, which changes from a functional female into a functional male. By the beginning of the second night, the flower is violet in colour, ravished, cold, unscented and unattractive. It opens for a second and last time, releasing the beetles covered in its pollen. The beetles then fly away to pollinate other white flowers. Water lilies amazed me not only by their beauty, but also by the complexity of their pollination system.

A small rural community stood at the far end of the Paracuuba channel. All its buildings were made of wood, with floors on stilts above the high-water level. In addition to houses, we passed a simple church, a primary school, a football field and a clubhouse. In fact this community was typical of many settlements in the Amazon and was practically identical to the one we were heading for in Manaquiri. Despite the early hour, the women of the community were already down at the water's edge, engaged in the never-ending task of washing clothes. The cleanliness they achieved using the muddy water was amazing. They looked up smilingly as we passed, while the numerous children, the smaller ones completely naked, waved appealingly.

Suddenly we were out onto the Upper Amazon (Rio Solimões). The view changed to a broad vista over an immense expanse of muddy water flowing majestically at about four knots. The distant horizon, uniformly low and flat, made the sky seem huge. We turned upstream, hugging the bank to starboard as close as possible to cheat the current. On port side the nearest land was Ilha Marchantaria, a partially cultivated floodplain island situated over a mile away in the centre of the river.

With the excitement of the Paracuuba channel behind us and the view on one side a long way away, most passengers drifted back to their hammocks. One of the musicians climbed onto the roof of the boat with a group of young people to sing sambas where there was less engine noise. However, the rest of the band tried to relax, knowing that the football party that evening would go on until daybreak.

One factor which helped us to relax was the knowledge that we would not be short of musical manpower. Our musical line-up contained musicians from two bands, including a saxophonist and a trumpet player. We had also brought several friends along to help out in the percussion section. As a result, there was considerable versatility as to who played which instrument and when. With so many musicians to choose from, it was not necessary for every musical number to include every artist. In this way, each performer in turn could take a break at some point during the show.

Lying in my hammock, I watched floating islands of grass, water hyacinths, tree trunks and other biological debris drifting downstream. Some of the floating islands were as big a football fields. In the rainy season there was always a lot of flotsam in the Amazon. Rainstorms flushed the aquatic vegetation out of lakes; and the rising river carried away any buoyant object that had been stranded on its banks during the previous year. Furthermore, wherever current flowed fast (often on the outside of bends), erosion occurred and the riverbanks caved in, dumping forest trees or crops into the river.

The "Three Brothers" passed a steep bluff that was being actively eroded by the rising river. The noise generated by the falling banks was awesome. When I heard it I was worried that the whole floodplain would disappear. However, I later realised that such a fear was ill founded, because the Andes, the ultimate source of the Amazon's mud, were still rising, so there was always a supply of new sediments. In fact, the less-noticeable process of sedimentation was building up new land on the floodplain all the time. In areas where current was slow, such as on the inside of bends, new banks were forming. Exposed in the dry season, the banks became colonised by plants, the presence of which further slowed-down next year's floodwater, favouring more sedimentation. Eventually the new land reached the height of the high-water mark, above which it could not grow by alluvial deposition. At this point it became indistinguishable from the rest of the floodplain.

From the "Three Brothers" I saw all the stages of the sedimentation process.

New mud banks were covered in grass. On slightly higher shoals a few pioneer tree species grew in addition to the grass cover. The pioneers typically included willow, *Cecropia* and *mata pasto* (literally "pasture killer"), a woody legume renouned for invading open spaces. Finally on the highest banks there were stands of mature floodplain forest, in which kapok trees with umbrella-shaped crowns and large buttress roots towered over the canopy of other flood-resistant species.

The swaying hammock, steady engine beat and distant sambas lulled me to sleep, only to be awoken at around 10.30 AM by people scrambling off the roof because of rain. Once everyone was inside, the boat's side tarpaulins were lowered to keep the rain out. They blocked the view and increased the engine noise, which resonated in the closed space, but in any case the heavy rain on the zinc roof was deafening. Nevertheless, the samba singers were not to be disheartened. Moving to the forward part of the vessel, as far away from the motor as possible, they crowded together, two or three per hammock, commandeered the band's drums and bellowed with increased gusto.

The singing stopped at lunchtime so that people could eat a watery fish soup accompanied by hot peppers and copious manioc flour. Because of overloading there were not enough plates for everyone, so the passengers dined in relays. While the meal was in progress the weather cleared, enabling us to roll the tarpaulins up and see that we were still chugging up the Amazon, but now on the south side, having crossed the river during the downpour.

Not long afterwards, we turned left into the channel leading to Lake Manaquiri. People were harvesting jute on the banks, wading knee-deep to reap the crop in already submerged parts of their fields. In order to obtain the longest fibres, they cut the plants as close to the ground as possible, which was a backbreaking job. They tied the severed plants into bundles, which they left to soak in pools in the fields, so that the soft tissues would rot away. Later they would pick up the course fibres and dry them in the sun ready for sale. In spite of the rain, we saw some of the coarse grey jute fibres hanging on the horizontal poles of a drying frame near one of the houses.

Shortly after 2.00 PM we arrived at the football field, a place which at low water one could reach by walking from the town of Manaquiri. At the time of our visit, however, the rising water had already flooded the footpath and one could only reach the field by boat. The pitch occupied a clearing on a promontory. It was surrounded by remnants of forest, in which local people still gathered Brazil nuts and had formerly tapped rubber.

The football clubhouse, situated near one of the goals, was an open-sided, wooden hangar designed for dancing. Its only internal divisions formed the bar and toilets. Several temporary refreshment stands had been erected nearby. There was no permanent habitation in the vicinity, but a floating shop consisting of a hut built on a heavy raft of sandbox-tree logs was moored next to the muddy slope leading to the field. Several general transport boats like ours, plus a number of canoes, were tied up at the water's edge.

As soon as the "Three Brothers" had moored alongside the other craft, the band started to unload its instruments and carry them up to the clubhouse. We set about the task immediately, fearful that the sloping muddy riverbank, slippery after the rain, might become impassable if it rained again. Wishing to keep our good clothes clean for the party, we changed into swimming trunks as the only practical way of dealing with the mud. Then we arranged lots of people around even the lightest piece of equipment and inched our way up towards the clubhouse, sticking to the edge of the track, where there were trees and shrubs to hold on to.

The return trip down the hill to fetch the next items was more carefree. We slid joyfully down the centre of the muddy slope straight into the water, where we washed the mud off and got ready to carry the next item. Occasionally someone took an involuntary tumble and mudbath, to the childish delight of everyone else. The excitement was heightened by the simultaneous arrival of two boats bringing the rival football teams. As each boat docked it tried to outdo the other in a noisy display of firecrackers.

Miraculously we managed to get the musical equipment into the clubhouse without problems; the black cladding of the amplifiers was covered in muddy hand marks, but nothing had been dropped hard or dunked in the river. We were pleased with progress so far.

Shortly before the scheduled 3.00 PM kick-off, another rainstorm began, accompanied by thunder and lightning, causing the start of the match to be delayed, while the public sheltered as best it could in the clubhouse and refreshment stalls. I was in the former. Thunder and the din of rain on the roof made it impossible to hold a conversation. Dejectedly we watched water cascade off the huts and form a lake in the middle of the pitch. Fortunately storms of such intensity rarely lasted long and by 3.30 PM the downpour had diminished to tolerable drizzle. The match began immediately, otherwise there would not be enough time to complete play before light faded with the 6.00 PM equatorial sunset.

The game was disappointing. After such heavy rain the pitch was in an atrocious condition. Players had difficulty keeping on their feet, let alone controlling the ball. The teams had started out in immaculately laundered uniforms, one side in purple and green, the other in yellow and black, but soon they were covered in mud and indistinguishable. Brazilians like and are famous for a fast, dry game with delicate ball control, dancing dribbles, rapid, secure passes, plenty of space and a minimum of body contact. Unfortunately the pitch at Manaquiri permitted none of this. Much of the match was an ill-coordinated scramble for a lifeless ball, sometimes resulting in dangerous collisions between players. European-style sliding tackles, not much appreciated in Brazil, failed to animate the cold, wet spectators. Furthermore, doubts about the legality of the rough tackles caused wrangles between the players, supporters and the referee.

The only exciting moment was a controversial shot at goal kicked from a distance of 20 yards with the goalkeeper prostrate in the mud at one side. The ball arched through the air, stopping dead on landing in the goalmouth. The attacking team was convinced it had scored. The referee, however, ruled that the ball had not crossed the line, meaning no goal. The decision caused uproar, stopping the game until spirits calmed. Because of the referee's verdict, the result at the end of normal time was a goal-less draw. So there had to be further play to try to break the deadlock.

The players were exhausted playing extra time in such heavy conditions, but despite their efforts, once again no goals were scored, leaving the match still drawn. The winner would be decided by shooting penalties. By the time the penalty shoot-out started, daylight was fading. The game had started late and gone on to extra time. The brief, tropical twilight meant that night would soon be upon us. The refreshment stalls had already lit their oil lamps and the portable generator was providing electric light in the clubhouse. Penalties were shot in the goal near the lights to get maximum illumination. One of the yellow-and-black team missed his footing in a powerful run-up, hitting the ball wide of the goal. All the other shooters scored. So there it was, the green-and-purple team were champions. Nevertheless, a win on penalties after extra time was not a convincing victory. Both teams knew that they were very evenly matched and that there was an element of luck involved. However, they were both proud to have triumphed over the forces of nature by putting on a show in such awful conditions.

In contrast to the football game, the party went tremendously well. It seemed that everyone wanted to forget the disappointments of the afternoon by making the dance as lively as possible. The rain stopped, meaning that locals who had stayed at home because of the storm now ventured out in the drier conditions. All through the evening boats bringing partygoers arrived out of the darkness. Practically none of the vessels had any navigation lights. Approaching motorboats could be heard a long way off, but canoes would materialise silently in the circle of light cast by the floating shop. Some of the dugouts contained whole families who, once on land, strung up hammocks in the trees for the children to sleep in, while the parents enjoyed themselves at the party.

The band's main preoccupation was to start as late as possible, so as to have enough energy to play all night long. In keeping with this strategy, we had a leisurely dinner at one of the little refreshment stalls and let a record player make background music until about 9.00 PM. We were able to procrastinate for a further hour, while the football organisers made long, flowery speeches and presented the trophy to the winning team, who were now refreshed and unrecognisable in their clean party clothes. By 10.00 PM, with no more excuses and the public getting restless, we started our all-night session of *forró* music.

Forró (pronounced "fo-HO") is a corruption of the English phrase "for all". The term dates back to the late nineteenth century, when English and American companies were building railways in northeast Brazil. From time to time the English-speaking supervisors held parties for their workers. Such parties were "for all". The music for these events had to be simple (for the musicians to play) and rhythmic (for the workers to dance to). It is amusing to reflect that more than a century after the railway building era, bands like ours chose their repertoires with the same two principles in mind.

Forró was a style, not a rhythm, in the same way that "country music" is a style not a rhythm. ("Country music" may include waltzes and two-steps). *Forró* tempos ranged from a very rapid stomp called *frevo*, through the medium fast *baião* (pronounced "ba-yon") and *xaxado* (pronounced "sha-sha-doh") to the slower *xote* (pronounced "shot").

Hoping to warm up slowly, the band started with a sequence of *xotes*. The dance floor immediately filled with the most diverse couples: young men and their girlfriends; husbands and wives; jolly, elderly aunts with insecure, neophyte nephews; old uncles with nubile nieces; young girls together; and parent-and-infant teams. It was obvious from the way so many people danced the opening medley, that the party was going to be long and lively.

The dance, *xote*, derived its name from the *schottische* (i.e. "Scottish") and stemmed originally from Europe. As might be expected, its rhythm and steps were simpler than those of Latin or African tempos. The basic figure consisted of two lilting side-steps in the same direction (open, close, open, close), followed by two steps back to the start. Instead of going from side to side, one could progress forwards and backwards, or turning. The dance was so simple that it was an excellent confidence-builder for learners. Every so often during the night we interspersed sequences of *xotes* into the programme to slow things down and get our breath back.

From the opening *xotes* we moved on to livelier rhythms called *lambada* and *merengue*, featuring the saxophone and trumpet. These instruments were not found in the original *forró* bands, which used only accordion, bass drum and triangle. Some traditional-style *forró* trios were still to be found in Manaus. They were easily recognisable by the instrumentation and the fact that the musicians usually wore leather hats from northeast Brazil. However, accordions were rare in Manaus. Consequently other instruments, particularly the electric guitar, saxophone and, more recently, electronic keyboards, had been incorporated into Amazonian *forró* music.

Soon the party was really wild and we had to reposition one of the amplifiers because parts of the wooden floor were vibrating excessively. Happy on account of the good sound and the public's response, the band played on in a euphoria that was aided by copious ingestion of a punch made from passionfruit and sugarcane liquor. A large cauldron of this brew somehow materialised in the centre of the orchestra.

Girl-watching was good too. *Forró* was an ostentatiously sensual dance style. The hold was offset, so that each dancer had one leg between the legs of his or her partner. As much movement as possible was then put into the hips, without kicking the feet sideways. Dancers increased the flexibility of their spines by putting their toes down before their heals, and by a relatively high position of the arms, which stretched the thorax. Even all-girl couples injected a lot of sexual suggestion into the dance, to the delight of male onlookers. However, within a short time all-girl couples became rare, because in the interior it was considered very bad form for a girl to refuse a dance invitation from a man.

Mesmerised by the swaying hips, I lost track of time and it seemed still early, when at 2.00 AM, the band made an interval to play a game of Bingo, the proceeds of which went towards our payment. The prize was a roast chicken with various garnishes. At the end of the game, the winner and his friends devoured the prize immediately. Another Bingo session took place at 4.00 AM, after which dancers became noticeably less numerous. Nevertheless, the party continued in high spirits until the sky started to get lighter at 5.30.

During the whole night only two problems were reported. The first concerned the lovelife of one of the musicians, who had found himself a good-looking, eager girl, the colour of dark honey. The band arranged a reshuffle, so that he could escape for a while. However, he returned sooner than expected, complaining that there was so much mud outside that he could find nowhere to lay his new love down to enjoy the wonderful things they both had in mind. On reflection this must have been a fairly generalised difficulty.

The second problem was a drunken squabble in one of the refreshment stalls. It almost ended in a knife fight and was typical of what can happen when men have had too much to drink. A lot of booze was sold at the party, mainly beer and punches made of sugarcane liquor. In addition, since salaries were low in the rural environment, by way of economy many men brought along their own liquor, often in the form of *conhaque* (a cheap distillate of sugar cane, only vaguely reminiscent of Cognac). Two young men, about eighteen and twenty respectively, having finished a private bottle each, were quite drunk, but still wanted more. So they retired to one of the small bars. Neither of them had the courage to admit that he was penniless and each hoped that the other would pay for the drinks. When the barman finally wanted his money, the two men started a violent argument about who had invited whom to drink.

The drunks exchanged progressively more obscene insults. The first few curses had to do with layabouts, male genitalia, hell and excrement. Then came stronger challenges, in which one of them suggested that the other was homosexual, cheated by his wife, and should make love to himself. The strongest oaths concerned calling the other's mother a whore and inviting him to indulge in anal sex.

The last round of invective was directed to the twenty-year-old, who, on hearing it, rose to his feet, drew a fish knife from his belt and in defence of his mother's honour threatened to kill the younger man. Fearing imminent violence, the 18-year-old rose too, his brown skin looking suddenly grey. For an instant they stood very still, glowering at each other across the table.

However, there is often an implied condition in a threat. In this case the threat was of the type, "If you don't retract that, I'll kill you." The younger man, having no knife, needed to avoid violence, but didn't want to lose face. So he said, "You what?" There then followed a dialogue rather like that between two people who are hard-of-hearing or have missed the point. The 18-year-old carefully did not repeat the insult, but neither did he retract it. He kept leading the other into conversational sidetracks.

A sizeable crowd built up around the incident. However, before the quarrel had chance to evolve further, the twenty-year-old's father, a wiry man with traits from northeast Brazil, stepped forward with considerable courage, authority and probably practice. He addressed his son with virtually the same insults as those causing the dispute and added others about real men being able to hold their liquor. So as to chastise the other young man too, he continued the harangue by exhorting his son to choose better company and to stop hanging out with penniless layabouts. As a finale, he announced that the family was leaving the party instantly (and in a quick aside agreed to pay the stallholder next time they met). With that, he proudly escorted his wife away, while his two other sons, one suspects not for the first time, grabbed their drunken brother and frog-marched him, still knife-in-hand, out into the dark and mud, to embark in a long dugout, in which they all disappeared into the night.

The crowd was left disappointed. It had been robbed of a juicy drama. However, the strategy of separating the potential combatants by several kilometres was very prudent. Nobody knew what might happen once the unarmed man got hold of a fish-knife or even a screwdriver, or, more dangerous for everyone, a revolver. Slowly, people started drifting back to the dance floor, where the band had continued playing, as was usual during such incidents.

As the sky started to become lighter, the musicians played two traditional close-of-party sambas, *"Vem Chegando a Madrugada"* (The Dawn is Coming) and *"Quem Parte Leva Saudades"* (Those Leaving are Nostalgic). The latter happens to be a stylised version of the Mexican song *"Cielito Lindo"*. Then the lead singer said a few quick words of thanks over the loudspeaker system, wished everyone "good morning" and switched off. The Manaquiri football party was over. Most of us rushed to our hammocks on board the "Three Brothers", in the hope of dozing off before full daylight made sleep more difficult.

At around 8.00 AM the boat's cook served coffee, after which we sleepily set about loading the gear ready for departure back to Manaus. We also had to carry on board the saxophone and trumpet players. They had stayed ashore after the party to celebrate their musical success by getting totally drunk on sugarcane liquor. By the time the boat was ready to cast off, at 9.00, they had achieved their goal and collapsed in a deep drunken stupor. Four of us, one at each limb, hauled them unceremoniously aboard and dumped them on the deck with the luggage and equipment, where they slept in bizarre, abandoned postures for the duration of the trip home.

The return voyage to Manaus was much quieter than the outward journey. Everyone was exhausted from the night's activities. I lay in my hammock in a kind of daydream, which was a poor substitute for real sleep. Nonetheless, excitement came as we approached the Paracuuba channel. Our boat received a tip-off from a craft coming upstream, that the marine authorities were checking vessels for overloading at the Manaus end of the short cut, a point where traffic was easy to intercept. With exactly the same passengers returning as on the outward journey, the "Three Brothers" contained about twelve people too many. There would be a problem if we were inspected.

The solution was simple. Shortly before entering the channel, volunteers equivalent in number to the excess passengers were put in the engine room. All the bags and equipment, along with the drunken saxophonist and trumpet player, were then placed on top of the hatch to make it difficult for the river police to check the space below. The volunteers would be liberated when we reached the Rio Negro.

Since I was awake at the time, I consented to be one of the stowaways. Laughing and joking we descended through the wooden trapdoor into the small, hot, smelly, deafening engine room. Most of us sat around the edge of the compartment with our feet towards the central motor and our backs leaning against the concave inside of the hull, but, as the space filled up, a young lady installed herself in front of me, using my legs as a backrest.

On closing the hatch we were plunged into pitch blackness. It was so dark that one could not tell visually if one's eyes were open or closed. The smell of hot oil was nauseating and my first thought was a hope that the exhaust system of the motor was gas-tight; otherwise we would all die of carbon monoxide poisoning. My next thought was that we would probably die of heat exhaustion, as sweat started to stream out of all the pores of my body. I suppose everyone else felt the same, but in the noise and darkness it was impossible to know how the others were faring.

When the boat started to rock in the turbulent waters of the Paracuuba channel, I put my hands on the shoulders of the young lady in front of me, to steady her. To my surprise she snuggled closer. Startled at the unexpected advance, I moved back a little. She snuggled again. Still cautious, I leaned forward and rubbed my beard gently against her neck. Now I knew she was certain whom she was approaching, since the other male stowaways, like their Indian forefathers, had no beards. This time I did not retreat from her advance. However, this was no place to take our new intimacy any further. It was too hot, noisy and likely suddenly to be exposed to the gaze of the public or the police. So we transmitted "patience" to each other and swayed on coyly.

After an incalculable period of time the "Three Brothers" reached the calmer water of the Rio Negro. The trapdoor opened and the "all clear" was given. The police had gone home. With happy shouts and heroic gestures, but visibly relieved, the stowaways climbed out of their hide. When I took my new friend's hand to help her up onto the deck, she did not let go. Manaus was in sight. We would not have to be coy and patient for long.

Chapter 9

Fig 9. Ox Dance (*Boi Bumbá*)   WK

June Parties

The next special dates in our band's calendar were in the month of June. The sudden flurry of musical activity in that month surprised me. I knew Brazil had a carnival that took place in the first part of the year, but I didn't know it also held important celebrations in June (with possible remote connections to the solstice). The habit of holding June parties *(festas juninas)*, was brought to Manaus by migrant labourers from northeast Brazil when they came to tap rubber in the Amazon in the late 1800's, early 1900's and during the Second World War.

June parties might be held on any day of the said month, but special attention was given to St. Anthony's day (13th), St. John's day (24th) and St. Peter's day (29th), as well as to preceding evenings and nearby weekends. Form varied considerably, but they often included: (1) a public dance in *forró* style, preferably with an accordion in the band; (2) special games for children; (3) bonfires; (4) fireworks; (5) traditional food; (6) unmanned hot-air balloons with live burners; (7) square dancing; (8) folk dances such as *boi bumbá* (ox dance), *pássaro* (bird dance), *cirandas* (circle dances) and *tribos* (Indian dances).

I soon discovered that in the same way that all sorts of social groups organised carnival parties, they also organised June parties. However, there was often a strong "neighbourhood" aspect to *festas juninas*, with celebrations taking place in the street, rather than in a commercial club. Driving around Manaus at night during the month of June, one was certain to come across bonfires blazing by the wayside and people performing square dances in the highway.

In addition to private parties, there were big festivals organised by the State Government. In Manaus, because of the city's large size, the state festivals included all kinds of folkdances, even dances from overseas, such as Arabian belly dancing and many dances from Portugal. On the other hand, the festivals in smaller Amazonian communities typically concentrated on only one form of dance. For instance, the town of Manacapuru, sixty miles upstream on the Amazon, was famous for circle dances, whereas the town of Parintins, three hundred miles away down the Amazon, was famous for the ox dance.

Our band, Cascavel, started the June-party season by playing for a street party in the Compensa district of Manaus on St. Anthony's Eve (12th June). This saint was to Brazilians what St. Valentine is to the English. On his day lovers and would-be lovers exchanged cards, love letters and presents. It was a time when girls in Manaus, in keeping with their highly romantic upbringing, were either extremely happy, because they had received the attention of the right guy, or very sad, because they hadn't.

Residents of an unpaved street near where I lived organised a party and wanted Cascavel to make the music. They were friends of the band, so we agreed to play unremunerated, just for fun, food and drink. (We often played free of charge as long as nobody was taking commercial advantage of our good will.) The cul-de-sac in which the festivities took place was so pitted near its entrance that no traffic came by, so it was not at all inconvenient to dance and light a bonfire on the carriageway. A lot of garbage that habitually littered the area was burned in the process.

Typical of Brazilian parties, the event was ostensibly for children, but adults took over later on. The children's main activity was to dress in peasant costumes and dance *quadrilha*, the Brazilian square dance. After this the adults danced *forró* until the party ended at midnight. As it was a weekday, people could not party into the early hours of the morning, since many had industrial jobs starting at 7.00 AM.

Before their square dance took place, the children amused themselves playing with the bonfire and fireworks. The cheapest form of pyrotechnics was a homemade sparkler improvised by igniting the wire wool used for scouring pots and pans. Kids robbed the material from someone's kitchen and fluffed it into loose ropes about two feet long. Taking a rope, they lit one end in the bonfire, held the other end and swirled it around fast, producing a yellow, sparkling flame. The torch had to be kept moving rapidly; otherwise it easily went out. The fun consisted of making luminous moving patterns in the dark. The game's mixture of danger and beauty completely fascinated the youngsters.

Another cheap and simple firework consisted of a pea-sized portion of gunpowder wrapped in soft paper. One could buy a box of fifty such explosive devices for next to nothing. Thrown forcefully at the floor or any hard object they exploded with a loud bang. Sometimes children wearing shoes detonated them by stamping on them. Some children had conventional fireworks. Bangers were preferred, but there were also fountains and rockets.

The square dancers (and, one supposes, their mothers) had put a lot of effort into having appropriate costumes. The boys wore deliberately tattered, brightly patched jeans, check shirts, red kerchiefs and straw hats. The girls sported bonnets or straw hats and wore old-fashioned, floral print summer dresses, gathered at the waist and cut short to display the thighs. Some versions of the Brazilian square dance included enacting a shotgun wedding, with one couple dressed up as pregnant bride and reluctant groom. However, the Compensa children kept their show simple and did not include that variation. When the modest, but joyful performance was over, the whole thing was repeated with the general public joining in. More women wanted to dance than men, so ladies danced with each other, or with small children. In spite of the improvisation, everybody enjoyed it.

Every family at the party brought along some item of traditional food for general consumption. They had previously made a list which avoided having too much of one thing and not enough of another. They arranged the food as a buffet on a white-clothed, large wooden table set up in the street. A single, naked light bulb, temporarily wired to a nearby house, swung precariously overhead, providing stark but adequate illumination.

The main food item was *vatapá*, a delicacy that appeared not only at June parties, but anytime poor people celebrated: weddings, birthdays, anniversaries or whatever. It was a dish renowned for being tasty, nutritious and cheap. It looked like ochre-coloured potato purée. To make it, dry bread (or wheat flour) was soaked overnight, seasoned with tomatoes, onions, green peppers, fresh coriander leaves and chives, then cooked in African palm oil *(óleo de dendê)* with prawns, coconut milk and garlic. As may be inferred from the use of ingredients from Africa and the coast, *vatapá* originated in Bahia, a state renowned for its beaches and afro-Brazilian culture. At the party our *vatapá* was accompanied, as usual, by copious white rice.

Other typical June party dishes on the buffet included *munguzá* (a frogspawn of white sweet corn cooked with milk, sugar and cloves), *mingau de milho* (runny corn-flour custard), *banana frita* (fried banana crisps), *tapioquinha* (sweet tapioca pancakes with grated coconut), *maçã de amor* (toffee apples), *bolo podre* (literally "rotten cake" – made with tapioca flour) and *bolo de macaxeira* (sweet-manioc cake). It is significant that half of the dishes mentioned were made from the cheap and abundant staple crop of the Amazon, manioc, a plant with many other names, including cassava, tapioca and gari in English, yuca in Spanish and mandioca in Portuguese. Manioc is so important in the Amazon that it merits some comment.

Although manioc is now cultivated all over the tropical world, it is native to the Americas, It is a root tuber which comes in two principal varieties, referred to as sweet and bitter. The sweet variety, called *macaxeira* in northern Brazil and *apaím* in the south, can be cooked and eaten like a sweet potato. However, the bitter variety, called *mandioca brava*, is potentially dangerous; it contains significant amounts of poisonous cyanide-producing chemicals, which in nature stop the plant being eaten by herbivorous animals. This sort of manioc has to be detoxified before consumption and is usually processed into a gritty flour called *farinha*. Tapioca is starch made from manioc tubers.

The children at the party drank a fizzy pop called *guaraná*. This was a nationally popular soft drink flavoured with seeds of the *guaraná* plant, a straggly bush cultivated extensively in the lower Amazon. An old man watching the children drink the pop, told me proudly that it was one of the few Amazonian products widely consumed in other parts of Brazil. In the commercial fizzy drink, he said, the seeds were so dilute as to be inert, but when commercialised in a more concentrated form, such as a powder, syrup or compacted stick, the seeds could be used to make a drink with aphrodisiac and other tonic properties. Later I checked his opinion against information in textbooks and learned that *guaraná* contained caffeine and produced the same effects as coffee.

Apart from the musicians, who received a crate of beer, adults at the party fended for themselves as far as alcoholic drinks were concerned. The nearby general store functioned as a bar, so men bought beer, sugarcane liquor and cheap south Brazilian wine, which they drank standing in small groups on the roadside or sitting on the front steps of their houses.

Cascavel's *forró* music was well received, with several local amateur musicians joining in to render their favourite numbers. It was a good opportunity for the band to practice its repertoire of June music – endless songs about balloons and bonfires – in preparation for its next paid assignment. The following Saturday we had been contracted to play at a big party held by the National Institute for Amazonian Research (INPA), where the lead singer and I worked.

The street party ended at midnight and shortly afterwards, pleasantly mellow on account of the mixture of cold beer and good music, I started to walk home. As I passed the dying bonfire, its glowing embers caused me to think warmly of the forthcoming INPA party. Not only was Cascavel going to play the music for it, but I was also scheduled to dance in the institute's square-dance team. Having just seen other people square-dancing, I was excited at the thought of taking part myself. In this mood the walk home passed quickly.

The National Institute for Amazonian Research (INPA) was a large research station set up in Manaus by the Brazilian Federal Government to coordinate academic interest in the Amazon. With over five hundred workers, it occupied several almost adjacent sites about five miles from town centre. It also administered three large forest reserves and a number of smaller field stations. At its inception, in the early nineteen-fifties, it studied only "pure" disciplines, such as botany, taxonomy, ichthyology and ecology. More recently, "applied" sciences had been added in an attempt by the government to see some economic return for its investment. Consequently there were now divisions researching forestry, timber technology, fisheries management and other practically oriented subjects. My department, called Alternative Energy Supplies, was one of these "applied" sectors.

By chance, everybody in my department at INPA was musical. My chief mechanic, Sr. Nagata, who had emigrated from Japan thirty years previously, played the trumpet. One of the two technicians was Nascimento, the lead singer of Cascavel. The other was Bosco, an amateur singer/guitarist specialising in the repertoire of the longstanding popular singer, Roberto Carlos. I found it pleasant running a department that could transform itself into an amateur musical ensemble. Whenever we worked in the interior, we would make music in our spare time, much to the delight of local people. As a result, we made friends quickly, even when we were doing research in remote communities where we initially knew no one. Because we played music, we were also popular guests at parties given by other sectors of INPA and were well known throughout the institute. It was therefore not surprising that INPA contracted Cascavel to play for its June party, nor that I was invited to take part in the INPA performance of square dancing.

For the month before the party the INPA square dance team practised twice a week after work. Each session lasted an hour and we danced on the asphalt five-a-side football pitch, which was also the arena for the final performance. A portable record player provided the music. Dancers without partners gradually formed couples as they got to know each other. I finished up paired with a Brazilian-born lady entomologist from São Paulo's large Japanese community. Since I was tall and Anglo-Saxon, whereas she was small and oriental, we made an exotic couple. The other dancers, liking the idea of racial mixing, as Brazilians do, decided that my partner and I should play the part of bride and groom, in the version of the dance with the shotgun wedding. As a result, instead of wearing a peasant costume like those at the Compensa party, I wore a dark suit, carefully patched and covered in dust to make me look like a socially inept country bumpkin, while the Japanese girl wore a white wedding dress, padded with a cushion to make her look pregnant.

In square dancing the steps are not critical. The figures – the complicated changes of partners and positions – are more important. To avoid our having to memorise the whole sequence of the dance, the figures were announced by a caller, who affected a comically exaggerated northeastern accent for the purpose. Many of the names of the figures were in French (as they are in American square dancing) possibly reflecting French colonial influences in northeast Brazil (and in Cajun America). We first practised the figures walking, setting them to music as we became more confident. Sometimes the confusion was hilarious. Nevertheless, we eventually learned a thousand and one ways of ensuring that everyone danced with everyone else and passed through all parts of the dance floor, which is what square dancing is all about.

Luckily for me, the INPA party was planned in two parts, so that the square dance did not conflict with playing in the band. The first half, from 7.00 to 10.00 PM, included the bonfire, sale of traditional food, children's games, square dance (to records) and a presentation by the *Tribo das Andirás* Indian dance group. The second half, from 10.00 PM to 2.00 AM, was the public *forró* dance with music by Cascavel.

On the night of the party I arrived at INPA's main campus at about 8.00 PM. to find the place packed. The institute was situated near a large, poor neighbourhood called Coroado, where many of the lower-paid employees lived in small houses lining narrow, rutted roads. Residing so close, the workers could walk to the party without having to brave Manaus' unreliable system of night buses. Furthermore, since INPA parties had a reputation of being good value for money, other Coroado families, alerted through the grapevine, turned out in force, even though they had no employment links with the institute.

In fact in some ways there were too many people. Long queues developed at the refreshment stalls, a situation exacerbated by the use of a cumbersome system of prepaid tokens. The procedure, common in Brazilian snack-bars, possibly served its intended purpose of minimising theft by the serving staff, but it was infuriatingly inconvenient for customers, who found themselves first going to the counter to see what was on sale, then to the cash-desk to pay for tokens, and finally back to the counter to exchange the tokens for goods. One possibly queued up three times in order to buy even the simplest thing.

In addition to the crowds at the refreshment stalls, another large crowd surrounded what was evidently a children's June-party game. Pushing my way into the throng, I discovered a greasy-pole contest. A smooth, vertical wooden mast about fifteen feet high, daubed with mechanical lubricating grease, had bunches of bananas, pineapples and papayas tied along its length. The object of the game was to climb the greasy pole to get some or all of the fruit. It was remarkably difficult. After some time, a team of three boys managed to reach the topmost bunch. One youngster stood on the shoulders of the second, hugging the pole for stability, while the third clambered up the human column so formed. All efforts drew enthusiastic shouts of encouragement from the bystanders, with resounding applause as the last fruit was unhitched.

The next game I saw was, *quebra pote* (break-the-pot). It was a form of blind man's buff, in which a blindfolded contestant armed with a stick tried to smash a ceramic pot hanging somewhere above his head. The contents of the pot, sweets and small change, were the reward for accomplishing the feat. The fun came from the onlookers trying to help the striker by shouting directions to him. As the striker had no reference point, he became very confused. Each child had three strikes until someone succeeded in breaking the pot.

I was absorbed in watching the vain antics of a *quebra pote* contestant, when my Japanese dance partner rushed up breathing heavily. She told me that most of the square dance team had already changed into their costumes, and that people were looking for me, because we were due to start soon. We walked briskly to the canteen, where temporary changing facilities had been installed.

Whereas English folkdancers have preserved their tradition by fossilising it, the people of Manaus had kept their square dance alive by lampooning it. They exaggerated everything: the raggedness of the jeans, the shortness of the frocks, the caller's accent, the men's bow-legged stance and drunken gait. To this day I still possess one red and one white sock I wore with my wedding suit as a satire of local peasants' social ineptness. Yet, although a parody of itself, Brazil's June square-dance has survived with tremendous vitality and popularity.

We put on a good show, performing our sets, lines, chains, squares, wheels, stars, spirals, shuttles and crosses, to finish up with the correct partner in the appropriate part of the arena. Halfway through the performance I was "married" to the Japanese girl, in a long speech full of ribald jokes about my honour and the bride's pregnant condition. The Master of Ceremonies read the bawdy prose at a rustic lectern across which a shotgun had been laid.

When we left the arena, the Andirá tribal dance team was preparing to enter. Known in folkdance jargon as a *tribo* (literally "tribe"), of truly Indian it had practically nothing. Andirá Indians became culturally extinct a long time ago. The dance was a candyfloss version of what they may have looked like. Genetically speaking, Indians were, however, well represented. The dancers were uniformly of small stature and brown in colour, the girls with the dumpy figures of their Indian ancestors and the young men with powerful shoulders, angular, Indian faces and straight, black hair. Nevertheless, if asked, none would have called himself Indian and most would have mentioned Portuguese, Italian or German grandparents.

Visually the *tribo* show was spectacular, although far from authentic. All the dancers wore some kind of plumary art. However, day-glow tints of orange, green, yellow and lilac indicated the use of industrially dyed chicken feathers, instead of quills from macaws, toucans, parrots and hawks, which true Indians used. Similarly, the great complexity of some of the halters, although beautiful, owed more to carnival than to tribal dances. The music was neither Indian nor special, consisting entirely of modern Brazilian saxophone *merengues*, not the haunting pipes-of-pan melodies that would have been more in keeping.

Notwithstanding the group's doubtful authenticity, the sight of the prettily adorned, half-naked young bodies moving rhythmically around the arena was an uplifting contrast to the dirt and disorder which permeated much of urban Brazilian life. Two parts of the presentation were particularly noteworthy, both danced by men. One was a well-choreographed, stylised representation of a stick fight, in which combatants whacked each other's sticks without smashing anybody's skull or fingers. The other was a dance with lighted flares, which, if not practised precisely, would have turned some of the more feathery participants into human torches.

I found it encouraging that a group of humble townspeople, in a country that largely despised its Indian heritage, should go to considerable trouble to try to recreate an Indian identity. Furthermore, the Andirá *tribo* was only one of many groups in Manaus that performed "Indian" dances. Lots of other *tribos* were scattered around the city's neighbourhoods. All had the names of extinct tribes from the surrounding area. One of the best known was the Barés.

By the time the Andirá *tribo* finished, it was time for the public *forró* dance to begin. Cascavel had installed its musical equipment during the afternoon, so we were able to start promptly. As soon as they heard our opening chords, people started dancing enthusiastically. The party had a good feeling about it. Most of those present, being co-workers, already knew each other. Moreover, since Nascimento and I were both INPA employees, there was already a sympathetic link between the public and the band. The presence of whole families increased the atmosphere of innocent fun. Whereas carnival was an opportunity for adult licentiousness, June parties were clean fun for families and friends. Nevertheless, as at all workers' parties, there were some people who welcomed the occasion to get to grips with paramours coveted in, but distanced by, the work environment.

I was vaguely reflecting along these lines, while beating out a frenetic *forró* rhythm on the electric piano, when suddenly a slender girl dancing not far from the band caught my attention. The dance floor was crowded, but whenever there was a gap between the couples, I saw beautiful, long legs stretching from crimson hot pants down to nimbly moving sports shoes. In spite of her flat footwear, the girl in question was a handspan taller than the other in high heels with whom she was dancing. To me at least, she stood out in the crowd.

When the interval came, I set about getting to know the dancing girl, taking the problem to Sandoval (the owner of the bar I had patronised while waiting for the carnival procession). I was godfather to his three sons, which made me his *compadre*. This special relationship made it easy for me to approach him on the delicate subject of women. In any case, our friendship had a broad base: he had previously been part of my research team, his brother was Nascimento (my technician, Cascavel's singer) and his sister worked in the INPA administration. Such family groups were not unusual in the Brazilian civil service; once one person in a family had landed a good government job, he or she found openings for the others. Federal employment offered tremendous security and reasonable rewards for very little onus.

Sandoval knew that the girl I was interested in came from Coroado, but did not know her name. He suggested that I ask his *comadre*, that is, his children's godmother named Alice, who was also an INPA employee and also present at the dance. Alice lived in Coroado and knew a lot of people there. While Sandoval and I chatted over a beer at a table on the edge of the dance floor, the eldest of my young godsons, still up at midnight, was dispatched to look for his godmother.

Alice was not hard to locate, since she was an immensely built, coal-black Afro-Brazilian. Although professionally she very probably suffered racial discrimination, she never showed any signs of resentment and her mood was invariably smiling and helpful. She came shambling powerfully across the empty dance floor, my godson scampering around her like a happy puppy. As she approached, she flashed her shining white teeth in a broad grin. Since I already knew her from the christening of our common godchildren, we needed no introduction. We embraced, I offered her a chair and she sat down. By the time I started to put my question, she had already poured herself a beer.

Yes, she knew the girl in hot pants and would be delighted to introduce us. Alice was happy that I liked Brazilian girls. It was commonly rumoured that she did too. My godson was sent off again, this time in search of the girl, whose name I now knew was Oneide.

A few minutes later, Oneide and her girl dance-partner accompanied our messenger back across the dance floor. Linked arm in arm, the two females approached shyly, giggling nervously to each other. As they traversed the open space, I was able to observe more clearly the girl who interested me. The more I saw, the more I liked. Oncide's graceful legs, which had first caught my attention, were matched by slender arms and neck, protruding from the crimson sleeveless bodice of a hot-pants suit. A magnificent shock of black hair framed her pretty face. Her smile was shy, but sincere. Her large black eyes mainly avoided contact, but occasionally flashed in a way, which inspired me to continue the quest of getting to know her.

Alice told Oneide I would like to meet her and introduced us. We fetched chairs for the two girls and Oneide sat next to me. Forced to plight my troth in public, I found it tough going. The many things I wanted to communicate were difficult to verbalise with others listening; so I limited myself to conveying the bare bones of my case: I was impressed by Oneide's good looks and dancing, and would like to have the opportunity of knowing her better. Since she had no telephone, I gave her my work and home numbers and she promised to call. She then excused herself, saying that friends were waiting for her. They were leaving, since her mother did not want her to be home late.

Others told me that after the interval the public continued to dance energetically and happily to Cascavel´s music. I must have played the piano, although I really don't remember. My thoughts were occupied by Oneide and the hope that she would ring.

On my way home the sight of a large, beautifully illuminated hot-air balloon drifting slowly across the night sky added to the romance of my reverie. Unmanned, decorative ballons with live-flame burners were a traditional element of June parties, even though they were illegal because of the fire risk. Numerous clubs, often with an influential membership, defied the ban and spent a lot of time, money and effort making and launching the spectacular, dangerous artefacts. The one flying overhead that night was about 5 metres in diameter. Besides the principal burner, it carried a large number of smaller lights and an intricate firework display controlled by a time fuse. I took the sighting as an omen of good luck and waited optimistically for Oneide to telephone.

The call came the following Monday at INPA. We decided that after work I should drop by her home, in a street virtually adjacent to the institute. In the evening I found the appropriate address, a humble house in unfinished rustic brickwork. There had apparently never been enough money to complete the construction. Gaps for the doors and windows were covered with rough boards, braced with poles at night against intruders. The building occupied practically all the available space within a wooden stockade. I clapped my hands, the Brazilian way of announcing a visit.

Oneide appeared in the dark hole of the doorway, looking like a fashion model using drab surroundings to emphasise her beauty. For a moment I was taken aback that such a badly built house could be home to such a well-built woman. Yet it was not the first time I had seen such a contrast. I was perpetually amazed that in the poor districts where Cascavel played, young people were good-looking, clean, well dressed and happy.

Flashing me a shy smile, Oneide asked me to wait a moment, while she secured the dog. The animal was an indispensable security measure, in view of the deficient structure of the house. I squeezed through the rickety gate into the narrow, unpaved, front yard, which principally contained an open oil-drum full of water for use during Coroado's frequent cuts in water supply. I kissed her politely on the cheeks. She led me inside the house and asked me to sit down.

The only piece of furniture in the minute front room was a ragged, cloth-covered armchair. I sat in it, while Oneide perched on one of its arms at a distance close enough to imply "I am your friend," but far enough away to convey, "I am not your lover."

We talked about a wide range of subjects, desperately trying to find some common ground. During the erratic course of the self-conscious conversation I learned several things about Oneide. She was completing her secondary education and attended the afternoon session of her high school. (With so many young people in Brazil, state schools used their buildings and staff for three different groups of students: one group studied in the morning, another group studied in the afternoon and a third group studied at night.) She was also a member of the Coroado folkdance team called Abelhinhas (literally "Little Bees") which was going to perform the following Thursday at a government-sponsored Folklore Festival of June-party dances. We agreed that I should accompany her and some of her family to the performance of the Abelhinhas.

Oneide called her mother from the depths of the dark house and introduced us. We discussed arrangements for the outing, after which the lady withdrew once more to her domestic activities. I also took my leave, since I felt uneasy courting a girl in a house containing her mother and no doors.

The following Thursday evening I drove my rusting VW minibus round to Oneide's house. She greeted me in strange attire, which was part school uniform and part bee costume. Then she disappeared to continue changing, leaving me to talk to her brother and sister. Two nubile girls dressed as bees and a third in ordinary clothes joined us to take advantage of my transport. Oneide's mother decided not to accompany us. I think she had never really planned to go, but did not want to give the impression of handing her daughter over on a plate. The rest of us set out.

The Folklore Festival took place on a huge traffic island, called Bola da Suframa, situated at the entrance to Manaus' industrial district. A large, floodlit stage had been built for the occasion on the lower part of the sloping terrain, with spectators occupying the high ground. Numerous bars and refreshment stalls selling June-party food lined the paths that criss-crossed the area.

Parking near to the festival was chaotic. When the traffic started to jam, I stopped the van in the first available space and we walked the remaining distance, picking our way through a crowded maze of parked and blocked vehicles. Oneide and the two bee girls ran off to the dancers' preparation area near the stage. Her brother disappeared too, presumably to meet his own friends, leaving me with Oneide's sister and the remaining girl. Though I would have preferred being with Oneide, I found the company very agreeable.

The three of us wandered to the higher ground and installed ourselves in an open-air bar, at a table with a reasonable view of the stage. The dance in progress portrayed *cangaceiros* (bandits from north-east Brazil, of whom Lampião and his wife, Maria Bonita, both shot by the police in 1939, are the best known). The male dancers wore military-style uniforms incorporating a highly decorated leather hat, cartridge belts around the waist and chest, and a rifle on the shoulder. They beat the floor with the firearm in some of the dance steps. The girls wore cowgirl-style fringed brown suede skirts with matching jackets. Their accessories included embroidered neckerchiefs, knee-length white stockings and sensible shoes. Their hair was done into plats or buns, the typical styles of *cangaceiro* women.

A simple, traditional northeastern trio of accordion, bass drum and triangle played the dance's loud *forró* music through several tons of sophisticated sound equipment provided for the event by one of Manaus' major electronics companies. The pretty, but somewhat long presentation featured the typical northeastern rhythms, *xote*, *xaxado*, *côco* and *baião*. The dancers performed competently, although, as may be expected from a group of non-professionals, they did not attempt anything too complicated. It was a perfect dance to watch intermittently, whilst chatting to my two companions and savouring the deliciously cold beer.

The next group, called *Pena de Ouro* (Golden Feather), presented a traditional ox dance *(boi bumbá)*. They entered the stage with tremendous energy and confidence, to the noisy accompaniment of a firework display. Since the ox dance told a story, the Pena de Ouro performance was more interesting than that of the *cangaceiros*. Its costumes were more varied and a lot of pantomime supplemented the dancing. Furthermore, the ox dance had its own specially composed music, played by a large drum band reminiscent of carnival but with a more Amerindian, less African beat. There were different melodies, rhythms and choreographies for each part of the ox story.

In the Amazon, the ox dance was the most popular of several June Party story-dances. Like virtually all Manaus' popular culture, it came from northeast Brazil, where there was a long history of cattle raising. The ox dance traditionally tells the story of Pai Francisco, a cowhand who kills one of the landowner's oxen so that his pregnant wife, Catirina, can eat it. When the crime is discovered, Pai Francisco runs away into the forest where he meets a group of Indians. Meanwhile, using various ribald remedies, a doctor resuscitates the ox (thereby enabling the dance to continue the following year). Francisco is rehabilitated; a priest blesses the Indians; and everyone lives happily ever after.

There were as many variations on this basic story as there were dance groups, but the Pena de Ouro presentation followed the traditional form fairly closely. Besides the five principal roles (Pai Francisco, Catirina, the doctor, the priest and the ox) there were three special solo female dancers: *a porta bandeira* (the standard bearer), *sinhazinha* (the land-owner's pretty daughter) and *cunha poranga* (the pretty Indian girl). There were also three large corps-de-ballet containing masses of participants: *os vaqueiros* (the cowboys), *os rapazes do amo* (the bourgeoisie) and *os índios* (the Indians). The first two of these corps-de-ballet had only male dancers, all dressed in ornate colonial costumes of conquistadors. They portrayed men on horseback by wearing amusing model horses around their waists. The dancers' legs protruding through the bottom of the model permitted realistic movement, so that from a distance the dancers really looked as if they were riding. The group that contained women was *os índios*. It was also the group with the scantiest uniform. This gave the girls an opportunity to show their bodies off to maximum advantage.

The most important personage in the dance was, of course, the ox. A dancer, called "the ox's brains", wore a hollow shell representing a large zebu ox (the most common race of cattle in northern Brazil). Considerable effort went into making the costume. The ox had eyes that rolled, a tongue that moved, nostrils that snorted smoke; and it could moo loudly.

In the time between seeing the Pena de Ouro presentation and writing this book, ox dancing *(boi bumbá)* has become such a cultural phenomenon in the Amazon that it is worth describing a few more details of the dance and its current importance.

Firstly, to appreciate the full humour of the ox dance, one has to understand the ambivalent symbolism of the ox. By its bulk, the animal is a strong male entity, yet by having horns, it is betrayed in love, a condition abhorrent to Latin *macho* men. "Wearing horns" is a metaphor used throughout Latin America – and formerly in mediaeval England too – to describe a man who is cheated by his wife or lover. The ox is a paradoxical figure like that of Shakespeare's Falstaff, a would-be womaniser, who is made to wear horns in "the Merry Wives of Windsor".

There is another joke, too, in Catirina wanting to eat the ox. The Portuguese verb *comer,* besides meaning "to eat", is also a slang term for "to make love to". Consequently, there is an underlying image that Catirina wants to make love to the big hunk of masculinity the ox represents. The humour is heightened by Catirina's already pregnant condition. In some versions the ribaldry is specific, she wants the animal's tongue.

These days, groups embellish the basic plot of the ox dance in many different ways. One variation popular with children has a set of dancers representing forest animals. Solo dancers may also depict rubber tappers, surveyors, prospectors, naturalists, missionaries, tourists and other stereotypes that appear in the forest. Participants may also weave historical scenes or legends into the framework of the traditional story.

The ox dance has been developed to its most spectacular level in the

Amazonian town of *Parintins* (population 30,000), where during the month of June all other civic activities stop so that two rival teams can dance competitively. One team is the *Boi Garantido* (Reliable Ox), with red and white uniforms. The other is the *Boi Caprichoso* (Capricious Ox), with blue and white uniforms. Every person in the town supports one team or the other. It is impossible to be neutral. Women supporting Caprichoso will even wear blue lipstick, so as not to use the colours of Guarantido. A huge ox dance arena *(bumbódromo)* has been built, rivalling the carnival stadium *(sambódromo)* of Rio de Janeiro. People come from all over the country to see the dance. Hotels are booked out and the town's harbour is packed with boats full of visitors. Naturally, as the Parintins festival has gained commercial importance, it has lost some of its folk character, but nobody can deny the deeply rooted popular spirit still present.

But I only learned these details later. When I first watched *boi bumbá*, in the form of the Pena de Ouro presentation, I just enjoyed the visual spectacle, the rhythmic music and the good company of Oneide's sister and her friend.

During the performance the two girls and I left our bar and strolled through the crowd, pausing to follow the show from time to time. I bought a hydrogen-filled balloon from a 12-year-old hawker and tied it to a length of fishing line I had in my shoulder bag. The balloon rose serenely in the balmy stillness of the night air. It was pretty and very appropriate for a June party, but impractical, because the tether kept catching in the dangerous web of temporary electrical wires supplying power to the wayside stalls. As a result, we stopped at another bar, where we waited for the presentation of Oneide and the Little Bees.

During the wait, I did a little mental arithmetic. The festival lasted two weeks and at least three dance groups performed every evening. There were about 80 participants on average per group. This meant that well over three thousand dancers took part in the festival. I found it amazing that amateur folk dancing could be so popular, especially when one considered that the dancers had probably already danced in carnival.

Finally the bee dance came. It was a curious phenomenon: a contemporary folkdance with no traditional base. A special category in the folklore festival catered for such performances, in which choreographers invented new dances to depict facets of current Amazonian life. INPA workers from Coroado invented the bee dance in the early 1980's, inspired by a former director of the institute – Dr.

Warwick Kerr – who was a specialist in bee keeping. They had danced it in slightly different forms every year since. Although accidentally instrumental in the introduction of African killer bees into South America, Kerr, a respected scientist, was remembered fondly by local people as one of INPA's best directors. He also happened to be the person who hired me, causing my move to Brazil.

The dance depicted the life of a beehive. The participants, adolescents and young adults, wore black and yellow, the most common bee colours. Respecting the gender of real bees, girls represented workers and boys drones. A particularly beautiful girl portrayed the queen and another the rival queen. Further solo performers depicted the sun, flowers and the beekeeper. Oneide was the standard-bearer. Her role involved dancing around the stage, waving an ornate, black-and-gold flag emblazoned with the group's name and coat-of-arms.

Like the ox dancers, the Little Bees entered the stage to a loud salvo of fireworks. Their story, less elaborate than that of the ox, held the public's attention by slick choreography, the beauty of the solo dancers (including Oneide) and clever lyrics clearly sung to the accompaniment of a well-balanced northeastern trio. The dance lasted 50 minutes, most of which time my eyes followed Oneide around the stage, although occasionally I simply leaned back, enjoyed the music and watched my motionless balloon in the starry sky. These moments of reflection gave me chance to appreciate how much gentler June parties were than carnival.

The bee dance was the last presentation of the evening and it ended at around 11.00 PM. As the dancers came off the stage, my companions and I went to congratulate Oneide and her friends on an excellent performance. For a while the Little Bees were euphoric, like any group of performers letting off steam after a show. Then suddenly the practicalities of life dawned on them and everybody wanted a lift home. The alternative to getting a lift was a long walk or a dispiriting wait for crowded late night buses. After impassioned arguments, in which I tried not to get involved (In any case, as driver, my seat was guaranteed.) sixteen young people, mainly dressed as bees, piled into my nine-seat minibus and we set off. Soon afterwards I was deep in Coroado's labyrinth of badly kept streets, dropping passengers in ones and twos until we got back to Oneide's house.

Her brother, sister and remaining friends discreetly said goodnight and left

Oneide and me alone in the parked vehicle. For the first time in the evening, I was able to appreciate at close quarters the bizarre beauty at my side. She was a surrealistic mixture of femme fatale and creature from outer space. Shapely legs sheathed in black fishnet tights protruded from a gold miniskirt. A black, short-sleeved leotard hugged her trim torso and black lace gauntlets adorned her wrists and forearms. She had removed the wings from her costume to enter the car, but her face was still made up to look like a bee. To give the impression of an insect, she had painted the entire orbit of each eye dark green and extended the colour backwards to the hairline, making her eyes look enormous and exciting. A pair of ball-tipped antennae sprouted from a headband hidden in her hair.

A female extra-terrestrial and her earthling admirer were ready for their own June party.

Chapter 10

Fig 10. Amazon Beach Party

WK

Amazon Beach Party

I played with the Cascavel *forró* band for a couple of years, until musical fashion started to change. It was the mid-1980s. The country, emerging from the isolation and protectionism of twenty years of military dictatorship, was opening up politically and economically and aligning itself with Europe and North America as a democracy. International recording companies realised that the time was ripe for pushing North American and European music into Brazil. The commercial advantages were clear; with production costs already covered by sales in the northern hemisphere, expanding into the Brazilian market without diversification increased profits substantially.

The foreign music industry declared war on Brazilian popular music in January 1985, with a two-week festival called "Rock in Rio", a tropical Woodstock with British and American pop idols televised nightly nationwide by Brazil's major TV channel. The shows took place in Rio de Janeiro's enormous soccer stadium. In addition to stimulating interest in foreign music, the concerts served as a huge publicity vehicle for all sorts of multinational companies wanting Brazilians to eat, drink, wear and generally consume standardised, international products.

Brazilian popular music in any idiom except rock suffered badly. Damage varied from region to region; only Amazonia's rural interior, unreached by television and never up to date with its stock of party records, remained unscathed. In Manaus the devastation was considerable. Even though many people preferred *forró*, there was a shortage of new *forró* songs to listen to. Recording companies released few *forró* records and radio stations broadcast practically none. Cascavel decided to follow fashion and change to playing rock music.

Faced with the unwelcome prospect of becoming a rock musician, I left the band. I do not like rock. For me it conjures up images of urban revolt, consumerism and tastelessness with which I do not identify. Having avoided it in

England, I certainly wasn't going to play it in Brazil.

I decided to take advantage of the changing situation and get back to singing in an unamplified, folk style. No commercial outlet for such music existed in Manaus, so I set about creating one. The new venture would hopefully: (1) allow me to play both Brazilian and foreign music, (2) be well remunerated, (3) be compatible with my full-time INPA job, (4) avoid late nights and (5) not require large investment.

In response to these criteria I conceived an evening tour for foreign visitors and called it the Amazon Beach Party. What I envisaged was basically a riverside picnic at which I could sing. The party would consist of three activities: a night-time boat trip through flooded forest to look for caimans, an Amazonian fish barbecue and finally music by a campfire on a beach. During the caiman-spotting my team of helpers would prepare the barbecue and during the music session they would clear everything away. It was conceptually a simple and compact event.

No permanent base was necessary, minimising overheads. The party could take place at any nearby rural location with road and river access. Furthermore it would only run if there were clients, making it practically impossible to lose money. A travel agent friend of mine liked the idea and we launched the venture together. He handled publicity and sales and I ran the operation. We were soon doing good business.

We were particularly fortunate in the site we found to hold the event. We had an Austrian friend named Schuster who owned a wooded piece of land with a sandy beach on the outskirts of Manaus. For a modest fee he let us use his property – and we only had to pay per person participating, so there were no fixed overheads. In addition to the natural beauty of the land, tourists loved seeing Schuster's massive timber house, built to an award-winning design by Severiano Porto, a Brazilian architect specialising in large, wooden structures. The building featured an elevated living space supported on heavy, hand-hewn columns that allowed air to circulate freely. The colonnade incidentally gave the beach party somewhere to shelter in case of rain.

We could take up to 40 guests, in other words, a bus full. The agent took reservations until 5.00 PM each day, at which time he phoned me to let me know how many to cater for. He then hired motorised canoes from Manaus harbour for caiman spotting, rented a bus and detailed a local guide to pick up the passengers. With that, his work was over, whereas mine was just beginning.

The first thing I had to do was to gather all the material and helpers and speed off to Schuster's. Since my working day at the research institute did not finish until 6.00 PM, time was always short. The secret of success was to have *caipirinha* cocktails ready for the arrival of the guests at about 7.30. As long as the waitresses served the welcome-drinks on time, I could relax in the knowledge that we then had one-and-a-half hours in which to prepare food, while the visitors admired the house and went looking for caimans.

Schuster had no mains electricity. For the last three kilometres of the 40-minute trip from central Manaus the tourist bus travelled on an unlit, unpaved road through trees. By the time they arrived, passengers felt they had penetrated dense jungle. An illusion. In fact the area was zoned for weekend-homes. However, enough of the original trees were still standing for the roadside vegetation to look like thick forest at night. In contrast, the riverbank opposite Schuster's beach had no road access and the forest along its edge was largely undisturbed, constituting an appropriate environment for the caiman search.

The bus, unable to pass Schuster's low gateway, stopped at the entrance to the property. Passengers alighted and somewhat apprehensively followed a flickering line of paraffin lamps to the house. The walk in dim light added to the excitement of the ride. The naked flames and forest sounds emphasised the feeling of primitiveness.

At the house the mood changed. Gas lamps there provided more light. People saw the building's majestic proportions and felt reassured that one could, after all, live well in the forest.

With an Austrian's love of large timber buildings, Schuster delightedly showed details of his house's construction to the guests: the various hardwood species used; the thousands of rustic wooden roof-tiles; and the hand-sawn, nail-less joints of the massive beams. He related the difficulties of coordinating two master carpenters and nine labourers during the year-long building period and recounted his battles in the constant war against termites.

The party included an endless supply of free *caipirinha* cocktails, the service of which began immediately. By the end of Schuster's explanations, most people had downed one drink, many were on their second and some were on their third. As the liquor descended, conversation and laughter increased, as did courage. Guests were now ready for the caiman search. They followed another romantic trail of oil lamps, this one leading to the beach, a natural sandy shore, weeded at the edges to make it even larger. The white sand showed up clearly in the dark. Cloudless nights were particularly beautiful. The moon illuminated the sand brightly and the stars reflected in the sheltered, perfectly calm river.

Large motorised canoes from Manaus were waiting on the beach. They had come from town centre up the Rio Negro and Rio Tarumã into Schuster's side-arm called Rio Mariano. The river journey took them about 50 minutes. Each craft had a driver and a spotter (catcher) and took about 10 passengers. Usually I left the caiman search to the boatmen, but on nights with few clients, for economic reasons, we did not hire boats and I led the search myself in one of Schuster's canoes driven by a helper.

At the beginning I had no idea how to find caimans. However, it wasn't difficult. Their eyes reflected clearly in the dark. They looked like bright rubies when light shone on them. Local boatmen, minimising capital investment, used ordinary hand flashlights, but I preferred to use a searchlight powered by a car battery. This proved more effective at long range and also gave enough light to pick out interesting features anywhere around us. The light beam hardly revealed the water surface, but it illuminated the crowns of the half-submerged trees that protruded above the invisible, mirror-like water. The treetops appeared to be fused with their own perfectly inverted reflections, producing a strange Siamese-twin landscape.

Until I gained experience, reflections other than those from caiman eyes confused me. In particular there were always lots of small spiders in the riverside vegetation, just above water level. Their eyes sparkled blue-green, whereas caiman eyes shone red. But it was not always easy to distinguish colour at low light intensity. Initially I often went after spiders by mistake. Worse still was to home in on discarded beer cans or other reflective litter.

Caimans were normally found lying in shallow water, resting lightly on vegetation or the bottom, with only their nostrils and eyes above the surface. Much less frequently we found them swimming or on land. Many writers maintain that from far away a spotter can estimate the size of a caiman by the distance between its eyes. Rarely was this true. A caiman's eyes are situated well on the side of its head, so that one seldom saw both its eyes. Two eyes could be seen only when the animal was facing directly towards or away from the observer.

I soon learned that to actually catch a caiman one needed good coordination between the catcher and the driver. Best results were obtained if the team had worked together before. The catcher could not shout instructions for fear of scaring the prey, so he had to use prearranged light signals to indicate left, right, fast, slow, stop and reverse. Frequently the driver did not see the animal, so the catcher had to indicate its precise location solely by use of the light.

A researcher at INPA explained to me why the driver had problems seeing the caimans that the spotter saw easily. This facet of caiman spotting was so important that I usually told it to guests at some point during the party. Basically he said that caiman eyes did not shine equally in all directions. Mirror-like crystals located behind the retina at the rear of the reptile's eye were what caused the light to be reflected. Their physiological function was to reflect any light unabsorbed by the retina back onto the retina. This increased the light intensity at the retina and helped the animal see in the dark. Any light unabsorbed by the second pass through the animal's retina left the eyes as a beam heading exactly back to where it had come from outside, i.e., directly towards the searchlight. As a result, the spotter, situated immediately behind the lamp, saw reflections easily, but people away from his line-of-sight did not.

At the Beach Party, to illustrate the directionality of the reflected light, I asked spotters, the first time they spotted a caiman eye, to pass the searchlight from passenger to passenger. Most people in the boat would have no idea what the spotter was getting excited about until they themselves held the searchlight. While holding the searchlight they would see the reflection, but not before or after.

The most common crocodilian we encountered was the spectacled caiman, which was not normally more than 6 ft long. One night, to everyone's excitement, we captured one measuring 7 ft. Most frequently we saw youngsters up to 3 ft long, i.e., up to two years old.

To capture small caimans the catcher lay over the front of the motorised canoe, travelling head first. He held a lamp in one hand, while his other hand was ready to snatch the caiman out of the water. A quick grab around the neck, from above, was sufficient to catch the beast. On getting close to their prey, many catchers preferred switching-off the searchlight and using a smaller light worn on the forehead or held in the teeth. This procedure not only left both hands free for grabbing the caiman, but also reduced peripheral illumination.

A more exciting catching technique involved using a waterproof floating flashlight and jumping onto the desired reptile. The catcher sprang into the water and jettisoned the lamp at the last second as he grabbed the caiman around its neck with both hands. This technique, pioneered locally by a Portuguese guide named Filipe Cirilo, considerably increased the catcher's radius of action. As a spectacle for impressing tourists, it could not be beaten. The splash, the sudden loss of light and the feeling of abandonment (as passengers realised the guide was no longer in the boat) made the experience unforgettable. The catcher had little to fear from the caiman, which would normally flee if it could. It would only bite if held in such way that it could not escape, but could still turn around. The principal hazards the catcher faced were spiny plants, submerged obstacles and surfacing under matted vegetation.

For catching large caimans we used a lasso consisting of a plastic-covered, 3/8-inch steel hawser, made into a running noose deployed at the end of a four-foot length of galvanised pipe. The catcher passed the noose surreptitiously over the animal's head and immediately tightened it. He needed both hands to do this, so he wore a light on his forehead or had a helper. A lassoed caiman would react violently for less than a minute, after which it became calm enough to be secured properly for safe observation and photography.

Whether they were small or large, we always released the caimans at the place we caught them, so as not to interfere with their territoriality.

People often asked me if light mesmerised caimans. I believe not. My impression was that two factors were important: firstly, the reptile simply didn't associate the searchlight with danger; secondly, the strong concentrated illumination caused temporary loss of the animal's peripheral vision. As a result, caimans neither expected nor saw the hands that caught them. In keeping with this theory, a catcher always held his lamp as far forward as possible, to avoid illuminating anything obtrusive, such as his hands or the prow of the boat.

Similarly, at the critical moment, just before capture, he never allowed passengers to use flashlights behind him.

At most Beach Parties we caught at least one caiman, but even if we didn't, guests always enjoyed the boat trip. Being away from city lights was an unusual and thrilling experience for most people. Navigating in the dark without buoys, compass, or radar was another. Just to be out in a boat near the forest at night had a unique fascination. Sometimes we would switch off the motor and paddle, gliding slowly between partly submerged trees, listening to the strange sounds of frogs, birds, insects and even an arboreal mammal, the *toro*-rat, which made a loud barking call as it moved around the branches of the riverside trees.

One night I caught a *toro*-rat with a caiman lasso. The animal tried desperately to scratch and bite me, but passengers were able to observe it closely. Its brown body, covered in smooth brown hair, was the size of a guinea pig and it had a long, thin tail.

Guests would return from the caiman search excited and hungry. They were now ready for the next part of the Beach Party, the fish barbecue dinner, an activity supervised by my new girlfriend, Paula.

When I started running the Beach Party, I was worried that I would have little spare time to spend with Paula. However, she responded magnificently to my new commitments, offering her services as chief helper and recruiting some of her single friends as hostesses. Not only did her involvement solve the problem of who would prepare and serve the food, but the party atmosphere was considerably enriched by the presence of a bevy of eligible young women.

In the colonnade of his house Schuster built two massive, rustic, wooden tables to accommodate Beach Party guests. The clients returned from the caiman search to find the tables decked with food ready for the feast to start. We ate by candlelight, which reflected romantically off the glasses, cutlery, plates and platters. The massive beams overhead completed the baronial-hall setting. People sat and helped themselves, while Paula and the girls circulated replenishing serving-bowls and wineglasses.

Since the Beach Party catered for once-in-a-lifetime visitors, with no repeat custom, the menu was exactly the same each night. The main course always consisted of barbecued *tambaqui* fish, rice, Russian salad, Amazonian vinaigrette sauce and *farofa* (manioc flour fried with bits of sausage and egg). The dessert was always fresh tropical fruit. The drinks, consisting of *caipirinha* cocktails, white wine and mineral water, all flowed in unlimited quantities.

The bill-of-fare was designed for maximum speed and minimum work. The only item needing cooking was the fish. All the other dishes were pre-prepared or just required mixing. Rice and *farofa* were purchased from a take-away restaurant on the way out of town. The fresh-fruit dessert required no cooking. Russian salad was made on the spot from tinned vegetables and bottled mayonnaise. Amazonian vinaigrette sauce, also made on the spot, consisted mainly of fresh tomatoes, onions and green peppers in a vinegar and olive oil base, along with chives, fresh coriander leaves, hot chilli peppers, ground black pepper, salt and a natural, red food dye called *coloral*.

The last-mentioned ingredient, *coloral*, (known in Spanish-speaking countries as *annatto* or *anchiote*.) was usually a novelty for the Beach Party guests, so I would take some time over dinner explaining it to them. First I would show them the commercial product in the form I had bought it at the market, that is, as a red powder. I would describe how people throughout Brazil used it to colour rice, meat, soups and sauces. Some of the older foreign guests would remember it as the substance used during World War 2 to colour margarine. Next I would show them the eye-catching, red, hairy, egg-sized pods, called *urucum*, from which the *coloral* powder was made. The pods came from a commonly planted small tree, often referred to in English as the lipstick tree. I would open one or two pods to show numerous small seeds inside, embedded in red paste. Indians today still use this paste as a crimson body paint. It may also serve as an insect repellent. To make *coloral* out of the seeds, all you needed to do was to dry them in the sun and grind them up. When I had finished the explanation, extraverts at the party would dip their fingers into the red paste and daub Indian designs on their faces with it. The dye washed off easily with soap and water.

Barbecuing the fish for the Beach Party was considered a man's job and Schuster's 50-year-old caretaker, Jorge, an archetype Brazilian with an Iberian father and an Indian mother, happily earned a little extra cash doing it. The only material he applied to the fish during cooking was the juice of fresh limes.

We always served only one type of fish and that was *tambaqui*, a species that rivals *pirarucu* and peacock bass as the finest eating in Manaus. I tried to buy it fresh for each party, but kept a frozen supply for emergencies. Medium-sized specimens, around 7 Kg in weight and 60 cm in length were the most convenient, although some examples in the market weighed 20 Kg and measured a metre. I always asked the fishmonger to remove the fish's gut and gills and cut the body into two sides, leaving the scales on. Sides cooked (and thawed, if necessary) faster than entire fish, while the scales gave the flesh mechanical strength during barbecuing. The skin peeled off easily when the fish was ready to eat.

Tambaqui was a giant, vegetarian member of the piranha family, netted in lakes near the Amazon. It had a piranha's broad elliptical profile, but instead of the piranha's renowned razor-sharp teeth, *tambaqui* had a dental arcade that consisted entirely of grinding molars, used to smash fruit and seeds from the flooded forest. Adapted to a food supply of a seasonal nature, *tambaqui* lived like a camel, that is, it fed voraciously when food was abundant (at high water) and lived off its fat for the rest of the time. The presence of the fat in its body made *tambaqui* particularly suitable for barbecuing. The fat melted during the cooking process, keeping the flesh succulent.

One day when I was shopping for *tambaqui*, the fishmonger unexpectedly offered me a shark. I refused the offer, since I didn't know any appropriate recipes. Nevertheless, intrigued, I opened his freezer. It contained a two-and-a-half-metre shark which had been caught in the State of Amazonas in the Rio Madeira about 1,500 miles from the ocean, an event widely reported in the press at the time. One supposes that sharks do not breed in fresh water, but they could evidently survive in it for a long time.

White table wine flowed freely at the Beach Party. It was inexpensive. It came from the extreme south of Brazil, especially the area around Bento Gonçalves, where the climate and soil were appropriate for growing grapes. Many Italian and German immigrant families were involved in making it. They produced agreeable (but not outstanding) table wines at reasonable prices. By looking for old stock in supermarkets, I could take advantage of high inflation and pay less than two dollars a bottle. At that price Paula and the girls could serve wine continuously, giving people a good party without penny pinching. Clients often asked me if the wine was local. My reply was invariably, "yes, if you call 3,000 km away local."

The fresh fruit we served for dessert varied from the familiar banana, pineapple, orange and water-melon, through Malay rose apple, mango, papaya, soursop, sweetsop and cacao to the little-known *pitomba* and hogplum. The choice depended on the season, price and where I did the shopping.

While guests were eating dessert, Jorge, no longer involved in cooking, lit the bonfire on the beach. By the time the meal was over, a cheerful blaze beckoned guests to the last part of the party, the campfire music session. We took the remaining wine, or another round of caipirinhas, and sat on tree stumps in a semicircle around the fire. Paula and the girls remained in the house to clear up, joining us as soon as possible. The horseshoe of tall trees around the beach formed a theatre. The fireside arena was the stage and the motionless, black Rio Mariano provided the backdrop. In this gorgeously romantic yet simple setting, I made or compared the party's music.

I was rarely the only singer. It turned out that Jorge wrote songs, which he sang to the accompaniment of a homemade banjo. Half-Indian, singing unpublished songs about local themes, and playing a unique instrument, he soon became an important part of the campfire show.

Jorge's banjo had several remarkable features. Its hand-carved neck had no metal frets, just wooden steps. He had made its body out of an old calcium carbide tin, covering it with a resonating skin of peccary hide and stringing it with nylon fishing line. In spite of the instrument's rusticity, it produced a faithful musical scale and harmonious chords.

In keeping with the roots of Amazonian popular music, most of Jorge's songs used styles from northeast Brazil, but he had others in *carimbó* rhythm from the State of Pará, near the Amazon estuary. I normally translated a summary of his songs before he sang. Providing the session didn't go on too long, guests were enchanted to listen to such authentic, personal and uncommercial music.

Nascimento was another helper who liked to sing. Although still active in the Cascavel band, he often came to help me at the Beach Party, where, besides singing and playing the conical drum, he mixed excellent *caipirinhas* and worked like a mule loading and unloading the party supplies. If I knew in good time that the party was fully booked (and therefore that there was plenty of money in the till) I hired yet other musicians to add to the show's variety. Sometimes there were also artists amongst the guests. I was always glad to incorporate them into the musical fun.

As master of ceremonies, if I hired local musicians, I always tried to get them to interpret as many different Brazilian musical styles as possible. Typically, guests requested samba, but they largely asked for it because they didn't know any other types of Brazilian music. My task was to broaden their horizons, because songs in a foreign language and all in one rhythm (like a marathon of sambas) quickly palled.

I liked to get the clients to sing communally if possible. This goal was not easy to achieve, because the Beach Party had participants from various nationalities with different languages. I would try to integrate the different groups by means of a judicious choice of music. I sang in English, French, German, Portuguese, Spanish, Russian and Italian if necessary. The dosage needed to be carefully managed, as the chemistry was not at all straightforward. Often two linguistic groups would come together through a song in a third, neutral language. For instance, French and Italians might enjoy singing the Hispanic song "*Besame mucho*". English and Germans might join together in the French-Canadian song "*Alouette*".

Group dynamics varied from night to night. Some parties became progressively livelier, ending in wild dancing. Others tended towards peaceful romance, with everyone dreamily watching the embers of the fire and listening to quiet ballads. In yet others, especially with groups of only one nationality, guests would joyfully sing their own songs, without accompaniment, remembering melodies and lyrics they had not sung in years.

When not singing or accompanying, I usually took a swim in the river. Floating in the dark water, watching the flickering campfire and listening to live music was intensely satisfying. Often I was tipsy by this time, the alcohol increasing my contentment.

If guests swam too, I counted the party a success. Communal swimming, whether in bathing suits, nude, or fully-clothed, symbolised the breakdown of inhibitions and people's total integration into the Beach Party atmosphere. The water temperature (at least 27C, 80F) was so inviting that we quite forgot that these were precisely the same waters in which we had been catching caimans earlier.

At 11.30 PM the party came to a close. The fixed finishing time was, from my point of view, one of the party's best features. In bars in town, musicians often had to continue playing to drunken stragglers well after the rest of the public had gone home to bed. At the Beach Party straggling was out of the question. Everybody had to leave together on the bus. The entertainment always finished on a peak, with no chance of a seedy decline afterwards. Despite the compliment implied by people asking for more, I never prolonged the party.

My helpers and I accompanied our guests back to the bus, partly out of genuine friendship, partly to ensure that departure was united and rapid. During the short walk up the drive, guests usually commented on the evening. Many told me that the Beach Party was the highlight of their Brazilian experience. An old Englishman, forgetting in his drunken state that the British never colonised Brazil, informed me that such a good party was one of the "nice consequences of the Empire". A group from Trinidad and Tobago, a country of idyllic beaches and plentiful rum, said there were no better parties in the Caribbean.

As soon as the bus departed, my team left too. However, the tourists had one last treat to see during their bus trip back to Manaus. They were usually able to see members of the spiritist faith putting out offerings *(despachos)* to their deities. Such religious ceremonies usually took place shortly before midnight, at places situated near crossroads, water and forest. These were precisely the conditions on the road back from the beach party.

On Friday nights, the time when spiritists were most active, our guests might see more than half a dozen *despachos* from their bus. The offerings were easy to spot because they always included candles burning in the darkness. The materials offered, usually arranged on a red cloth, depended on the financial means of the believer and the magnitude of the favour desired. Simple offerings consisted of a few candles, with maybe an open bottle of sugarcane liquor, wine or champagne, and possibly a cigar or two. Big offerings included flowers, food and freshly slaughtered chickens or goats, the blood of which was collected in brown earthenware bowls.

The prettiest offering we ever saw on the way back to town consisted of several hundred closely spaced candles along the water's edge on each side of the Tarumãzinho waterfall (7 km from Schuster's). On another night we found an intriguing offering that included a frilly red-and-black satin dress. Had the owner of the dress – evidently, from the colours, a fan of Rio's Flamengo soccer club – done a strip tease for her deity and gone home naked? I suspect not. In contrast to the dramatic way in which the cinema portrays voodoo, the spiritists we saw along the Beach Party road habitually went about their business in a quiet, orderly fashion.

For tourists the *despachos* were an unexpected bonus, something else to photograph, but for me they were another reminder of just how widespread spiritism was in Brazilian society. Since the time Alice's mother incorporated the spirit of Preto Velho, my experience of black magic had grown considerably.

For instance, I learned that my maid ran spiritist sessions to supplement her income. Then I discovered that many of my work friends resorted to spiritism to solve emotional problems. Furthermore, I observed that some of my rich acquaintances called in mediums to cure sickness, which they attributed to witchcraft. And once, when I had a legal problem, a black-magic priestess I happened to meet outside the courtroom introduced me to the judge before the hearing started. I'm sure she helped my case.

Even in my present middle-class home, I one day returned unexpectedly early to find my Brazilian houseguests kneeling on the living-room floor around a red, candle-bedecked carpet, chanting in Yoruba. Yet more dramatic was the quiet Sunday afternoon when my maid became possessed by a violent spirit and lay kicking and screaming in her room, terrified by hallucinations. She wrecked her meagre furniture and only calmed down after punching out two windows, cutting her wrists badly enough to require stitches. Neighbours who came in response to her screams recognised her possessed state and knew a huge repertoire of charms and incantations to counteract the bewitchment. They evidently considered black-magic events to be part of everyday life.

Occasionally, out of curiosity, I went to black-magic rituals, of which the largest and most colourful I attended was the annual homage to Iemanjá, the goddess of water. The ceremony took place, as it did every year in Manaus, on the Ponta Negra beach near the Hotel Tropical on New Year's Eve. As a water goddess, Iemanjá was a deity whom sailors and fishermen revered. Logically, with so much water in the area, she was very important in the Amazon. Around 10.00 PM her worshippers, dressed mainly in white, crowded onto the beach, where, by groups of about twelve to twenty people, they arranged offerings of candles, champagne and flowers in large model boats. The most evident member of each group was a girl dressed as Iemanjá in a light blue dress so long that it spread over the sand. A cut-glass tiara with a starfish in the centre held the girl's specially groomed, long black hair in place. For over an hour she stood perfectly still at the head of the offerings, looking towards the water, while the others chanted to the accompaniment of at least one drummer. At midnight, amid a salvo of firecrackers, the faithful carried the boats with the offerings and candles down the beach and set them adrift on the water. In the process they immersed themselves in a cleansing ritual, bringing the ceremony to a close. Iemanjá's candle-lit boats floating down the dark Rio Negro made an unforgettable sight.

The Beach Party ran brilliantly for about eighteen months, but towards the end of its second year it collapsed. Greed fuelled by success caused the downfall, which started when I went on a month's holiday to Europe. During my absence, my partner kept the party going and in the process enjoyed pocketing what would have been my share of the profits. He liked his increased income so much that when I returned, he didn't want me back in the business. I was shocked and disappointed. In the past we had worked together successfully, splitting the costs and proceeds fifty-fifty. To me there seemed no need to change the situation.

In view of the conflict, I sold out to my ex-partner. There wasn't much to sell: forty plates, knives, forks, spoons and glasses; assorted bowls and trays; some oil-lamps, candleholders and a couple of gaslights. The total value was only a few hundred dollars. I really had no option but to sell out: I couldn't run the party without the supply of guests he provided, whereas he could run the party without me, by hiring a cook, musicians and helpers – as he had done during my holiday.

I considered starting another party with a different travel agency, but rejected the idea. There was no guarantee that the same thing would not happen again and initially any new party I ran would have to compete with the old one that had the good reputation I had built up. It was time to do something else.

In spite of the bitterness I felt at my partner's greed, my recollections of the Beach Party are principally of happy times: the excitement of catching a big caiman; laughter around the baronial tables; nubile girls serving copious wine; a circle of jovial faces lit by campfire flames; a multinational chorus, with a backing of frogs and insects, intoning a bizarre repertoire ranging from "Waltzing Matilda" to "*Garota de Ipanema*" in styles from sea shanties to sambas; not forgetting warm water and fellowship as people shed their inhibitions and their clothes to join me for a swim.

I had gained a lot of experience, including discovering the conflict between friendship and business. I had learned to catch caimans and to love the river by night. And sometimes I made more money on the beach than in my research job. As for music, the party's *raison d'être*, my repertoire had increased in quantity and quality, and was more eclectic than ever.

In the end my ex-partner didn't find anyone with the right flair to keep the party going routinely – and it petered out. There was for me a kind of grim satisfaction in the news. But the best compensation for the party's demise was the joy of once more spending quiet evenings alone with Paula, without forty guests and half-a-dozen helpers as chaperones.

Chapter 11

Fig 11. Cisne's

WK

River Trips

With the demise of the Amazon Beach Party, I lost a substantial source of income, so I looked around for other ways of earning cash in my spare time. (I still had a regular job as a research worker.) After considering various ideas, I decided to renovate my old wooden riverboat and sell weekend trips in her.

My vessel was called Cisne's, a name I liked because it contained elements of English and Portuguese. ('s is a typically English construction; *Cisne* is Portuguese for "Swan"). But I didn't choose the name; it was the Manaus Port Authorities, who christened her like that. Under her previous owner she was a commercial cargo boat called Cisne. When I changed her registration to the pleasure-boat category, a yacht happened already to have the name Cisne, so the authorities simply added 's to the name of my boat, to avoid the cumbersome paperwork of changing her name officially. The resulting linguistic mixture seemed very appropriate for a Brazilian boat owned by a foreigner.

Cisne's was diesel powered, 33-ft long and functioned like a camping-car. There was only one permanent bed, a double one built in an alcove over the rudder mechanism. The other beds were collapsible, transforming into seats or tables during the day. The boat could accommodate a total of seven in rustic comfort, with no privacy. It appealed to young people and families.

In view of commitments at the research institute, I ran trips mainly at weekends, leaving town on Friday evenings and returning on Sunday evenings. The excursions, sold informally with no publicity, were soon booked out weeks in advance, making money and providing lots of fun.

The passengers on the first charter typified my clientele. A young German co-worker at the research institute wanted to show the river to his parents, who were visiting from Europe. His work, like mine, left him free only at weekends, so we made a deal and I took the group out. Once I had run one successful trip, word spread quickly through the five-hundred-strong research community and demand for my services grew rapidly.

As a former passenger-barge captain in France, I have a great love for inland waterways. However, I soon learned that boating in the Amazon was quite different from boating on the French canals. European steel barges, designed to pass through standardized locks and bridges, all had the same dimensions and looked alike. Amazonian boats, with no constraints on width or height, were all shapes and sizes; moreover, being made out of wood, they required a special type of maintenance.

The absence of locks on Amazonian rivers, compared to a lock every two or three kilometres on the French canals, also meant that a trip in the Amazon had quite a different style from that which I had been used to in France. On the French canals passengers could easily get off the vessel at one lock, walk or bicycle through the countryside, talk to the locals and meet the vessel further along the way. In the Amazon there were no natural breaks – and no automatic, easy contact with locals. From Manaus one could navigate for days, even weeks, without stopping. An Amazon boat captain had to make deliberate stops, otherwise his passengers would see nothing in detail.

I soon got to know the local waterways, preferring, like most pleasure-boat pilots, to cruise the clear, black, slow-moving Rio Negro and its tributaries, rather that the faster-flowing, muddy Amazon. Although the poor, acid soils of the Negro basin were not good for agriculture, they supported a luxuriant forest and made cruising the black river preferable in several ways. Among the advantages of the Negro, compared to the Amazon, were: (1) fewer inhabitants and therefore less destruction of the forest on the banks, (2) practically no mosquitoes, (3) sandy beaches instead of alluvial mud, (4) water more attractive to swim in, (5) easy navigation with not much current and (6) no floating grass or tree trunks to interfere with the navigation.

The main problem on board Cisne's was to avoid other weekend boaters, of which there were a lot. In view of the limited possibilities of getting out of town by road, many people from Manaus took to the water on Saturdays and Sundays. Some set out in luxury motor-yachts equipped with sophisticated accessories such as micro-light floatplanes and motorized beach tricycles. Middle-aged men in swimsuits, sunglasses and gold necklaces cruised in high-speed launches with young bikini-clad paramours. There were water skiers, jet skiers, even a rowing club and, on breezy afternoons, wind surfers. At the same time, hoards of poorer people set out in commercial transport boats that ran services to nearby beaches.

The only class of leisure craft not well represented in the central Amazon was large sailboats. The average windspeed in Manaus was too low to make it worthwhile investing in any sailing vessel larger than a surfboard. Even in colonial times Portuguese master mariners sailed across the Atlantic, but used Indian paddlers to get around in the central Amazon.

In the process of avoiding other weekenders, I began to find little creeks close to Manaus where one could enjoy solitude and wilderness despite intense urban activity not far away. Many pleasure boats helped my evasiveness by being gregarious amongst themselves. Those whose vessels were primarily status symbols liked to show off, for which an audience was required. Thus large motor yachts often headed collectively for the same venue, such as Lake Tupé, where they could be seen by one another. Runabouts tended to head for closer beaches, such as Areial or Praia da Lua. Shunning these and other Meccas, I would navigate in small side arms through flooded forest, where big, fast boats could not enter, and I would content myself with a small patch of sand instead of the large beaches favoured by Brazilians. By judiciously applying these tactics I could usually escape the crowd.

Typically on a Friday evening Cisne's travelled a few hours in darkness. After a little practice, I could find my way from the mooring in the Rio Tarumã to virtually anywhere in the Lower Rio Negro area, even on nights with no moon. Only once did I loose my way; I was caught in fog, a rare phenomenon sometimes occurring around midnight as mist rolled off the forest into the smaller tributaries. I simply tied the boat to a tree and we slept where we were, to continue after sunrise. Fog never persisted beyond breakfast time.

Passing the night in the boat while it was moored to a random tree in a deserted creek was in any case a delightful experience. One of Cisne's most enjoyable features was the perfect silence once the main engine had been switched off. The boat required no noisy machines to keep its basic comforts operational. The lights ran off batteries, the refrigerator was an ice box and the plumbing worked by gravity.

In spite of the proximity to Manaus, the lower Rio Negro offered lots to see and do. Typical things to show visitors were: *floresta de terra firme* (highland forest); *igapó* (forest flooded by black water); *campinas* (sandy areas with special vegetation); *buritizais* (swampy areas covered by pure stands of *buriti* palms); peasants' homes (with Brazil nuts, fruit trees, rubber trees, manioc plantations and occasional cattle); fishermen and their catch; boat building; Indian ceramics; caimans; dolphins; waterfalls; and beaches. Visitors also liked fishing for piranhas and swimming – though usually not in the same spot.

Some of the attractions were seasonal. For instance, at low water (September to February) there were a lot of waterfalls where streams on the beach dropped off a rock layer that was submerged at high water. Beaches, too, were more numerous and bigger when the water was low. On the other hand, at low water it was impossible to navigate through flooded forest; all the trees were high and dry. (No trees germinate under water, even if they subsequently tolerate being under water for substantial periods. Hence the so-called "flooded forest" occurs on land that is dry for part of the year and should really be called "seasonally flooded forest".)

Since most of her passengers were friends of mine, Cisne's was a jolly boat. I often sang for or with my guests in the evenings. The inaugural trip found me mellow with *caipirinhas*, sitting in the Paricatuba waterfall, about two hours upstream from Manaus, gazing at the campfire's reflection in the dark water and singing *"Auf de schwäb'sche Eisebahne"*, with an attempted Schwabian accent, to the amazed amusement of the German passengers. The multilingual repertoire I had developed at the Amazon Beach Party served me well, not only on that occasion, but on many others.

My first longer trip with Cisne's was also the first time that I took passengers from a travel agency. A friend of mine in the travel business heard that I had a small boat and asked me to run a weeklong trip for some clients of his, namely a Swiss doctor and his French-speaking family now living in the USA. The trip he proposed coincided with Christmas and New Year, so the seasonal holidays from my permanent job allowed me to be available. I thought the passengers would be an interesting group and the timing was right, so I agreed to take them.

For me this was a very different adventure from my weekend sorties. Firstly, as it was longer in duration, it would automatically take me into areas I did not know. Secondly, if we got into trouble, I did not have any pre-established link of friendship with the passengers to help solve the problems. Thirdly, I had to provide the meals. (Previously my clients brought their own food and catered for themselves and for me.)

To deal with the catering problem, I looked to my girlfriend for help. By this time I was going out with Arlete, a young lady from a well-to-do family in the city of Belém. Amongst her many attributes, Arlete was a great cook. She had a natural flare for producing the right amount of tasty food at the right time. I invited her to come on the voyage as cook and companion. To my delight she accepted.

We were inexperienced and did not know, for instance, how long we could keep food in the tropical heat without a conventional refrigerator. People told us that a block of ice would last for about five days in a medium sized polystyrene box, depending on how often we opened the lid. They said we should work with two boxes; one would be the "working box" containing food and ice, while the other would be a store of ice opened only occasionally to replenish the working box.

The plan with the ice would certainly work for the first few days, but we were still uncertain about the last couple of days. We had to be certain of having a supply of interesting food even if the ice should run out. Our answer was to turn to traditional solutions. For instance, the famous Brazilian black-bean dish, *feijoada*, used salt pork, which did not require refrigeration, so it featured on the menu towards the end of the trip. Likewise, on one of the last days Arlete prepared tasty fish balls from *piracuí*, an easily preserved protein-rich powder that Indians made from dried catfish meat. Last, but certainly not least, like many local boats, we took along a live chicken to slaughter and eat when required.

The clients were due to arrive in the early hours of a Saturday morning, on a flight that originated in Miami and had Santa Cruz de la Sierra, Bolivia, as its final destination. A guide from the travel agency would meet them at Manaus airport and bring them to the boat, which was moored on a beach on the outskirts of the city. Arlete and I were on board, ready and waiting to greet them. We waited and waited. No news. Finally I hitched a ride to the nearest telephone to find out what had happened. It turned out that there had been a tremendous thunderstorm in Manaus at the moment the plane was due to land. Since there were few passengers for Manaus, the pilot had decided to continue straight to Santa Cruz de la Sierra rather than wait for the weather to clear. My clients were in Bolivia, at the airline's expense, and would not be arriving in Manaus for another two days.

That, of course, gave us a chance to stock up with ice again, thereby pretty well guaranteeing that there would be no problem with food storage. However, because the menus had been prepared in advance and the provisioning done in accordance with the original plan, it still seemed a good idea to take the live chicken along with us.

Finally the Swiss doctor and his family arrived and we set off. The route I chose involved crossing the Rio Negro and then proceeding upstream close to its southern bank. The river was five miles across where I intended to cross it. I could see bad weather brewing in the distance, but imagined that we would get across and be in sheltered waters on the other side before the storm broke. We were already two days behind schedule and naturally anxious to get going.

How wrong I was with my weather prediction! Cisne's was not a fast boat. Furthermore I had set a diagonal course across the river, so that the five miles bank-to-bank was probably more like eight miles on our heading. That represented over an hour's navigation in Cisne's. We were half way across the river when a tempest of strong winds and driving rain hit us. The waves became bigger and started to come dangerously close to swamping us. One of the first things I had done on purchasing Cisne's was to raise its roof a handspan so as to make more headroom for foreigners (who were on average taller than Amazonians). However, the drawbacks of a higher roof now became all too apparent: the boat was more top-heavy, righting itself more slowly when rolling. In addition, there was more side area to catch the wind. The situation was especially dangerous because, with so many supplies on board, Cisne's already rode low in the water. It was the beginning of the trip and we had with us everything we needed for the next several days. In fact we were transporting so much stuff that even before starting out we had put some food, an ice box, the tools and the chicken into a large wooden canoe that we towed behind us. Although serving as extra space, the prime purpose of the canoe was to make side trips, such as spotting caimans, in places that Cisne's couldn't reach.

The passengers didn't seem to be worried by the storm, whereas I was desperate to stop the boat's excessive rolling. I decided to heave-to, hoping to ride the storm better with the waves coming directly from forward. Now, instead of dangerous rolling, we had violent pitching. Cisne's coped better with the waves in this position, but suddenly the out-of-phase pitching of the boat and the canoe caused the towrope to snap and the canoe started to drift away astern. Should we turn around to recover the canoe and risk putting the waves on the beam again? Or should we stay safely head to wind and risk losing the canoe? It was not an easy decision, but I turned Cisne's around and went back for the canoe. The hair-raising manoeuvre was eventually successful. However, when the towrope broke a second time, I decided it was too risky to try again, and we abandoned the canoe.

We stayed head to wind for about twenty minutes before conditions calmed down enough for us to run safely for shelter in a creek on the south side of the river. The waters of the creek were so calm that one could hardly believe how rough the weather had been on the open river. Arlete made afternoon tea to pass the time while we waited for the storm to abate completely. Then we set out to try to find the drifting canoe. The Swiss passengers took all this very serenely. They seemed to conform to their country's stereotype in not demonstrating strong emotions: they had not let the episode with the Bolivian airline perturb them and I suppose that the doctor dealt with life-and-death situations routinely in his professional life. The family said they had come to the Amazon for an adventure and they were glad to be having one.

After tea we set out to look for the canoe in the huge expanse of the lower Rio Negro. We tried to retrace our course and reach the position where we thought the canoe had broken loose. Then we motored downwind, searching with powerful binoculars, which the doctor had brought along for bird watching. Finally, much to our relief, we discovered the canoe, oriented across the wind and riding easily over the remaining slight swell. As we approached it, we found that there was surprisingly little water in it and, best of all, the chicken was alive and well. The bird lay on the floorboards clucking away as if mumbling under its breath that he was glad to see us but critical of the whole procedure.

After this adventure the chicken became part of the family. We gave him the most common name of riverside men, Raimundo. At the end of the trip no one could bear the thought of slaughtering Raimundo to eat, so we gave him away to a local peasant. Although he probably finished up in the cooking pot, at least he gained a little extra time to enjoy the banks of the Rio Negro.

The rest of the trip was peaceful and very agreeable. We spent New Year's Eve on a small, uninhabited island with a beautiful sandy beach and no mosquitoes –

a chance to sing a folksong or two in English and French. Wildlife was scarce, but right at the end of the excursion, as we disembarked, we found a deadly fer-de-lance snake on the path between Cisne's and the car. The landowner killed it instantly with a machete. Then, as we drove to the airport we saw a sloth crossing the road. The sloth, adapted to living in trees, moved slowly and awkwardly on the asphalt, so we had plenty of time to stop and take close-up photographs. It often happened like that on excursions – one rarely saw animals, but then they appeared when you least expected them.

Taking all things into consideration, the voyage with the Swiss family was a success. Above all, Cisne's had not sunk during the storm. However, she did sink – in calm water at her moorings – several months later. I wasn't there to see her go down, but getting her back afloat turned out to be a fascinating exercise.

I had gone to Europe on holiday and left Cisne's tied up for safekeeping at a jungle lodge in a lake on the south side of the Amazon, a two-day boat trip away from Manaus. Although all the workers at the lodge knew that my vessel was there to be looked after, no individual person took responsibility for it. As a result, through a combination of leaking seams, rainwater and neglect, down she went and nobody told me.

After my return from Europe I went to the lodge to pick up my boat, only to find out that this would not be possible. The workers showed me the scene of the accident. The vessel's roof was about four feet below the surface of the lake. In the strong sunlight through the dark, clear water I could see fish swimming in and out of the cabin. They were angelfish and their beauty completely repressed my anger at the workers' negligence.

That night I talked to several people about how to recover my vessel. A master carpenter who looked after construction and maintenance at the lodge said that the job would require fifteen men for a day. That was not as onerous as it may sound, because in the interior a labourer's wage was only two dollars a day. In addition, he said, I should give each man a bottle of sugarcane liquor (unit price about a dollar). In this way the men could party as they worked. I would also need to bring a change of oil for the motor. It sounded like a bargain and I told him to organise the gang.

I returned to Manaus to continue my weekday research job and went to the lodge the following weekend with the cash, booze and oil. Early on Sunday morning the work gang appeared. They were all local men, who knew each other and generally met on Sundays to play football. They were going to have some fun and earn a little spare cash with my project before playing their habitual game.

They explained to me how they intended to recover my boat. One man would dive down and tie a stout rope to the stem post. Then they would drag the vessel along the bottom of the lake into the shallower water of a side arm. Once they could get the gunwhales just out of the water, they would start bailing and the boat would rise. The plan was conceptually simple but not so easy in practice. There were many underwater obstacles to manoeuvre around. Changing direction meant coordinating the whole gang to pull from a different position. As the day wore on, they started opening the bottles of sugarcane liquor. Whether this made them stronger I cannot say, but it certainly made them happier and louder. When they finally got the hull to the surface of the water they all jumped into the vessel with buckets and started throwing water out as fast as they could. Eventually Cisne's started to rise. They immediately put chocks underneath her and stakes to stop her keeling over.

When I returned the following weekend, they had changed the engine oil and Cisne's was ready to travel again. There was surprisingly little damage. When I first left the vessel at the lodge, at the beginning of my holiday, I had removed most portable things like mattresses, cooking utensils, alternator and battery. The gas cooker was still on board, but it dried out without problems. The cabin walls were oily and needed a coat of paint, but they were still intact. The carpenter told me the caulking was old and that Cisne's was leaking badly. He advised to be very careful on the voyage back to Manaus, otherwise she would sink again.

I set off alone, driving the boat for an hour and then pumping water out by hand for ten minutes. This became a routine until suddenly the pump developed a problem for which I needed a spare part. I was in a dilemma. If I left the boat to try to get the spare part, she might sink while I was away. Yet if I stayed on board and didn't repair the pump she would sink anyway. Finally I managed to improvise a repair and got pumping again. All through the night, when it was too dark to navigate, I still had to wake up hourly and pump. On the afternoon of the second day I arrived at a boatyard on the Manaus waterfront and asked them to haul Cisne's out of the water straight away and caulk her. To my great relief, the slipway was vacant and they hauled her out immediately.

Soon I was back in business operating my weekend trips with people who contacted me through the research institute. Many of my clients were biological specialists, some of whose knowledge gradually rubbed off on me. With each cruise I learned a little more natural history, which I could then share with the next clients. A Viennese professor taught me to recognise the commonest frogs. A German researcher explained to me the physiology of submerged plants. A French botanist from the Michelin Tyre Company's rubber plantation in Bahia showed me how to distinguish the true rubber tree from its cousins. American ornithologists taught me the English names of the birds, and so on.

As my knowledge increased, I began to be considered an "Amazon specialist" (which paradoxically in nature tourism means "Amazon generalist"). Within a short time a local company organising biological tours contacted me to work as a free-lance guide. Soon others approached me too, offering more work than I could possibly undertake while employed at the research institute.

These developments took place in the eighties, a significant decade for anyone like me working on energy supplies. The world price of oil, high since the mid-seventies, dropped dramatically in 1983, putting petroleum back at the centre of the energy scene and making research into alternative energy sources less important.

Suddenly no funding was available for my INPA studies. This disappointed me immensely, since I passionately felt that the river-powered generator I had invented showed tremendous promise. Not only could the invention produce useful amounts of electricity, but river current data indicated that it could function practically anywhere along the Amazon. I was heartbroken not to be able to finance long-term performance tests in a permanent floating installation.

The frustrations were two-fold. On one hand, a lot of interesting travel and natural history work was available, which I could not undertake because of my obligations at the research institute. On the other hand, my research work could not progress because of lack of funds. In short, I was wasting my time.

When British writer Anthony Smith invited me to accompany him on a steamboat down the River Araguaia (a southern tributary of the Amazon) to make a film for the BBC, the lure of excitement, action and travel, compared to stagnation at INPA, was irresistible. I resigned from research and made myself available for the steamboat adventure. While waiting for it to take place, although running Cisne's occasionally, I worked mainly on other people's riverboats, specialising in the role of naturalist rather than trip operator.

The riverboat on which I worked most frequently as a biological guide was the Tunã, a now defunct double-decked vessel, 26m long. It was faster, more spacious and more comfortable than Cisne's. Having a full-time nautical crew, the craft could navigate long distances at night, leaving plenty of time during the day for the two guides to lead the twenty passengers on local visits. It catered largely for tourists from North American and Europe.

The Tunã's standard 4-day itinerary provided an opportunity for tourists to enjoy and learn a lot about the biology of the Rio Negro. The clients went out by motor canoe mornings, afternoons and at night, so there was a good deal of close contact with nature and local life. I learned more and more as I tried to find answers to the endless questions that passengers asked. We would walk in the high forest, canoe through the flooded forest, fish for piranhas, swim in the river, visit local farmers and craftsmen and go out at night with a searchlight looking for nocturnal life.

I particularly liked the night-time excursions. They were richer and more varied than those I had done in the past. We almost always saw the spectacled caiman, which I already knew well, but the trips on board the Tunã also provided opportunities literally to get to grips with black caimans, smooth-fronted caimans, birds, snakes, iguanas and opossums, none of which I had handled previously.

With regard to the kind of caimans found, I learned that there were good reasons why I had previously seen spectacled caimans rather than black caimans. Black caimans had been hunted to the verge of extinction because of their large size (up to 15 ft in length). They were so large that immature adults were shot before they had chance to reproduce. Without a supply of new eggs, populations declined rapidly. However, more recently there are signs that the decrease in numbers of black caimans may be reversing, especially in protected areas like the Anavilhanas Archipelago. Some government officials are even considering legalising the controlled hunting of caimans, at least in selected areas, such as at Nhamundá on the lower Amazon.

We saw smooth-fronted caimans (maximum size 4½ ft) much less frequently than either spectacled or black caimans. They were not particularly rare, but they inhabited smaller creeks and streams with difficult access. Like spectacled caimans, smooth-fronted caimans reproduced when still too small to be shot for the (illegal) skin trade. Hence hunting did not threaten their reproduction. They were the liveliest type of caiman to catch by hand. They struggled strongly to try to escape and their very bony skin made them hard to grasp.

Another new experience for me was discovering places where young caimans had just hatched and were still clustered together near the nest site. From a distance the searchlight picked out myriad red-dot reflections, each one representing the eye of a 9-inch, baby caiman. The hatchlings were easy prey. Just with one hand one could catch several of the tiny creatures.

There were frighteningly big caimans too. One night a local fisherman took Tunã's clients and myself by motor-canoe into the centre of a lake near Novo Airão (about 100 km up the Rio Negro from Manaus). He wanted to show us how to attract large caimans by imitating their mating call. Conditions were favourable: the searchlight produced lots of red reflections on the banks of the lake, indicating that there were plenty of caimans around us. Stopping the boat and switching the motor off, the fisherman announced that he would make the caiman mating call. He then made a kind of stifled coughing sound. I had seen guides do this before to no avail and was sceptical about the whole concept. However, this time it really worked. Within thirty seconds, the longest caiman I have seen outside a zoo came swimming sinuously across the surface of the dark lake, attracted by the prospect of finding a mate. Estimating the reptile's size to be around 12 ft, and fearful of the consequences of its imminent sexual frustration, we started the motor and fled. Thus the most memorable of my caiman spotting experiences was also the briefest.

I learned to catch birds by hand at night, snatching them out of the vegetation while standing, kneeling or lying on the front deck of a motorised canoe. Nocturnal species, such as nighthawks and potoos, were easy to spot in the riverside trees, because their open eyes reflected the searchlight. Sleeping diurnal birds, such as kiskadees and kingfishers (in the trees) and blue gallinules and wattled jacanas (in the floating grass), were more difficult to find, because they had their eyes shut.

Catching birds gave visitors a chance to observe some interesting biological adaptations: the nighthawk's funnel-like moustache for deflecting flying insects into its wide mouth; the potoo's immense eyes enabling it to see in the dark as well as we do in the day; the kingfisher's large bill for catching fish; the jacana's long toes for spreading its weight lightly over the floating vegetation.

Catching two or three nighthawks at a time particularly impressed passengers. It was not as difficult as one might suppose. On cooler nights, young band-tailed nighthawks often huddled together on their favourite perch and could be seized as if they were a single bird. The catcher required no special visual acuity, just practice.

All birds, irrespective of species, flew away safely after observation. Nighthawks lost a few feathers (possibly a defence mechanism making them harder to grasp), but I never saw one that couldn't fly away well on release.

Nocturnal snakes, which we caught with a braided nylon noose deployed on a tubular plastic handle, were another popular item to catch for closer inspection. The species we most frequently saw was the Amazon tree boa, which is non-venomous and rarely grows more than two meters long. We would find them in the branches of the vegetation overhanging the water, where they preyed on bats, birds and frogs, which they first seized with their sharp fangs and then asphyxiated by constriction. They were easy to spot. Snakes have no eyelids, so their eyes were always open and capable of reflecting the light from our searchlights. They were particularly common when the water was high.

Whenever we caught a tree boa, it would make an aggressive display, opening its mouth wide to show its fangs and making rapid darting movements as if about to strike. The catcher had to be careful handling the snake, because the fangs, although not poisonous, could easily draw blood. A further need for caution arose because the species varied considerably in colour and markings, possibly leading to misidentification with lethal consequences. Catching a snake with a lasso was easy. Releasing it could be more difficult. Wary of the possible dangers, I always favoured cutting the noose as the simplest and quickest way to liberate the animal.

My lack of courage with regard to handling snakes stems from the time I was bitten by one – one of the most frightening events of my life. The accident happened while I was trying to catch an emerald boa (a close relative of the tree boa mentioned above). Although I aimed to seize the serpent just behind its head, I missed my aim and finished up grabbing about four inches too far back, giving the snake enough of its neck free to be able to turn and bite me, drawing blood. Startled, I used my other hand to adjust my grip. The snake bit that too. Dropping the reptile and sucking my small puncture wounds, I hoped, suddenly with desperate uncertainty, that I had identified the snake correctly. I couldn't help remembering that not long ago a director of Brazil's leading snake research institute at Butantã, had been killed on a picnic with his family by a deadly coral snake, which he misidentified. He thought it was a harmless false coral and picked it up. It reacted and bit him fatally. My panicking brain kept reminding me that if he, an expert, could get it wrong, so could I. Too far from civilisation to seek medical help, I looked at my watch, telling myself that if there were no medical problems within twenty minutes, things would be alright.

I was deeply shocked and feared for my life, but I could not objectively tell if my nervous agitation and palpitations were caused by panic or by the bite. At the same time I endeavoured to convince the tourists who were with me that nothing of consequence had happened. In the end my worries subsided and all was well. However, my confidence had been undermined. For a long time afterwards, I would only catch snakes if I had a lasso.

Lassos had to be well made. Once I pulled a small, unidentified snake down inside the handle of one that wasn't. Removing the animal in the dark near people was difficult and potentially dangerous. Using a good lasso increased one's catching radius and was safer than hand-grabbing. One could use the same lasso to catch a variety of animals, including iguanas and opossums.

Another activity I liked when I worked on board the Tunã was walking in the forest. At some point in the voyage the riverboat would stop and the guides would lead the twenty passengers on the so-called "jungle walk". Ideally two guides accompanied the walk, one a local person from the forest and the other a trained biologist. In this way the clients received a practical and an interpretational vision of the rainforest and its natural history. With my botanical training, I was the academic guide. My good friend Chico was often the local guide.

I could describe hundreds of "jungle walks," but the one on which Dr. Kramm lost his glasses is a good example. It started in the typical manner. The Tunã stopped in front of good-looking forest on the north bank of the Rio Negro near the mouth of the Rio Cuieras. The boat had been in the area before and Chico had already made a trail into the high forest. To reach the walk the sailors ferried the passengers and guides ashore in large motor canoes.

The first question from the passengers came during the canoe ride: "What is the difference between Rainforest and Jungle?" At least I knew the answer to that one. I replied that "jungle" was originally a word from northern India describing the kind of thicket vegetation in which one would shoot tigers. By extension it had become a popular word in English for any dense tropical vegetation. "Rainforest," on the other hand, was a more academic term, which specifically referred to natural forest growing in areas of high rainfall (more than 1500 mm of rain per year) with no pronounced dry season (more than 50 mm of rain in the driest month). Basically scientists studied rainforest, whereas journalists got lost in the jungle. I explained that I would review some of the characteristics of rainforest during the course of the walk. With that, our group left the canoes and Chico led the way inland.

In order to reach the forest on the land above the high-water mark, the group had to walk through some seasonally-flooded forest that was currently dry. When we reached the high-water mark, I asked the passengers to look around and observe the vegetation closely. Although, with the exception of Dr. Kramm, none of the passengers on the walk were botanists, everybody could appreciate that the vegetation in front of us on the high land was different from the vegetation behind us in the zone subject to flooding. I drew passengers' attention to a few, easy to recognise differences. For example, the Brazil nut tree (which had large, wooden, ball-shaped fruit-pods) only grew on the high land. On the other hand, the pot-bellied rubber tree (with light, smooth bark and its leaflets in threes) only grew in the seasonally flooded area. Similarly we found the fern-like ground cover, a species of *Selaginella,* only on the high ground and the large, spiny *jauari* palm only in the seasonally flooded area. Dr. Kramm, who was a botany professor on holiday from his university in Germany, made a much longer list of which plants belonged to which zone.

Chico, machete in hand, led us further into the highland. He had made the track on a previous occasion, but occasionally he needed the machete to clear fallen debris to let our line of tourists through. Once we were well into the forest we stopped again to look at the plants. I harvested a palm leaf more than a metre long and a similar-sized elliptical leaf of a species of *Heliconia.* The passengers appreciated that the leaves I harvested were bizarre compared to the leaves they habitually saw in northern temperate regions. They agreed that my leaves looked "tropical." I asked them to imagine other obviously "tropical" plants. Besides palms, their suggestions included bamboo, banana, sugarcane, sweetcorn and *Philodendrons*. Even without any formal botanical training, the passengers instinctively – and correctly – chose examples from the group of plants that have only one embryonic leaf in their seeds – the so-called monocotyledonous plants. (Most "conventional" plants have two seed-leaves in their seeds and are called dicotyledonous.) To formalise their observations and get walking again, I explained that in the colder regions of the world monocotyledonous plants tended to be small – like tulips and daffodils; whereas in the tropics they could be gigantic – like coconuts and bamboo.

When we came to a tree-fern I stopped the group again and did some more theorising. First I asked the passengers to look at the forest floor and notice that practically no sunlight came straight through the canopy. This meant that in general the area of leaves in the forest was much greater than the surface area of the land on which the trees stood. The dense canopy was important in reducing the temperature at ground level. It also protected the soil from the mechanical impact of heavy rain. Moreover, it retained and re-evaporated rainwater, and transpired water from the soil through the trees into the atmosphere. I tried to help people realise that the forest made its own climate – it was cooler and wetter than a pasture would be. Half the rain that fell on the forest came from the forest.

Next I asked passengers to look at the tree nearest to them and then to look at the second-nearest tree and decide whether the two trees were of the same or different species. The result was overwhelmingly that the trees were different. This contrasted sharply with what would happen in a European forest. If they stood near an oak tree in England, there is a very good chance that the next-nearest tree would also be an oak. The tropical forest was characterised by great biological diversity, whereas temperate forests contained only a few species.

Nevertheless, I told them – and this was impossible to illustrate, but they should keep their eyes open – the renowned diversity of the tropical rainforest was deficient in one group of trees. There were no conifers in the Amazon: no firs, no pines, no spruce. They might see Caribbean pines in plantations or Norfolk Island Pines (and others) in gardens – but not in the forest.

Finally, I turned to the tree-fern and mentioned one more point before moving on: all the vegetation tended to be woody. "That's obvious," most people thought, "the forest is made of trees and the trees are made of wood." But before they had the opportunity of expressing these thoughts, I pointed out that it was not just the trees that were woody: vines could be woody (e.g. Jacob's ladder vine), grasses could be woody (e.g. bamboo) and even ferns could be woody – like the tree-fern by which we had stopped.

We continued our walk, stopping from time to time while Chico talked about medicinal plants, pointed out important timber species, showed us useful fibres and resins, demonstrated how to make shelters and animal traps and lots more. In this way he and I punctuated the walk and kept the group together.

When we reached a rotting dead branch lying on the ground, I stopped the group for a discussion of soil fertility. I crumbled some of the rotting wood and showed people that it was extensively penetrated by the roots of nearby trees. If these roots came out of the soil into the dead branch – I reasoned – it was because the rotting branch contained more nutrients for plant growth than did the soil itself. In other words, the main source of nutrients for the growth of the rainforest was the rotting biomass and not the soil. This had important negative implications for agriculture. If one cleared forest to make farms, one removed the source of rotting biomass and only infertile soil remained. One should not expect agriculture in the area to be very productive.

The forest only survived by recycling itself. Passengers could see that recycling went on fast: there was practically no humus layer underfoot, meaning that the recycling of dead material was going on as rapidly as growth.

To conclude my theorising, I mentioned a second and perhaps more important implication of recycling: on a net basis one should neither expect mature forest to produce oxygen for the world nor to clean up carbon dioxide from the air. Certainly, photosynthesis makes biomass, produces oxygen and absorbs carbon dioxide. However, rotting eliminates biomass, uses up oxygen and liberates carbon dioxide. If the total amount of biomass in the system remains constant, so must the amounts of oxygen and carbon dioxide.

While I was talking, Dr. Kramm had been photographing some ants. In the process, he inadvertently happened to disturb a colony of wasps in a nest hidden underneath an overhanging palm leaf. Suddenly the wasps started to attack us all, at which everyone screamed and fled away through the jungle as quickly as possible back to the canoes. Some passengers were so excited that they didn't stop at the canoes; they just ran straight into the water, where the wasps couldn't reach them.

When things had calmed down, we took stock of the situation. The number of actual stings was few and of those stung no one suffered a strong reaction. But in the melee Dr. Kramm had dropped his glasses. While the rest of us continued with our next tourist activity, Chico went back into the forest to look for the glasses. He didn't find them, but we promised that we would look for them again in the future.

In the following weeks we looked for the glasses systematically – to no avail. Months later, when I had long given up hope, I found them. I sent them by mail to Dr. Kramm's address in Germany. He was so grateful and pleased with the service that he wrote me a nice letter of thanks. Thereafter we exchanged more correspondence and he subsequently became one of my best friends.

I often think about that walk. We only went about half a mile into the forest before fleeing. Nevertheless, in a very short distance we had seen the main features of rainforest and how it worked. But nature had given us an extra lesson without needing an explanation from Chico or me: she had shown us how important the insects are in the forest – and there are more species of them than of all other organisms put together.

The riverboat Tunã had a pleasant sun deck situated well away from the noise of the engines, so there were plenty of opportunities for me to sing during the voyages. Its owners came from France, so I often sang songs in French. I particularly enjoyed songs by George Moustaki. Some of his songs were popular in Brazil and I identified with him – a bearded, romantic foreigner with a liking for the tropics. He expressed these sentiments brilliantly in songs like "*Mon Hamac*", "*Donnes du Rhum á ton Homme*" and his French version of Tom Jobim's bossa nova hit, "*Aguas de Março*". Singing "*Ma Liberté*" or "*Le Métèque*" while cruising through the forested channels of the Rio Negro thrilled me immensely. I think passengers liked it too.

For lazy sunsets with English speakers, the song "Summertime" from Gershwin's "Porgy and Bess" fitted wonderfully. With its talk of jumping fish and its tropical mood, the song could easily have been written for the Amazon, although it was actually set in Charleston, America. For more lively occasions, sea shanties suited the nautical atmosphere. Furthermore, I easily sympathised with their typical themes of pennilessness, drink, travel and the attractions of the girls on shore. During storms on the river I often led sing-alongs to keep spirits up. As high winds seldom lasted for more than an hour-and-a-half, my repertoire never ran out before the end of the bad weather. The songs Brazilians most liked to hear me sing were a set of sambas I wrote in Portuguese describing Brazil seen through foreign eyes. *"Samba Sotaque"* (literally "Samba with a Foreign Accent") was usually their favourite.

Working on board the Tunã not only extended my experience as a naturalist, but also broadened me socially. It brought me into contact with a class of people I seldom met in Manaus, namely, successful independent women. They were rare in Manaus, where men overwhelmingly occupied the best jobs. The spectrum of guests on board the Tunã reflected more egalitarian societies in Europe and America. There were often lady passengers from these areas travelling independently. They tended to dance less sexily than the girls of Manaus, but refreshingly always split the bill if we went out partying after the cruise.

Chapter 12

Fig 12. Sketch of Steamboat

WK

Media and the Steamboat

Many foreign journalists, writers, broadcasters and filmmakers pass through Manaus. The city is a natural hub for a visitor wanting to get into the heartland of the Brazilian Amazon – and globally there is a large, fashionable demand for documentary material about rainforest biology, deforestation, Indians, herbal medicine and so on. I have met a lot of people from overseas on Amazonian documentary assignments and worked with some of them.

Getting involved with visiting media-men's projects always turned up something new for me. For instance, a meeting between Robert Richter, an independent filmmaker from New York, and ex-workmate Philip Fearnside, the INPA specialist on deforestation, made me aware of some of the numbers relating to the amount of CO_2 in the atmosphere. Philip's calculations showed that burning fossil fuels would be in the long run a much greater source of atmospheric CO_2 than deforestation ever could be. Burning the whole Amazon forest down once-and-for-all would produce CO_2 approximately equivalent to 12 to 20 years' worth of world emissions from fossil fuels.

Priit Vesilind, a reporter from National Geographic Magazine, provided me with a chance to learn more about Amazonian agriculture. By interviewing people who owned farms that they had carved recently from virgin rainforest, Priit hoped to identify factors determining the success or failure of such farms. He took me along as interpreter and guide on part of his mission. Since I was doing the translation, if there was something new to be learned, I was bound to hear about it. I suggested to Priit that he and I should visit a government scheme that was settling people in the forest at Rio Preto da Eva, about 60 miles east of Manaus. I knew a lot of people there through INPA. Priit agreed and we went on a short visit.

The visit to Rio Preto turned out to be an enlightening excursion, because we met a poor family and a well-to-do family, farming almost side by side. The farms were so close together and the terrain so similar that one suspects that differences in the two families' backgrounds, attitudes, access to capital and choice of crops – not physical factors – were what determined the vastly different living standards we encountered on the farms.

The poor family lived in a small wooden house surrounded by a manioc plantation, which was their main source of food and revenue. They grew a few other useful plants, including herbs for cooking and medicine, some vegetables and a selection of fruit trees. The head of the household, Raimundo, hunted in the adjacent forest and kept chickens. The river was too far away for fishing. There were no machines. Raimundo's equipment consisted of a hoe, axe, machete, rifle, wheelbarrow and basic carpentry tools. He considered himself well off. Originally from the desperately poor northeastern state of Maranhão, where he could not farm due to lack of water, he thought himself a king in the Amazon, just because he had a stream running through his property. Raimundo was a typical *caboclo*; he worked hard, but could never accumulate enough surplus to become rich.

The well-to-do family was headed by Francisco Schwab, a Brazilian of German descent from São Paulo. Francisco, previously an industrial worker, had put his life's savings into his farm and its equipment. He also rented-out his house in São Paulo to provide a small income, while waiting for his crops to mature. Determined to make a commercial success of his Amazonian venture, he reviewed every operation on the farm for cost-effectiveness. For instance, when clearing forest, he initially tried to sell logs to sawmills. The receipts didn't cover the cost of the truck used for transport. From then on, whenever he cleared forest, he just saved the timber he needed for fences and construction and burned all the rest. Looking at the economics of his citrus plantation, he noticed the high cost of buying grafted seedlings. In response, he learned first to economise by grafting his own seedlings, and later made a profit selling grafted seedlings to others. He knew through personal experience the price and benefits of fertilisers and pesticides. He did not plant manioc, the traditional crop of the Amazon; he considered it gave a poor economic return for a lot of hard work. Yet, he was not afraid of hard work. (He just didn't like getting little for it.) Priit and I arrived at his farm on a public holiday and found the whole family, Francisco, his wife and two teenage daughters, at work sorting oranges for sale in Manaus.

Oranges were Francisco's main crop. He also grew some other types of tropical fruit and raised cattle. A sceptic might have thought Francisco was still living off his initial capital, but I believe not. In the five years since we had first met, his material well being had improved noticeably, evidenced by a new brick house under construction next door to the old wooden one and a new truck parked near his dilapidated old pick-up.

The principal difference between Francisco and Raimundo, apart from the amount of initial capital, was that the man from São Paulo treated farming rigorously as a business, whereas the man from Maranhão was accustomed to a life of subsistence outside the economic system.

In the article he wrote, Priit did not specifically mention Francisco's success. I felt this was a pity, because one hears so much about poor farms like Raimundo's. The success of hard-working, well-capitalised owner-farmers, like Francisco, should be noted.

On the road to Rio Preto, Priit and I also passed several prosperous fruit, vegetable and chicken farms belonging to Japanese immigrants and their families. We stopped at a couple to interview their owners. The farmers' parents or grandparents had come from Japan as part of a now-extinct Brazilian government immigration programme to strengthen and diversify Brazil's agriculture. The Japanese community grew a lot of the vegetables consumed in Manaus, and a similar community supplied the city of Belém. The key to the success of the Japanese and to the success of Francisco Schwab, was to shun manioc production, identify more profitable sectors of the market (such as fruit and vegetables) and work intently to meet demand. The immigrants' positive results were remarkable enough to be epitomised in a local joke: Question – How do you grow good tomatoes in the Amazon? Answer – Plant them on a Japanese farm.

Most media projects were interesting. However, film work, despite its glamour, easily became tedious; it required lots of repetition for retakes, cutaways, sound recordings and so on. In any case, filmmakers always shot vastly more film than they ever used in the final product. Making the Los Angeles CBS TV film, "Two on the Town: Up the Amazon" would have been an instance of tedious shooting, had it not been for light relief provided by mishaps during the sessions. The stars, Melody Rogers and Bob Chandler had to explore the Amazon looking perpetually cool, well-groomed and successful. When the moment came for Melody, in solar topi and pink Reeboks, to do an imitation of Tarzan's Jane swinging through the jungle, the "vine" (actually aerial roots of a

Philodendron species) broke in mid-swing, unceremoniously depositing our heroine, unharmed but indignant, on the muddy forest floor. There was no retake, since the "vine" had fallen down on top of Melody, but the hilarious first take not only broke the tedium of the filming, but was actually used to brighten up the final film. Another blunder occurred during the evening caiman-spotting excursion; the catcher by mischance dropped a live caiman inside Melody and Bob's canoe. That sequence too was used in the final copy.

No single communicator had a greater impact on my life in the Amazon than the British writer and broadcaster, Anthony Smith. It was he who triggered my leaving INPA by inviting me to join him in a steamboat adventure. I first met him when he was travelling with his then producer, George Monbiot, reporting for a BBC Radio series called "Forest Frontier". Anthony interviewed virtually every English-speaker at INPA, including me. When we talked about ways of seeing more of the forest, I volunteered to take him out in my boat and he accepted.

Our friendship burgeoned from then on. He liked steam engines; I had written a paper on steam power. I liked hot-air balloons; he had flown a hydrogen balloon in East Africa and built an airship in England. Each of us worked to some extent with Amazonian natural history. We both wanted more experience of the Amazon and felt we could work together.

Anthony had already written a book called "Mato Grosso" based on his participation in a Royal Society and Royal Geographical Society expedition to Brazil. He was now planning a new adventure, using a series of steamboat trips as the *leitmotif*. The idea was to build a steam-powered craft to a novel design allowing the vessel to be dismantled and portaged into regions that conventional craft could not reach. He would make trips, say, on a white-water river, a black-water river, in a lake system, in a gold-mining area, in an Indian reservation and so on until he had enough material for a comprehensive description of the whole Amazon. The steamboat would be an autonomous vehicle, fuelled by driftwood from the riverbanks, and the "romance" of steam power would add charm to the final narrative. It sounded a terrific project. So when he invited me to take part, I readily agreed, even though details, particularly how to finance the venture, still had to be worked out.

Well over a year later, Anthony, back in England, succeeded in getting BBC TV to sponsor the steamboat's construction and the filming of its first trip. The film would be screened as part of the nature/travel series "the Natural World". Although it was not a millionaire project, there was a lot of work in front of us; we had to build, test and equip the boat, transport it to the starting point, do the voyage, and finally dismantle, transport and store everything ready for the next adventure. Involvement in the project demanded too much of my time to be compatible with my job at INPA, so I resigned from my research post. This was not a heart-rending decision, because I was frustrated in my scientific research by lack of funds, due to the economic crisis that Brazilian governmental institutions were suffering at that time.

Anthony wanted his steamboat to combine ease of dismantling, portability, light weight, stability, shallow draft and maximum living-space. In response to these requirements he gradually conceived an intuitive, catamaran design, which he formalised in a sketch on the back of an envelope. This picture showed a vessel consisting of a frame-tent mounted on a platform over two aluminium canoes. Behind the living area was the propulsion unit, which was probably the world's only steam-powered outboard motor. A flexible pipe from the fixed, wood-burning boiler supplied steam to the moveable engine mounted on a swivel between the floats. The helmsman steered the craft by turning the whole engine and drive shaft unit to the left or right. He could also swing the engine and drive shaft unit vertically, to raise the propeller in shallow water.

Based on Anthony's sketch and descriptions, an English engineer in São Paulo worked out a detailed design for the craft. This man was Jonathan Thornton, an Englishman who had been in Brazil for 15 years. Jonathan was well known in ballooning circles in Brazil and knew Anthony through ballooning activities. He was a partner in an engineering company manufacturing high-pressure hydraulic equipment, so he had access to all the tools necessary for building a steamboat. Hence he was a terrific asset to Anthony's project; and finally joined us on the voyage.

The fourth and last member of the steamboat crew was 25-year-old Bruno Sellmer, who also lived in São Paulo. He was the expedition's still photographer. As the only native Brazilian on board, he also looked after public relations. The common denominator between Bruno, Jonathan, Anthony and myself, apart from the steamboat, was an interest in ballooning. We three Englishmen were balloon pilots and Bruno worked in a ballooning company. Anthony had promised the BBC that a hot-air balloon would be taken along on the steamboat trip.

I went to São Paulo to help build the steamboat, staying at Jonathan's large, suburban house, in the yard of which the craft gradually took shape. Much of the construction involved routine manual work. However we managed to make it more agreeable by occasionally going ballooning. While we were building the steamboat the first ever Brazilian National Balloon Festival took place, with the presence of nine balloons and all four steamboat crewmembers.

Preparations for the expedition became more intense when the boiler and engine arrived by airfreight from England. Because Brazil did not allow the importation of used machinery, we had to allege that the imported equipment was brand new. Paradoxically, the second-hand engine, a Stuart Turner design from 1906, aroused no suspicions at customs because it looked clean and shiny. On the other hand, the new boiler, built specially by the London Living Steam Museum in Kew, was sooty and full of ash from tests. The customs officials took a long time to be convinced that it had never been used outside the factory.

With the arrival of the propulsion system we were able to see the complete craft on the water for the first time. She had considerable visual appeal. The outboard-motor configuration displayed the copper pipes, naked cranks and reversing valve-gear of the compound-double engine to maximum advantage. A crooked chimney and an aluminium lookout tower added a touch of fairytale charm.

It was good television. However, there were three serious problems. Firstly, in spite of the lightness of the hulls, the enormous weight of the boiler and engine meant that the vessel's freeboard was low, with a serious risk of shipping water and possibly sinking in wavy conditions. Secondly, the boat's maximum speed was around four miles per hour, not a good prospect if ever we needed to travel any distance against the flow of a river. Finally, if it rained, lowering the walls of the tent produced so much windage that the vessel became difficult to control.

In spite of the problems, we decided we should proceed with making the film. We dismantled the steamboat in São Paulo and loaded it into a furniture van, along with all the expedition's other equipment, including my guitar and two extra boats to be used by the film crew. Of course the extra boats never appeared in the film, which featured only the steamboat.

Accompanied by a fleet of private cars, the furniture van headed for Barra do

Garças, a small town on the River Araguaia, two-day's drive north of São Paulo. Anthony had been there twenty years earlier, when writing his Mato Grosso book. He had decided that the first steamboat trip would take place from Barra do Garças, down the River Araguaia as far as we could go, possibly to the River Tocantins and the Tucurui hydroelectric reservoir, or maybe even further, round the dam to meet the Amazon at Belém. The cars accompanying the van carried the steamboat crew (Anthony, Jonathan, Bruno and me), the film crew (director, cameraman and sound engineer) and various well-wishers from São Paulo.

Filming started during the drive. The documentary began when the van left the basin of the River Plate and entered the Amazon basin, about 17° south of the equator. At that latitude the dry season of the southern winter was already well under way, meaning that red dust covered the roadsides and produced a dramatic plume behind the moving van, providing some fine visual effects for the film. The area's drought-resistant vegetation (known as *cerrado*) formed an appropriately exotic background for the pictures. It gave an impression of African "bush"; many of its sparse, low, gnarled trees had waxy leaves and corky bark.

The area where we started filming constituted the southern equivalent of the northern savannah belt I had observed near Boa Vista on my job-hunting trip. The road in the south was made of the same red laterite as in the north, producing the same omnipresent dust. No mountains in the south were as high as those in the north (which are the highest in the country). Nevertheless, near the van's route, the Serra do Caiapo rose to 1010m. As we dropped down its escarpment towards the River Araguaia, we were treated to spectacular views of a broad river valley shimmering in the afternoon sun.

Later in our trip we could build or dismantle the steamboat in about five hours, but at Barra do Garças the initial assembly took two days, even with numerous helpers. There were lots of last minute details to attend to. We fitted splashboards to the floats in a literally stopgap attempt to reduce the risk of sinking. The compass and radio were installed for the first time. However, some jobs, like wiring the navigation lights and the alternator, still had not been done by the time we set off.

The steamboat's departure from the beach was not, however, swift and decisive. The necessities of filming were such that the moment had to be recorded from the beach, from a high bank, from on board and with various close-ups. We therefore found ourselves pushing off, steaming away and then going back to the beach again to shoot the next angle. We pushed off four times in all. Only when we passed the first set of rapids were we sure there was no way back.

That night, camping on a sandbank, we took stock of the situation. We were fortunate in many respects. Firstly it was dry season. Locals informed us it would not rain in the next four months, meaning river level would be low, giving us lots of spacious sandbanks to sleep on under the stars – we would not have to sleep huddled for shelter under the roof of the steamboat. Another favourable aspect of the season was the relative lack of biting insects. Furthermore, the dry riverbanks contained a plentiful supply of driftwood to fuel our engine. Things looked hopeful, in spite of less than 6 inches freeboard at the stern, a top speed of only four knots and no means of charging batteries for the radio. Glad to have started the real adventure, we settled down to sleep, vaguely aware of the hum of some distant farm's generator.

The following day was typical. The sun rose at around 6.00 AM and shone from a clear, blue sky until around 6.00 PM. We breakfasted, loaded the steamboat and set out as soon as the steam pressure in the boiler reached 100 psi. From time to time we stopped to gather wood for fuel, or to film anything strange or beautiful. The river was wide and shallow, with winding channels bordered by sculpted sand banks and gallery forest. We met practically nobody, although occasionally the noise of machinery and glimpses of cattle indicated that there were big farms hidden behind the riverside trees. We prepared and ate lunch on the move. While the portable cooking stove was alight at midday we boiled river water to drink later.

Just before nightfall we selected another pleasant sandbank on which to camp. As soon as the boat's engine stopped, we quickly removed the burning wood from the firebox to prevent the boiler from boiling dry and exploding. (While the engine was turning, its automatic pump kept the boiler full, obviating this danger.) Thus started a daily ritual we called "the eternal flame": in the evening the boiler fire was shovelled out to become our campfire and in the morning we put the still-burning campfire back into the firebox.

Wildlife was abundant. We often saw spectacled caimans and sometimes black caimans. The most impressive birds we saw were jabiru storks, which stood over four feet tall. We regularly passed them in large numbers at the water's edge. Hoatzins (strange, shy, pheasant-like, herbivorous cuckoos, whose young can swim and have claws on their wings) showed themselves occasionally, but more often one could tell that they were in the riverside trees by their flitting movements, a noise like husky breathing and a strong, fetid smell. We frequently heard howler monkeys before dawn, but only saw squirrel monkeys. The largest mammal we observed was a brocket deer, although many other furry quadrupeds, including *capivaras*, tapirs and jaguars, left tracks in the sand and mud near our campsites at night. We encountered two snakes, both in the non-poisonous boa family: one was a twelve-foot anaconda, which slid down the sunny bank into the water as we approached; the other was an emerald boa about 5 ft long, which apparently spent the night with us on our sandbank. Fresh-water turtles regularly basked on waterside logs and stones.

Filming animals from the steamboat was not easy. In normal operation the engine made very little noise. However, whenever the cameraman required us to slow down or stop, the unused steam quickly built up in the boiler and blasted off, scaring the creatures away. If the fire were doused to prevent this happening, it later took us at least half an hour to raise steam to travel again. In other words, too much or too little steam pressure usually prohibited a second shot. The problem of equating boiler fire with steam demand in stop/start conditions was something I had not been aware of when I had written an academic paper about wood as a fuel. With more hands-on experience, some of the romance of steam power disappeared.

Many local people considered fish to be the most important wildlife of the River Araguaia. Although the producer did not feature fishing in the film, we passed a few lodges and boats that catered for Brazilian and foreign sport fishermen who trolled for peacock bass or angled the giant catfish *piraiba* and *pirarara*. Occasionally we met commercial fishermen. One of the techniques they used for catching catfish was new to me. It consisted of putting piranhas as live bait on large hooks hanging about a metre below floats made of five-gallon plastic drums (one hook per float). A fisherman would bait about a dozen hooks and release the floats in the current. He then drifted downstream in his boat close to the floats. If one of the floats started to agitate violently, it meant that a large catfish had snapped the bait and become hooked. The fishermen lassoed the bobbing float and eventually dragged the hooked catfish into his boat. If after a while there were no strikes, he checked the bait, regrouped the floats and tried again.

Local authorities controlled fishing on the River Araguaia quite thoroughly. Officials twice searched our vessel for illegal nets – the bag containing the balloon looked suspiciously as though it might hold a poacher's net. However, we later found out that most of the government controls of fishing were carried out on land rather than on the river itself; checkpoints on access roads prevented vehicles from transporting prohibited quantities of fish out of the area.

Although we tried angling for the best game fish, we were much better at catching piranhas. We caught lots of the red-bellied ones, especially in the backwaters behind sandbanks. Barbecued piranha became a frequent dish for supper. Anthony wanted to demythologise the legendary piranha danger by being filmed swimming while the rest of us were catching piranhas. One day we did it. In the final film the sequence lasted about three minutes, but with retakes, cut-aways and dialogue, shooting took over two hours. During this time Anthony was constantly in the water – and Bruno and I caught a bucketful of piranhas. First we used salami as bait. When that ran out, we sacrificed one or two of our catch and used pieces of dead piranha. The film sequence graphically illustrated Anthony's correct assertion that piranhas ate lots of dead meat, even of their own kind; however, they did not attack large healthy animals. Anthony's only discomfort in the water came from harmless, minnow-like fish called *piabinha*, which pecked innocuously at his body-hair and nipples. Between shots Anthony was to be seen in the water, his hands covering his breasts, like a topless model posing for a modest pin-up photo.

Notwithstanding the expedition's capability to survive by eating piranhas, we actually carried enough food to eat handsomely for a couple of weeks or longer. As it turned out, about once a week we arrived at small towns where we could shop, at least for basics. With no ice on board we used a lot of tinned foodstuffs. Their weight, although considerable, was insignificant compared with that of the steam engine.

The riverside towns, although sleepy, had a lot of history. Aruanã was the first one we visited. It amazed us by having several old steamboat boilers decorating its main square. Local people told us that the immensely heavy pieces of Victorian ironwork were salvaged from boats of a steamboat company on the River Araguaia that went bankrupt in 1900. They said that previously the river had been an important trade route through the interior to diamond mines situated upstream from Barra do Garças. The riverside Indian tribes had been pacified relatively quickly, but when the gem deposits ran out, traffic on the river declined.

Later, when we arrived at the Tucuruí hydroelectric dam, we saw another manifestation of the former importance of the river as a trade route. Outside the power company's best hotel stood an ancient, wood-burning locomotive, a relic of a railway that once carried goods and passengers around rapids situated where the dam is now. The railway used to connect boat services on the upper and lower sections of the river.

But that was still weeks ahead. As we drank cold beer in a bar on the waterfront at Aruanã and looked first at the ancient boilers and then at the deserted river below, we realised that not only steamboats, but through-navigation in general had disappeared. Our expedition was reliving not one, but two traditions: firstly steam power and secondly long distance travel. We suddenly felt twice as happy with our adventure – and doubled our consumption of beer.

After the drinks, we went shopping in Aruanã and happened to meet a Carajás Indian girl working at the supermarket checkout. She belonged to a community of about thirty Indians living in an enclave on the outskirts of the town. Cheerful and uncomplicated, she taught us the Carajás names for familiar objects and spoke of her life in and outside the tribe. It transpired that she was about to marry a Brazilian man. On marrying him she would cease to be an Indian in the cultural sense, typifying the fate of her people. Many of the town's inhabitants had the same features, skin colour and history as she had. They were assimilated Indians. Significantly, like many young Carajás integrating into Brazilian society, she did not wear the tribe's traditional, black, circular marks on her cheeks. With her integration the number of tribal Indians in her community would diminish. But although Indian culture was dying, at least individuals were not. Whoever feels sad at the demise of Indian ways should remember our friend from the supermarket and her evident happiness at the prospect of marrying the man she loved. Other towns we visited later had already gone through the same assimilation process as at Aruanã: their older inhabitants could remember the time when Carajás Indians lived nearby in small enclaves that had gradually disappeared.

Large groups of Carajás Indians did still live on Bananal island, which we passed several days later. Often claimed to be the largest river island in the world, Bananal contained an important Indian reservation. It was the home of several tribes, some of which were politically well-organised and not always friendly to whites. Local people advised us not to camp on the Indian side of the river, advice that we followed rigorously. Nevertheless, one morning we awoke to find Indians visiting us; our camp was full of Carajás men interested to know who we were, what our strange-looking boat was and trying to sell us a couple of turtles they had angled using hearts-of-palm as bait. The Indians were friendly, although their etiquette included a tendency to poke into everything we possessed. We served them hot chocolate, but it was clear by mime that they would have preferred alcohol.

When they showed no signs of leaving, we took the opportunity of filming them, to which they responded enthusiastically, although they had no patience for retakes. Only two of them spoke Portuguese, but they told us that they did not like the fact that all interactions between whites and Indians had to pass through the government Indian agency FUNAI. They considered that FUNAI did not resolve their problems and at the same time it prevented them from working out their own solutions. (I have met Indians from the Tikuna, Tukano, Waimiri-Atróari, Satarê-Maué and Carajás tribes, but have never yet met an Indian with a good opinion of FUNAI.)

As a goodwill gesture we bought the turtles from the Indians, who paddled away, probably to buy sugarcane liquor with the payment. We of course released the turtles as soon as our visitors had left, but we felt a certain sadness in the event. The turtles were free again, but the Indians were likely to become slaves to their love of alcohol.

As a geographical feature, Bananal Island was a disappointment. Our maps showed the River Araguaia dividing into two arms, which joined again after flowing around a piece of land the size of Wales. But at low water, as we saw it, the right hand (eastern) channel was so shallow and overgrown that no craft larger than a dugout canoe could have gone down it. We even had to make two passes to be sure we had found the entrance.

We continued down the broad, left-hand (western) channel, through vegetation still predominantly composed of gallery forest on the banks and *cerrado* further inland. Sometimes palm groves or pasture extended down to the water's edge. The palms, although referred to locally as coconuts, were actually *babaçu*, a species common in areas cleared by fire. In a few regions "vines" grew in such profusion that their weight had brought down tall trees, leaving a low, uneven canopy covered in creepers. This type of vegetation is known technically as "liana forest."

After more than a month's slow navigation it was clear that the steamboat would not reach the Tucurui hydroelectric dam within the time available to the film crew. However the producer felt that steaming up to the dam would make such a visually dramatic end to the film that he decided we should gain time by dismantling the boat, transporting it by truck and reassembling it at the hydroelectric reservoir. We succeeded in fulfilling his wishes – in spite of the scarcity of roads and vehicles.

The producer was right. Piloting the steamboat up to the 8,000-megawatt dam so that we could touch the concrete and see through the spillway arches to the old river valley 160 feet below was an awe-inspiring experience and produced great pictures. The spillway design made the view particularly impressive: the rivers feeding the reservoir had highly seasonal flow rates, sometimes transporting immense amounts of floodwater. To cope with these floods, Tucurui had a spillway larger than that of any other dam. There were 23 steel spillway gates, each 20 m wide. We approached the top edge of these gates in water so calm it was hard to conceive the record-breaking power underneath. The upper lips of the gates projected only a foot above the surface of the reservoir and were the only barrier between us and the drop beyond.

To take aerial pictures of the dam, the film crew finally decided that the hot-air balloon (which had been brought along for this purpose) was too difficult to manoeuvre; so they rented a helicopter. They soared, hovered and dived, obtaining superb aerial shots, in which the immense power and modernity of the dam contrasted sharply with the puny, old-fashioned steamboat. Behind the scenes, the helicopter and the balloon offered a similar comparison.

It was the end of the trip. We were no longer camping, but housed in the hotel with the old steam locomotive in front. However, we had not finished filming. Anthony wanted to do a sequence about Brazil nuts and the producer wanted some shots of trees that had been killed by flooding. We were able to fulfil both these wishes by taking a boat trip up the reservoir.

During construction of the dam, engineers had cleared the forest near the powerhouse so as to reduce the amount of corrosive hydrogen sulphide produced by rotting vegetation. Removing the trees also reduced the risk of debris entering the turbines. However, further away from the dam the trees of the forest had been left standing. As we steamed upstream from the dam into the reservoir, we entered a huge area of dead forest, killed by flooding. The trees, highland species incapable of surviving in waterlogged conditions, formed a sad landscape of leafless skeletons protruding out of shallow areas of the lake. Some of them were immense. Occasional orchids, aroids, bromeliads, ferns and other epiphytes survived on the otherwise bare branches as melancholic reminders of the forest's former exuberance.

Not all of the consequences of flooding were negative. For instance, the lake provided easy access to virgin forest on its banks. Researchers were now able to drive in the comfort of a fast boat to places which were formerly impossible to reach conveniently. Some biologists were already taking advantage of such access and doing fieldwork in the area. As part of its public relations efforts, Eletronorte, the power company, maintained several biological research stations on the edge of the lake.

Another activity facilitated by improved access through flooding was a unique logging operation that harvested valuable timber submerged in the reservoir. In this enterprise a diver used a pneumatically powered chainsaw to cut the trunks of valuable trees that had been flooded. The logs were then floated out to a sawmill. Lack of access was one of the reasons more trees were not harvested conventionally before the reservoir was filled.

After filming the dead trees in the lake, we continued upstream to one of the research stations, where we shot Anthony's sequence about Brazil nuts. Near Manaus I had often shown tourists the round crowns of Brazil nut trees protruding above the forest canopy. However, the Brazil nut trees we encountered on the edge of the Tucuruí reservoir were much bigger than any I had seen near Manaus. Many were over 10 feet in diameter. Furthermore, the whole forest had a luxuriant aspect. We knew immediately that any footage we shot in it would make a visually attractive sequence for the film. Sounds were good too, with the screaming piah piping out its loud, insistent wolf-whistle, the most typical birdcall of *terra firme* forest.

Anthony wanted to illustrate how Brazil nuts fell to the ground in wooden pods like cannonballs and to show how hard it was for an animal to open the pods to reach the 12 to 20 nuts inside. Finally he would conclude that rabbit-sized rodents called agoutis were the only animals in the forest capable of opening the pods and deduce that the dispersal of Brazil nut trees in the wild depended on having agoutis in the forest. It was a nice ecological story and easy for the viewing public to understand. However, in the end we were not able to use all the film material the cameraman shot, as it took Anthony and I a full ten minutes to chip one of the cannonballs open with a machete. By the time we succeeded, we could not contain our laughter at our frustration and could only admire the gnawing power of agoutis.

On our way out of the forest we found several empty Brazil nut pods, all with holes made by agoutis. The hole was always at the top of the pod. Our guide told us that if we were to invert the pods, hiding the holes, the following day we would find the pods once more with the holes uppermost, having been turned over by agoutis. Apparently the rodents liked to be able to recognise empty shells from a distance, so as not to waste time revisiting worthless fruit.

During the boat-trip back to the dam I caught a beautiful peacock bass by trolling with a metal lure. Such game fish, relying on vision to feed, had proliferated very successfully in the clear waters of the reservoir, where they saw prey easily. (The river lost its turbidity by sedimentation as it entered the lake.) With no means of cooking the fish, because we now dined at the hotel, I gave my trophy to the doorman, who later reported that it was delicious.

By now the film crew felt they had shot enough material to make their film. They had filmed the start of the journey at the southern edge of the Amazon basin; they had filmed the completion of the journey at the Tucuruí dam; and they had filmed lots of nature, landscape and local colour in between. Their story had a beginning, a middle and an end; so they lost no time in packing up and returning to Britain to begin editing. Jonathan left too, to organise a balloon contest. Suddenly, of the original seven travellers, only Anthony, Bruno and I remained to dismantle the steamboat and ship it via Belém to Manaus for storage.

Once the dismantled steamboat and all our other equipment had been safely loaded on board an 18-m cargo boat in Tucuruí, Anthony departed too. Only Bruno and I remained to accompany the material to Belém and to arrange for its onward transportation to Manaus. This last task provided a dramatic, Brazilian finale to the steamboat saga. It is a pity the others missed it.

Shortly after nightfall, twenty-seven hours after leaving Tucurui, the cargo boat carrying Bruno, me and the equipment docked at Porto do Sal (Salt Port), a set of rickety wooden piers in a poor district located just upstream from the centre of Belém. The vessel was scheduled to remain at the quayside for a few days, so Bruno and I, having plenty of time to unload our things, went to stay with Arlete, my girlfriend in Belém. Her feminine company was a tonic after six weeks with only men on the steamboat. Moreover her car, telephone and local knowledge were invaluable in helping Bruno and I to make arrangements.

ENASA, a shipping company that operated a fleet of large cargo catamarans, agreed to transport the dismantled steamboat and equipment from Belém to Manaus on board a vessel currently moored in the deep-water docks, about two miles away from Porto do Sal. Fine – thought Bruno and I – we'll ask the skipper of the Tucuruí boat to bring his vessel alongside the ENASA catamaran and we'll transfer our material conveniently from one boat to the other. For legal reasons this turned out not to be possible. The Tucurui captain informed us that although he had carried our large items on the roof of his boat (They were too big for the hold), it was, in fact, illegal to stow cargo on the roof. Since there were plenty of river police in Belém to check us, he had timed our journey to arrive in Belém at night and he would not venture from the quay with our equipment by daylight.

We discussed the possibility of moving the material between the two boats by truck. This was technically feasible, but expensive, because members of the stevedores' union would have to be employed at the port, even if they did no work.

The Tucuruí skipper and a cargo agent finally worked out a plan. The skipper would bring his illegally-loaded boat alongside the deserted docks near the ENASA catamaran by night, avoiding both the river police and the stevedores. Bruno and I would unload the material in the dark and sleep by it on the dockside. At first light the agent would open the warehouse and we would put our things inside before the stevedores arrived. It was an ingenious plan, but not without its drawbacks. Besides being illegal, it could only be carried out at high tide; at low tide the quay would be too high to unload the Tucuruí boat without a crane. We looked at the tide tables and decided to risk it the following midnight.

Arlete drove Bruno and me down to the Tucuruí boat at Porto do Sal at around

11.00 PM. There were already a number of young sailors on board and we cast off immediately. The short journey in front of the downtown area to the main docks took us past some of Belém's famous landmarks. The first was the Old Fort, set on a promontory separating the Salt Port from the central waterfront. The silhouette of the fort's cannon-topped ramparts stood out against the glow of the urban sky. Meanwhile, at the Porto do Açaí, adjacent to the fort, riverboats were taking advantage of the high tide to unload baskets of the small, purplish-black *açai* palm berries used to make Belém's favorite fruit-juice. Next we passed the fish wharf, where galleon-like fishing boats with motors and sails were getting ready to take the tide, as were pram-fronted motorboats that transported hand-made pottery from Marajó Island. Then we sailed in front of the much photographed, four-turreted, wrought-iron Ver-o-Peso market, perhaps Belém's best-known building. It looked more sinister at night than it did by day, but the recently restored promenade and restaurant area beyond it was attractively well-lit. Our destination was the ominously dark area in the distance: the main commercial dock.

We arrived to find the dock eerily silent and the wharf unoccupied except for the large ENASA catamaran moored in front of the first warehouse. The hangar-like buildings and their overhanging roofs shaded the quay from the street lamps, making the place inky black. For several hundred yards not a single light bulb penetrated the Stygian gloom. Slipping in behind the catamaran, our boat tied up and we started unloading straight away. No one wanted to make the job longer than necessary. We used no torches and tried to be as quiet as possible, but lack of light meant we moved clumsily, clattering metal objects and cursing as we bumped into unseen obstacles. The danger of alerting a trigger-happy guard loomed urgently in our minds. (Bullets flew easily in this country.) Even if shots were avoided, getting caught might mean a major hassle with the authorities. Yet with each item unloaded it became more difficult to turn back. Guards were visible, chatting in an illuminated area, far away at the other end of the docks, near the gates. Since they were in the light and we were in the dark, they could not see us. However, when one of the watchdogs started barking insistently, we knew discovery was inevitable. The glow of a torch started to approach along the quay. Eventually we made out the silhouette of a man and two Alsatian dogs. Prudence dictated that we try to placate the apparitions before they had chance to become aggressive. It was a job for someone with a native command of Portuguese. Bruno rose to the occasion. Still unobserved, he walked towards the man with the dogs; called out to him; and gave a reasoned account of why we were unloading a boat in the dark. The watchman cast his light towards the voice and eventually saw Bruno, who showed him the rest of us, nervously unloading the last items.

Once he had reassured himself that we were in fact putting things onto the dock and not stealing, the guard could not have been nicer. He kept the dogs under control and never even hinted at a bribe. (I suspect, in retrospect, that the shipping agent may have tipped him earlier.) Our fear subsided and our adrenaline levels started to return to normal. The Tucurui boat departed and Bruno and I slept soundly alongside the pile of equipment until dawn.

The rest of the operation went according to plan. By the time the stevedores arrived, the material was already inside the warehouse and Bruno and I were checking the bill of lading with the shipping agent. What a strange collection of goods we had: 4 aluminium canoes   (2 modified as steamboat floats), 4 hardwood bridge struts, assorted aluminium tent poles, tent fabric, various marine-ply deck boards, 1 aluminium ladder, 1 Stuart Turner 6A steam engine with drive shaft and propeller, 1 engine cradle, 1 firebox, 1 boiler (the heaviest single item), several sections of pizza-oven chimney, 1 complete hot-air balloon, 6 oars, 4 crates of camping, nautical and maintenance equipment. In total it weighed about three-quarters of a ton.

Because some items, if listed separately, might be taxable when transported across the Pará-Amazonas state border on the six-day voyage from Belém to Manaus, we declared all the equipment in the non-taxable category of "house moving". In view of the fact that the steamboat had been our home for six weeks, the classification seemed most appropriate.

We had just finished the paperwork when Arlete arrived to drive Bruno and me back to her apartment for a shower and breakfast. As we pulled away from the warehouse, I was beginning to put steamboats out of my mind and get back to modern life, when an ancient steam traction engine preserved as a monument at the dock entrance caught my eye. Making Arlete stop the car, Bruno and I got out to admire the machine's finer features, the significance of which we now appreciated fully: the reversing valve gear, the all-important boiler sight-glass, the pressure gauge, safety valve, automatic water-pump, lubrification system, etc. We were glad to see that all along the thousand-mile route we had travelled, people fondly remembered the steam heritage; the town of Aruanã had preserved some ships' boilers, Tucurui had preserved a locomotive; and Belém had preserved a traction engine. Travelling by steam seemed very appropriate for a voyage down the Araguaia.

Bruno went back to São Paulo and I stayed on in Belém for a few days, enjoying Arlete's company before returning home. Overtaking the ENASA catamaran by air, I was waiting in Manaus when the expedition's equipment arrived. Thereafter I continued to work as a naturalist and reassembled the steamboat in my spare time.

One evening, after sundown, I was sitting on the veranda of my modest two-bedroomed bungalow on the outskirts of Manaus, enjoying the cool and quiet which darkness brought, when I received an unexpected telephone call from my friend Bill in Germany.

"Hello, John," he said, "I just switched the television on and there you were, on a sandbar, singing with a guitar by a campfire. You were on a trip down the Araguaia River in a steamboat."
"Oh yes?" I asked excitedly, "What was the song?"
"Romaria," he replied, "in Portuguese."

I was overjoyed. I had not yet seen the film myself. I didn't even know the producer had finished it – and I didn't know its contents. On several evenings the film crew had recorded me singing by the campfire, but there was no certainty they would use any of the material. After all, less than 5% of all shots finished up in the final programme. Nor did I know when and where the film would appear on television. I knew that sooner or later BBC 2 would show it in the "Natural World" series, but I had no idea which American channels would screen it, and had not even considered possibilities like the British Forces' Network in Germany, which Bill watched. The song the producer featured struck me as particularly appropriate. The title meant "pilgrimage" and I felt I had completed a musical pilgrimage across the Amazon basin. I had started on the northern edge of the basin, unable to speak Portuguese, singing for rough gold-miners on my first night in Brazil. Now I had reached the south side of the basin, singing in Portuguese for the BBC.

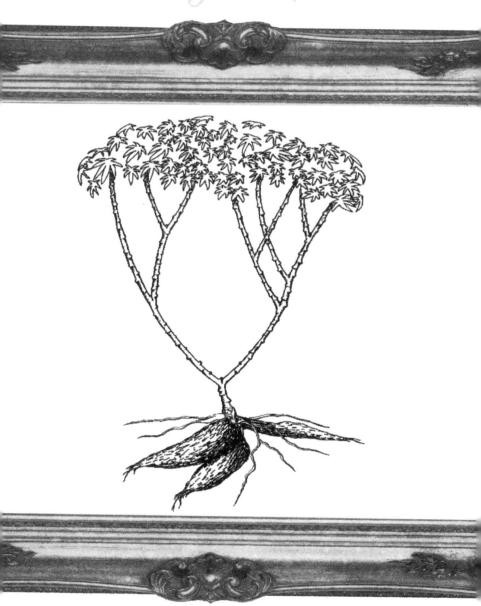

Chapter 13

Fig 13. Manioc Plant with Tubers

Amazon to Orinoco by River; Back by Sea

After I had gained experience as a naturalist working on local riverboats, I received an offer to work as a naturalist on board a small adventure cruise ship that was sailing from the Caribbean to the Amazon. The itinerary sounded fascinating. I was to embark at a port near Caracas in Venezuela. There was a chance to snorkel in the clear Caribbean waters of Bonaire and Tobago. We would visit the delta of the Orinoco River and its Warau Indian inhabitants. There was an inclusive charter flight to see the tallest waterfall in the world, Angel Falls, located in southern Venezuela. Next came a stop at the infamous French penal colony at Devil's Island and finally there was the prospect of navigating nearly a thousand miles up the Amazon to arrive back home in Manaus. For me, as a budding tropical biologist, the trip was a remarkable opportunity to see new areas and ecosystems. I accepted the offer enthusiastically.

Not only was the cruise going to be exciting, but I planned to have an extra adventure on my way to the ship. At the beginning of the cruise, the shipping company needed to fly me from Manaus to Caracas, a straight-line distance of about 2000 km. In the absence of a direct flight they wanted to send me through São Paulo and Miami, a journey of about 11000 km. Their proposed route spent far too much time in the sky and would have been very expensive for them. Give me a thousand dollars – I told them – and I will make my own way overland to Caracas. They agreed.

It was the perfect occasion for me to fulfil an old dream. I had long wanted to travel along the Casiquiare Canal, the little-known natural link between the Rio Negro and the Orinoco River. I had often thought of taking my own boat up there, which was perfectly feasible, but it was a long trip for my small, slow boat, not to mention the problem of having to bring the boat back once one had accomplished the journey. Travelling along the Casiquiare Canal as part of my itinerary to join the cruise ship was a chance to do a one-way trip. But of course it would have to be done on local riverboats. I felt sure that I would be able to find boats along the route and now had money in my pocket to buy passages on them. The essential elements of the plan were to leave Brazil by boat going upstream on the Rio Negro, traverse the Casiquiare Canal by boat and travel downstream by boat on the Orinoco as far as Samariapo near Puerto Ayacucho, from where it would be possible to reach Caracas and the ship by bus.

What I particularly liked about the scheme was that after my journey from the Amazon Basin to the Orinoco Basin by river, the cruise ship would bring me back by sea. I would thereby have navigated almost all of a gigantic aquatic loop that many people living in Manaus found hard to envisage. Most of my friends here could not imagine that they lived on an island. Nevertheless, because the upper Orinoco River splits into two, with most of its water flowing north to the Orinoco Delta and some of its water flowing south to the Amazon Delta, the land between the two deltas must be an island. Admittedly, it's a rather strange island. Most of it is occupied by the mountains of the Guiana Shield, but Manaus is also on it. Think of it this way – I would tell my doubting friends – if you were to leave Manaus on foot and try to walk as far as possible on dry land, you would eventually be stopped by either the Rio Negro, or the Casiquiare Canal, or the Orinoco, or the Atlantic Ocean or the Amazon. In other words, your starting point in Manaus was completely surrounded by water.

Long before I had any contacts with cruise ships, I had done some research in Venezuela about conditions along the Casiquiare Canal. Venezuelans in Puerto Ayacucho informed me that big boats transited the Canal mainly during the high-water period, that is, from May to August. At that time of year both Colombia and Venezuela used tanker barges from the Orinoco to transport fuel to riverside settlements in the Rio Negro basin. However, for the rest of the year the water in the canal was shallower and only small craft could get through. That suited me fine. My trip was planned for early August, so I could expect to find a big boat and easy navigation.

In the eighteenth century, there was a lot of academic discussion in Europe as to whether the Casiquiare Canal really existed. It was not easy for scientists to believe that the Orinoco (or any river) could actually run onto its own watershed and consequently divide. Alexander von Humboldt was the first European explorer with sufficient prestige to convince western academics that the Casiquiare Canal was a reality. In the year 1800 he made a long excursion on the

Orinoco and its tributaries. During these travels he and his Indian guides carried his boat overland from a tributary of the Orinoco to a tributary of the Amazon and then paddled back to the Orinoco via the Casiquiare Canal. It was historic achievement, although Humboldt was quite modest about it, affirming that he had not "discovered" the Canal. He said that all he had done was to put it accurately on the map – the local people certainly knew it was there. In his journal, besides reporting on the Canal itself, he recorded many aspects of the biology along the way. In particular he graphically described the large number and variety of insects that tormented him during the trip. Black flies and deer flies attacked him during the day and mosquitoes attacked him at night. Suitably forewarned, I made a special mosquito net for my hammock.

I gave myself seventeen days to do the whole trip from Manaus to Caracas. The first part of the trip would be easy; a commercial riverboat left Manaus once a week heading up the Rio Negro to São Gabriel da Cachoeira, the last Brazilian town on that river. The journey took three days. After that I would have two weeks to find a way through to my destination in Venezuela.

Unfortunately I had to take with me more luggage than I would have liked. I needed to carry a lot of slides and books for my job as a naturalist on the cruise ship and, as usual, I couldn't bear to travel without my guitar. So, there I was, ready to face the Casiquiare Canal, with a rucksack on my back, a bag of academic natural history material in one hand and a guitar in the other. I hoped I would find transport easily, because I couldn't walk far with all that weight.

As planned, three days after setting out from Manaus a riverboat dropped me in São Gabriel da Cachoeira, the end of the territory I already knew and consequently the start of the adventure proper. I learned that there was a bus setting out the following day for the Brazilian frontier post, Cucuí, situated where the Rio Negro enters Brazil from Colombia (West bank) and Venezuela (East bank). I checked into a simple hotel to pass the night and caught the bus.

Cucuí was the only place to which one could take a bus from São Gabriel. There were no other roads: none into Venezuela, nor into Colombia, nor back in the direction of Manaus, nor even eastwards towards Roraima (in spite of an optimistic dotted line on some maps indicating the proposed North Perimeter Road). The road to Cucuí was an unpaved strip of compacted red laterite, cut through what had recently been virgin forest. Rain more profuse than that in

Manaus had severely eroded some of the embankments, but in general the driving surface was relatively smooth. Occasionally we crossed rustic wooden bridges spanning beautiful black rivers. For safety reasons, the passengers got out and walked over these bridges, while the bus crossed empty.

The road ran near Brazil's highest mountain, Pico da Neblina (literally "Foggy Peak"; 3014m high), situated further east along the border with Venezuela. It was impossible to see the peak from the road, but notices along the roadside indicated that we were in the Pico da Neblina National Park. At a particular bridge the driver pointed to the river we were crossing and told me that climbers took boats upstream from there to get closer to the mountain before attempting to reach the summit on foot.

An isolated signpost marked where the road crossed the equator. Nothing else in the landscape suggested that our bus was leaving the southern hemisphere for the northern one. The seemingly endless forest ahead looked exactly the same as that behind. No wayside tricksters tried to make me believe my bathwater would now drain clockwise instead of anticlockwise – and the vines in the forest continued twining around their supports in the same direction, whether I looked north or south.

The bus arrived in Cucuí in the mid-afternoon. Although the road had taken me away from the river and closer to high mountains, I was now back on the banks of the Rio Negro and definitely in lowlands again – my map showed only 80m above sea level in spite of being literally thousands of kilometres inland. The landscape was flat except for one feature, which one could not miss: the Cucuí Rock. This was a huge, sheer-sided, more or less conical, granite mass. From anywhere in or around Cucuí it caught one's attention. The land surveyors who drew up the borders between Venezuela, Colombia and Brazil could not have chosen a better marker for the triple frontier. It was unmistakable and could be seen from miles away. It actually stood just inside Venezuela, where in Spanish its name had a different spelling, being called the Piedra Cucuy. (There is no y in Portuguese.) I got my first view of it just after bright sunshine had dispelled an afternoon shower. The sun's rays bounced off the wet granite slabs, turning the whole rock into an immense lighthouse. I appreciated the giant navigational aid and felt encouraged to continue my journey by boat.

Cucuí was a military frontier post. There was no town as such. Nevertheless, as often happens where there are large numbers of soldiers with time on their hands, an embryonic collection of bars, shops and other services had sprung up. Presumably it would eventually grow into a town. There was already a guesthouse, a pleasant, airy wooden building with a nice veranda and big wicker easy chairs. It was set a short distance from the river in an agreeable green paddock, over which one could not help but see the enormous bulk of the Cucuí Rock. Cucuí was my travel target for the day. Having reached it, I checked into the guesthouse, content with my progress so far.

Just before the sun went down, the owner of the guesthouse took me out for a sightseeing trip on the Rio Negro. We embarked in his aluminium outboard motorboat, set off up the river and then switched the motor off, so that we could drift slowly back. In the rich light of the sunset the panorama was serene. Under a blue sky, green forest flanked the smooth black river, from the middle of which one could see three countries.

The most evident military post was that of Brazil. In Venezuela one could see just a handful of buildings and in Colombia none at all. On each side of the river a white obelisk flanked by two flags stood in a small clearing marking the exact position of the border. Brazilian and Colombian flags flew on the west bank and Brazilian and Venezuelan flags flew on the east bank. No authorities asked us what we were doing or challenged out right to be in the area. In particular, the quiet of the Colombian sector made it hard to believe that civil war and horrendous violence occurred in other parts of that country.

The following day I set about finding a boat to leave Brazil and head further up the Negro. After breakfast I walked to the riverbank and chatted to the Brazilian military authorities. Their checkpoint, at which all vessels leaving Brazil had to stop, made a perfect place to meet boat captains and hopefully negotiate a voyage upstream. Fortunately, by this time I had lived in Brazil long enough to have acquired a Brazilian passport. This helped me enormously, because the officials told me that a foreign passport would need to be stamped in São Gabriel da Cachoeira, which now lay a day's trip behind me. With my Brazilian passport I was legally ready to leave the country. All I needed was a vessel.

Shortly after 9.00 AM a type of craft known locally as a *bongo* pulled into the checkpoint. It was a large dugout canoe with a flat zinc roof and a 40-HP outboard motor. The skipper, a Colombian Indian, got out to do the necessary formalities, while his two female companions, who turned out to be his wife and her sister, remained in the vessel. He was dressed in blue jeans and a T-shirt and had an honest aspect. Judging by the large amount of merchandise in the *bongo*, he appeared to be a trader. Feeling that I could trust him, I asked him if he would take me upstream and we negotiated a reasonable price.

His name was Miguel and he lived in an Indian community on the Guainia River. He said he would take me to San Felipe, the Colombian town on the Rio Negro opposite San Carlos in Venezuela, from where, he thought, I would probably find a boat heading through the Casiquiare. He did not want to get involved with authorities in San Felipe, nor in San Carlos. He would simply drop me on the riverbank at San Felipe and continue his way upstream, leaving me to deal with the Colombian immigration officials on my own.

We set out immediately. I occupied the middle of the *bongo* well in the shade of the roof. I had a little wooden seat and could also recline on sacks of manioc flour that Miguel had bought in São Gabriel and was transporting to his tribal village. Miguel sat behind me at the tiller of the outboard, while the two women sat in front of me, one on each side of the vessel, leaning on the poles that supported the roof. Noticeable items of cargo included several barrels of fuel, spare parts for generators and boat engines, as well as a large circular pan for making manioc flour.

The sun shone intensely all day from a clear blue sky, so I was extremely glad to be accommodated in the shade. Even under the roof I could feel the sun's glare reflected off the smooth black water as we sped upriver between banks of largely undisturbed forest.

Shortly after leaving Brazil we called at a simple Colombian border post located in an isolated riverside building that had formerly been a guesthouse for tourists. The fine wooden establishment had beautiful views of the river, but civil unrest in other parts of Colombia had killed its tourist trade.

There were no bureaucratic problems and we soon continued upstream. Because Miguel was Colombian, he kept to the west side of the river, where the land and waters were Colombian. Had he been Venezuelan, he would have kept to the east side, where the land and waters belonged to Venezuela. From time to time we passed small Indian communities consisting of groups of low, zinc-roofed brick buildings or thatched adobe huts. The settlements had the same primitive aspect, whether they were situated in Colombian or Venezuelan territory. However, the area was only sparsely populated. I felt rather vulnerable in this lonesome place. I had a lot of cash on me (in case I got stuck somewhere and needed to rent an air taxi to speed things up) and I never carried a weapon. It would have been easy for Miguel or anyone else (the FARC?) to rob me. In the end, the day – and indeed the rest of the trip – passed off peacefully.

We stopped at one of the Colombian Indian communities to buy *patauá* palm berries. These fruit resembled plums in size and colour. Miguel wanted to buy some to take home to make a nourishing drink by dissolving the skin of the fruit in water. The Indian who sold them to us went by the unlikely name of Kennedy and I had no difficulty understanding him as he spoke Spanish very clearly. He had plenty of the *patauá* berries already packed in 20-kg papoose-like baskets woven from palm fronds. To show us that his produce was tasty, he gave Miguel and myself some juice he had just made. It was a tawny-coloured porridge that was savoury rather than sweet. We drank it heartily. It made a nice change from the monotonous food we had been eating in the *bongo* all day – *xibé* – handfuls of raw manioc flour washed down with gulps of water we scooped out of the Rio Negro with a calabash.

Encouraged by the fact that we liked his *patauá* palm juice, Kennedy proudly invited me to see how he made manioc flour. After eating *xibé* all day, I felt that I already knew a lot about manioc. Nevertheless, I welcomed the opportunity to stretch my legs after sitting in the *bongo* for so long. Miguel said we had time and the three of us strolled off together.

Kennedy's village consisted of a rectangular group of houses arranged around a central beaten-earth area that served as soccer field and plaza for civic occasions. We walked away from the houses into dense secondary forest growing in an area that had once been cultivated. Finally we came to a clearing about an acre in size, where a crop of spindly bushes 2-3m tall grew haphazardly amongst the charred remains of felled trees. The bushes had knobbly stems and dark green, hand-shaped leaves. This, said Kennedy beaming at me, was his manioc plantation.

Kennedy cut the top off one of the bushes and holding the cut stump pulled the roots out of the ground to show me the tubers from which he, like most

Indians from North Argentina to South Mexico, made manioc flour. There were five or six tubers about the size of large parsnips that had grown horizontally just below the surface of the ground. He pointed to a portion of stem in the centre of the clump of roots and explained that that part was the remains of the piece of manioc stick that he had originally planted. Nobody used seeds, he said. Farmers just took a piece of stem and buried it in a shallow hole. It easily sprouted to develop into a new manioc plant.

Having seen the plantation we walked back to the village, where Kennedy wanted to show me the actual process of making flour from manioc tubers. His house stood on the main square and had a thatched shack at the back. In this shack his entire family was involved in making flour. Holding up a tuber like the one he had shown me in the plantation, he explained (rather over-enthusiastically I thought) that I would die if I were to eat it directly. It had to be detoxified, which was done by converting it into flour. The process required several steps: peeling, soaking, milling, pressing, sieving and drying. He introduced me to the various members of his family who were doing these tasks. The women and children were peeling the tubers with knives and machetes. I was alarmed to see small infants using machetes that I considered to be dangerously large. The peeled tubers were put to soak overnight in a swamped canoe lying in shallow water at the edge of the river. Kennedy's brother was milling the soaked tubers from the previous day. His mill consisted of a rotating wooden roller with saw blades set in it, driven by a belt from a small petrol engine. The motorisation surprised me, as I thought the Indians would grate the tubers by hand, using traditional wooden boards with pebbles set in them. In the next step (pressing) the family did, however, use the traditional tubular basket press *(tipiti)* for squeezing the milled manioc, rather than using the more modern lever press. They also had fine-quality basketry sieves for removing fibres from the pulp after it came out of the press.

A fire with almost no smoke burned in the centre of the hut, heating a 5-ft diameter circular pan of the type Miguel was transporting in his *bongo*. Here, Kennedy exclaimed triumphantly, was the final stage of the process. As he spoke he made a theatrical flourish and presented his cousin who was using an old canoe paddle to swish damp pulp around in the hot pan. In about twenty minutes, he said, the pulp would dry out completely and become hard and gritty. He gave Miguel and me some of the dry product to try. It was quite tasty, but we ate it only out of courtesy, not mentioning that we had been eating manioc flour all day.

During all Kennedy's explanations Miguel, who of course knew everything about manioc, had been quietly deferent. Now he and I thanked Kennedy for his trouble and took our leave. We rejoined the women in the boat and continued our journey upstream. Shortly before sunset we started to see lots of houses on the riverbank and Miguel pulled into San Felipe. He dropped me ashore and pulled away immediately, leaving me on my own to walk up the bank to a military pillbox occupied by Colombian soldiers. To my surprise, a young conscript came out to help me with my bags. Another conscript, festooned with machine gun ammunition and a hand grenade, greeted me courteously and checked my papers. On seeing my Brazilian passport, he gave me a strong hug and exclaimed that Brazilians and Colombians were brothers and that they hated Venezuelans. Personally at that moment I was not thinking about national stereotypes – I was worried that we might explode if he squashed his ammunition in our strong embrace. The imaginary danger passed and I was heartened by the friendliness and simplicity of it all. He noted my passport number in a big book, after which the first conscript helped me to carry my luggage to a nearby guesthouse.

I had expected San Felipe to be a much bigger place than it was. The size of the city's name on maps had given me the impression that there ought to have been more than the one street I found. The complete absence of traffic, because there were no roads to anywhere else, emphasised the feeling of a tiny place with not much happening.

There were a number of other guests in the guesthouse to which I was taken. They were mainly traders who drove *bongos* around the area. After a simple, wholesome dinner of chicken, rice, beans and (yet again) manioc flour, we sat together drinking and chatting. I found the stories fascinating. Obviously Colombia, Venezuela and Brazil had different products at different prices. This promoted cross-border commerce, some of which was legal and some of which was not. The *bongo* drivers said that smuggling was commonplace and that the authorities often turned a blind eye to it if it was done on a small scale. For instance, all *bongos*, irrespective of nationality, tried to get hold of cheap Venezuelan petrol.

One racket involved smuggling Brazilian cigarettes to Brazil. How could that be? I enquired naïvely. The answer was quite simple. The cigarettes were exported from Brazil at a low tax-free price, then smuggled back without paying taxes. Sometimes the cigarettes never left Brazil and people made money just by falsifying the export paperwork. The *bongo* drivers were aware of a more sinister traffic in Colombia, involving drugs (out) and arms (in), but they gave the impression that as small traders they tried not to get involved. If in some isolated headwater a band of insurgents, drug traffickers or pirates asked a *bongo* driver to "donate" a tub of fuel or other merchandise, he would hand it over with a smile and promise to forget the incident. That was the way to survive in the lawless environment.

The following morning, after a good night's sleep, I said goodbye to Colombia and took one of the many small aluminium outboard motor boats that ferried goods and passengers across the Rio Negro to San Carlos on the Venezuelan side. San Carlos was a larger settlement than San Felipe. The two towns were situated exactly opposite each other on the banks of the river, not more than 200 metres apart. As I had done in San Felipe, I walked up the shore to check in at a military pillbox manned by conscript soldiers. The Venezuelans greeted me with far less enthusiasm than the Colombians had. The heavily armed men who questioned me were barely literate and I wondered pessimistically whether they made as many mistakes with their sophisticated weaponry as they did with a notebook and pen.

In contrast to the brutish Venezuelan conscripts, the military commander I spoke to shortly afterwards was courteous, well educated and could not have been more helpful. In excellent American English he informed me that they did not stamp passports in San Carlos, but he would write an official document stating the objectives of my trip and indicating that I had passed legally through the area of his jurisdiction. Armed with this document, he assured me, I would have no difficulties registering with Venezuelan authorities further north. Mercifully he was right.

Since San Carlos was situated only about 15km from the southern end of the Casiquiare Canal, I felt myself to be within striking distance of my objective and waited eagerly for a boat going there. In the end I waited for the rest of the day – in vain. There were plenty of passengers travelling north, but they were all going up the Guainia River to Maroa, over the watershed by road to Yavita and then down the Rivers Temi and Atabapo to reach the Orinoco. In terms of reaching the Orinoco, their route made good sense; it was shorter and had more settlements along the way. It was exactly (but in the reverse direction) the route Humboldt had used to get his canoe overland from the Orinoco to the Rio Negro. But I wanted to retrace the next part of Humboldt's itinerary – the longer part – the part where he paddled his canoe, without portaging, back to the Orinoco.

After a frustrating day waiting on the riverbank, I chatted in the evening to merchants and anyone else I thought might be able to help me get going the following day. Finally I found a man who was willing to take me the 35km or so from San Carlos to Solano, the nearest settlement inside the Casiquiare Canal. There I would wait again, but at least all traffic on the Casiquiare would go past Solano, including any boats coming from the Rio Guainia.

I met my boatman early the following day and soon realised that he was more of a sharp businessman than a sailor. He was improvising the trip by borrowing an aluminium boat from one person, an outboard from another, fuel tanks from yet others and so on. However, by mid morning we embarked in the launch and sped off up the Rio Negro.

The Negro looked much the same as it looked further downstream, but there were more rocks in it, with large rounded granite outcrops on the shores. After about an hour the boatman announced that we were entering the Casiquiare Canal. I looked around and hardly noticed that we were at a confluence and were taking the right fork of the junction. The arm we entered seemed about as big as the one we avoided. Neither of the arms was called Negro; ours was the Casiquiare Canal and the other was the Rio Guainia. In accepted nomenclature the name Negro terminated at this point (or started if you were coming downstream).

After about another hour's travelling, we reached Solano, a small Indian village with a military checkpoint. Here my boatman introduced me to the soldiers on duty and left me in the care of a group of civilians with whom I could have lunch.

The Venezuelan Government had at some point invested quite a lot of money in Solano. It had built houses and a school for the Indians, presumably to encourage them to stay in one place, under control, rather than have them wandering back and forth over the Colombian border with its problems of illegal incursions, smuggling and drug traffic. However, it appeared that after construction there had been no money for maintaining the buildings and most of the houses were in poor condition. In any case, the Indians preferred to sleep in their well-ventilated, thatched huts, which were cooler at night.

My new companions invited me to the yard of an abandoned brick house, where they had prepared a meal over an open fire. It was Saturday and they were in party mood, drinking cheap red wine in flagons, while they ate rice, plantains, manioc flour and chicken. I was happy to join in, safe in the knowledge that even though I could not see the river, someone would let me know if a likely boat came by. After lunch I moved back to the riverside and relaxed in the shade of an immense kapok tree. The tree was large and old and reminded me that Humboldt had mentioned such a tree two hundred years previously.

In the mid-afternoon, a large, empty, flat-decked motorised barge with a forward loading ramp for vehicles pulled into Solano. It was flying a Venezuelan flag and was heading up the Casiquiare. In view of the various pipes and stopcocks around the edge of the deck, I recognised it as an oil tanker. By its size I guessed it was capable of carrying about two hundred tons – that meant it was by far the biggest craft I had seen on the river above São Gabriel da Cachoeira. The local Indians knew the vessel and told me that it was returning empty to the Orinoco, having delivered a cargo of diesel to the Venezuelan town of Maroa on the Rio Guainia.

I immediately liked the vessel. It had robust, practical, square lines. The railings and cabin trimmings were gaily painted in red and it looked clean. It was different from oil barges in Brasil, which were typically dumb barges pushed by a pusher tug; this one was self-propelled and therefore had its own wheelhouse, built on a flying bridge over the rear part of the deck. Twin 350-HP Scania motors manoeuvred it gracefully into the bank in front of the military checkpoint.

When the skipper, a wiry, moustached *mestizo*, stepped ashore to do the formalities, he told me that his was not a passenger ship (by which he meant that he had no cabins and he would not feel duty bound to get me to my destination within a particular time-frame). Nevertheless, if I gave him something to cover the cost of my food, he would be glad to take me through the Casiquiare to his base at Samariapo, which was the downstream limit of navigation on the Upper Orinoco. He already had four passengers from Maroa on board on these conditions. I naturally took up the offer.

I could not believe my luck. Here was a sturdy vessel going exactly where I wanted to go. I could string my hammock in the corner of the front railings, well away from the noise of the engines. If it rained I could move in under the bridge, where it would be noisy but dry. There would be food prepared by a cook, as well as a shower and WC on board. There was shade from the sun in the wheelhouse as well as on the side walkways and rear veranda. And there would be plenty of room to walk around the main deck. What more could one want? It was better than a *bongo* – and the price was right.

We set out without delay and motored for about two hours before tying up for the night as the sun set. A sailor put a rope around a tree on the bank and tied it to the forward quarter of the barge. The vessel hung stationary in the open water, maintained well away from the bank by the action of a noticeable current flowing towards the Rio Negro, which now lay substantially behind us.

Just as we were making fast, a similar tanker to ours, but flying a Colombian flag, passed us. It too was coming from the River Guainia and was returning empty to the Orinoco. It was the only vessel we saw on the Casiquiare Canal.

As it grew dark I expected to be plagued by the mosquitoes that Humboldt had written so profusely about. However, to my astonishment there were none. Lying comfortably in my hammock without having to use the mosquito net, I wondered why my experience was so different from Humboldt's. Time of year could have been a factor: I was there in August, whereas Humboldt had been there in April and May. Also, he slept on the bank under the trees, whereas I was sleeping on a boat in open water. Anyway, I was pleasantly surprised – in general there were no problems with insects until I disembarked in Samariapo, where biting black flies were abundant.

The next morning we set out as soon as it got light and navigated almost continuously until dusk. During the day we made only two short stops. The first stop was ostensibly to buy fish from Indians, but it seemed that the captain actually wanted to visit some friends. Buying fish would have been quite appropriate in view of the fact that the place was called Tucunaré – the Tupi-Guarani name for the Peacock bass – a fine sport fish. I could not find the settlement on my detailed map made by the Venezuelan government, but it seemed to coincide with a location shown as "El Mango". During our short visit there, for the first time in my life I saw an Indian use a blowpipe.

While we were waiting for the captain to visit his friends, I took a stroll behind the cluster of houses. The Indians I had seen on the waterfront had been wearing western clothes, but behind the houses a young, naked Indian boy was walking around the yard, shooting birds in the fruit trees with a blowpipe about nine feet long. He was successful and had killed a couple of small specimens. It reminded me of my childhood in England, when some of my friends would take air pistols and shoot birds just for the fun of the hunt.

The motive of the second stop was to harvest *açaí* palm berries in order to make a drink similar to Kennedy's *patauá* palm juice. (The major difference was that *açaí* juice was deep purple in colour, whereas *patauá* juice was tawny-coloured.) One of the crew spotted a magnificent bunch of ripe, almost black berries at the top of a tall, slender *açaí* palm a long way ahead. We put the bow of the barge into the bank and a sailor leapt ashore, grabbed some herbaceous undergrowth, twisted it into a coarse rope, tied his feet together and climbed the smooth palm tree with incredible speed. He ripped the bunch of palm berries off, threw them down to the other sailors below and slid quickly back down. We were on our way up the Casiquiare again within three minutes.

The vegetation continued to be reminiscent of that of the lower Rio Negro. For much of the time I felt I could have been travelling along one of the channels through the Anavilhanas Archipelago just above Manaus. The Canal was broader at its lower reaches than in the upper ones, but for most of the way it was at least fifty metres wide. Nonetheless in certain places it narrowed down between big rocks that produced violent eddy currents. These were the sites of rapids that at low water would impede the passage of boats as big as ours. However, in August we had plenty of water and the captain kept his two motors running at full throttle.

The sailors of the barge made some extra money recycling aluminium. In Maroa they had collected lots of aluminium scrap, especially empty beer cans, old outboards and other machines made predominantly out of aluminium. They had brought the material on board in big sacks. Whenever they felt bored, they emptied a sack out onto the deck and sifted its contents into categories. They smashed the cans down to the size of discs using a sledgehammer and carefully dismantled the machines, so as not to leave any steel or other non-aluminium components on the carcasses. Then they packed the cans, bulk aluminium and non-aluminium waste back into three separate bins, ready for sale in Samariapo. Venezuela had a big aluminium industry and I was heartened to see that aluminium recycling had reached even the remote interior of the country.

The third day we did not stop at all and by the afternoon we reached the Orinoco. The landscape opened out into a more populated, pastoral scene. The broad Orinoco flowed from right to left in front of us and the mountains of the Cerro Duida could be seen across it in the distance. We turned left and picked up speed as the current changed from facing us in the Canal to behind us in the Orinoco. I looked back to take my last view of the Casiquiare. All I could see was a mouth in the riverbank where water flowed into a channel that disappeared into the forest.

I had just completed a journey along a remarkable natural waterway linking two of the mightiest rivers in the world. I was happy to have got to know it. I now knew that it was not part of a swamp that leaked out onto both sides; its water came from the Orinoco; it was a year-round tributary of the Rio Negro and never reversed its flow. I was pleased to have experienced first-hand that at high water it was transited by 200-ton barges. Loren McIntyre, a modern explorer who retraced Humboldt's journey and produced an excellent photographic book about it, states that the Canal is 328 km long. It was certainly a lonely place. We saw inhabitants mainly near the Rio Negro end of the Canal and saw nobody at all during the last 24 hours of our transit. Apart from the Colombian tanker on the first evening, we saw no other traffic.

On the Orinoco we met high-speed aluminium passenger boats and oil tankers operating between Samariapo (downstream from us) and Tama-Tama and Esmeralda (upstream). With more water under the keel we did not need to stop at night. We also ran into heavy rain, which meant that I had to move my hammock to a position under the flying bridge, near the engines. Fortunately I had brought earplugs along with me, so I was able to sleep through the noisy night. In this way we sped non-stop down to Samariapo, which we reached in the late afternoon of the following day. Here 64 km of rocky rapids impeded navigation to Puerto Ayacucho, from where it was possible for other barges to navigate the rest of the Orinoco down to the Atlantic Ocean.

I had accomplished the journey faster than expected, so I spent my spare time in the Samariapo area investigating the rapids of the Orinoco and looking at many pretty waterfalls on the smaller tributaries. Local rafting companies offered exciting trips on certain sections of the rapids, but they unfortunately had no convenient departure that I could join in. The landscape of the area was basically rocky savannah with patches of rainforest.

Finally it was time for me to join the cruise ship. I continued north by bus to Caracas, enjoying some excellent birdwatching through the windows as the vehicle trundled across the Llanos, the fertile plains on the west side of the Orinoco valley. I boarded the ship without any hitches and still had quite a lot of money left in my pocket as I did so.

The ship took me into the Orinoco Delta and into the Amazon Delta. It was a splendid opportunity to compare the lower reaches of these two mighty rivers, which had many geological and biological similarities, but many cultural and historical differences.

The most obvious similarity between the estuaries of the Orinoco and the Amazon was that they were both muddy (even though each river had important mud-free black tributaries that flowed off the Guiana shield). In both cases, the mud came predominantly from the Andes. The Orinoco received mud mainly from the Colombian and Venezuelan Andes via tributaries on its left bank, whereas the Amazon received mud mainly from the Peruvian and Bolivian Andes via its headwaters and its major tributary, the Rio Madeira.

The most obvious physical difference between the two rivers was that the Orinoco was located entirely in the Northern Hemisphere, whereas most of the water in the Amazon came from the Southern Hemisphere. This meant that the two systems were out of phase; when it was rainy season in the Orinoco basin, it was dry season in most of the Amazon basin and *vice versa.*

In terms of ethnicity and history, the Orinoco estuary was very different from the Amazon estuary. We saw the difference quite clearly on our excursions from the cruise ship. Many of the inhabitants we met in the Orinoco Delta were Indians, whereas we saw no Indians in the Amazon Delta. Historically, the Orinoco River was not the key to Venezuela's development. The modern wealth of Venezuela lay along the coast, particularly in the rich oil fields of Lake Maracaibo. Hence, (until the recent development of heavy industry in Ciudad Guyana) the mouth of the Orinoco suffered little European influence. From our ship we were able to visit Warau Indians living on the islands of the Orinoco Delta in much the same way that they had done for centuries. They built thatched houses with few or no walls, paddled beautiful dugout canoes, spoke Warau and slept in fine hammocks made of fibres from what they called *moriche* palm (the same species Brazilians call *buriti*).

On the other hand, in Brazil, the mouth of the Amazon was the main access to literally millions of square miles of hinterland. Portuguese colonisers, followed more recently by Brazilian rubber tappers, made a huge impact on the Amazon Delta, producing a great deal of ethnic conflict, racial mixing and cultural change. On the lower Amazon rural populations had changed so much that on our excursions no one we met called himself an Indian, even if he looked like one.

Brazilians had a special word for people from the interior who looked Indian but were not. They called them *caboclos* (from a Tupi-Guaraní word meaning "forest dweller"). I learned that *caboclo* was a term that foreigners should use with caution, because, like the English word "peasant" it could be neutral and just mean a simple person who lived in the countryside, or it might be pejorative ("country bumpkin") or eulogistic ("son of the earth"). It also had racial overtones ("not pure white") as well as economic ones ("poor"). *Caboclos* were quite simply the mixed-blooded rural poor. They spoke only Portuguese and didn't like to be confused with Indians.

In spite of not speaking an indigenous language and not structuring their society along tribal lines, the *caboclos* we met in the Lower Amazon used a lot of Indian technology, including cultivating manioc, growing a wide variety of fruit trees, catching shrimps in cylindrical basket traps and fishing with poison. On one of the excursions from the ship I saw fish-poison for the first time. A *caboclo* who lived on the banks of a creek showed me a bundle of inch-thick khaki-coloured roots from a leguminous vine he called *timbó*. At high tide, he said, after fish had swum into a particular side arm, he was going to erect a fence across the entrance to the arm and poison the fish inside the enclosure. He would beat the roots so that their toxic sap dissolved in the water. The moribund fish would float to the surface, where he would give them the coup-de-grace with his machete. The poison did not make the fish dangerous to eat.

I had hoped that the cruise ship would give me an opportunity to see the renowned Amazonian tidal bore called *pororoca*. I had heard that, as the rising tide invaded shallow channels, noisy waves, 4 to 8 ft in height, raced inland at 6 to 9 knots. However, after reading the ship's navigation manual, I learned that the tidal bore was not as common as some reporters have described. The manual said that the bore only occurred in specific places. It took place principally in watercourses open to the sea near the Canal Norte in the zone from Maracá Island to Janaucu Island. It did not occur in the Rio Pará (the waterway near Belém), nor in any channel more than seven metres deep. So one would never see it from a cruise ship. Where the phenomenon occurred, it was most likely to take place at the equinoxes, because equinoctial tides were particularly high. It was more common at the March equinox than at the September equinox, because in the first half of the year winds coming off the sea from the northeast helped to push the wave inland. (People do surf the *pororoca*, but the wave they most frequently ride is the on the Araguari River.)

After a couple of days the ship left the tidal Amazon Delta area and headed upstream towards Manaus. I would be home soon. But there was still one last treat in store for me on the Lower Amazon. In front of the city of Santarém, roughly halfway between the Atlantic Ocean and Manaus, the ship turned left and made a detour into the clear, greenish waters of the River Tapajós. There we spent a day on the beautiful white sand beaches of Alter do Chão, a former fishing community, now a charming weekend resort visited mainly by people from Santarém.

Our trip up the Tapajós took about an hour-and-a-half and we anchored in front of the pretty hamlet of Alter do Chão. The landscape was flat except for an isolated hill that stood out above the plain. Going ashore in our small boats, it was hard to believe that we were in the Amazon; the water was clear and the sand dazzling white. It seemed as if we were in the Caribbean. There was plenty to do. The town housed a cultural centre with a fine collection of Indian crafts. The hill offered panoramic views to those energetic enough to climb it. Street vendors and artisans from various parts of Brazil and even from other countries sold their wares in the main square. The bars served cool refreshment and the water was delightful to swim in.

To complete the Caribbean atmosphere, after sundown the ship's crew prepared a wonderful barbecue dinner with a bonfire on a beach well away from the town. They also engaged a team of young dancers from Alter do Chão to perform folkdances by the fireside after the meal. While we munched our luxurious barbecue of beefsteak, lobsters, spare ribs, lamb chops, hamburgers, sausages, local fish and so on, the dancers arrived and started to set up their show. Their dance repertoire would include *carimbó* rhythms, typical of the State of Pará, as well as music from the *Çairé*, a local folkdance somewhat similar to the *Boi Bumbá* of Parintins, but having a dolphin, not an ox, as the main character.

When dinner progressed from the main course to desserts, the dancers were more or less ready to start, but suddenly they became aware of a problem with their sound system. The CD of their music would not play. I suspect it was a pirate compilation that had not been copied correctly. Probably, having been contracted at short notice, they had not had time to test the disc before coming to the beach. To make matters worse, no other Brazilian music was available: the ship had not yet called at any major Brazilian cities, so that neither passengers nor crew had yet purchsed any commercial CDs – and our part of the beach was a considerable distance from the village, so that we could not send someone there quickly for help. I pointed to the guitar and the dance group agreed that we should try to improvise some live music.

Although we had made the barbecue a long way from the village, a number of villagers had come to our party. Some had come to watch the dancers. Some had come to watch the foreigners. Some had come to make their last sales of craftwork before their potential clients departed for good. Others hung around just to get a free meal from the left-overs after the passengers had dined. The dancers and I started to look urgently for musicians in the Brazilian entourage.

A young man accompanying one of the girls in the dance group turned out to be a powerful singer. He knew the songs the dancers needed and even which keys they were in. A handicraft salesman had a beautiful base drum that he had been trying to sell all afternoon. (The drum was a magnificent instrument made out of a palm trunk, but nobody would buy it because its skin was made of jaguar hide, which made it ecologically incorrect and impossible for a foreign tourist to get through customs.) Another vendor had a triangle, with which he usually advertised his presence in the street. Other instruments brought along by vendors included decorated European recorders, Andean pipes of pan, Afrobrazilian *berimbaus* (bow harps) and Indian whistles and shakers. Once the locals realised the urgent need to improvise an orchestra for the dancers, they passed out the available instruments to anyone who had a notion of harmony and rhythm.

Led by the strong singer, our makeshift band successfully produced an appropriate dance repertoire in spite of the strange array of instruments. The singer bellowed loudly, I hammered out the harmony on the guitar, while the jaguar-skin drum provided the basic beat. Recorders, pipes and whistles ornamented the melody and the whole sound was reinforced by myriad percussion instruments.

The dance performance lasted forty-five minutes and the orchestra stayed the course. It was not the finest musical event, but it was certainly one of the most enjoyable. It reminded me nostalgically of the time when I had run beach parties professionally. I loved the bonfire. I loved the dancers. I loved the lack of electronics. I loved watching the musicians pump out music as though their lives depended on it. And I loved being able to jump into the warm waters of the Tapajós when it was over.

Two days later our ship tied up at the floating docks of Manaus. My trip from the Amazon to the Orinoco by river and back by sea had reached its end. The circle was complete. I had seen the strange phenomenon of two river systems linked by a natural canal. I had met Venezuelan Indians and Brazilian *caboclos*. And I had found it worthwhile carrying the guitar all the way.

Chapter 14

Fig 14. Vision

At Altitude in the Andes; High in the Lowlands

After the Orinoco trip, somebody must have spread my name through the adventure cruise ship industry, because I started to receive invitations to work as a naturalist on other vessels. As far as I could, I accepted the new offers. I liked the work. Typically an adventure cruise ship in the Amazon would cruise along the river, dropping anchor twice a day, once in the early morning and again in the late afternoon. After anchoring it would put a fleet of inflatable rubber boats into the water and each naturalist would drive a boat and take about ten passengers to explore the riverside. One had great freedom and it was a joy to share one's knowledge with the passengers and to discover new things together. Of course in the inflatable boat you were exposed to the tropical sun, rain, heat and humidity, but back on the ship you had air-conditioning, hot showers, a laundry, a bar, gourmet cuisine, a library and an interesting team of co-workers. Furthermore, the new offers gave me the chance to extend my cruising territory into new areas. Soon I was heading regularly up the Amazon to Peru.

All adventure cruise ships tended to come to the Amazon at the same time of year, typically around March and April. The timing of the vessels had nothing to do with the particular attractions of the Amazon – the Amazon could be visited all year round. It had to do with the fact that the ships also worked in the Antarctic, which could only be visited in December, January and February. Like some giant marine migration, the ships left the Antarctic at the same time and called into the Amazon as they made their way north for the summer.

Obviously I could only work on one ship at a time. However, lots of job offers meant that I could chop and change; I could travel for a while on one ship and then switch to another, taking the opportunity to do some personal exploration in the free time between leaving one vessel and joining the next. In this way I managed to arrange enough free time in the upper Amazon to fulfil another old dream – to travel from the Pacific Coast over the Andes to the Amazon.

I had already been in the Andes. I had been to Machu Picchu, the fabulous Inca ruins in South Peru. Like most people who went there, I had flown to Cuzco and taken the quaint little train that finally reached the ruins by following a cascading river in a deep valley between snow-covered mountains. It was spectacular, beautiful and full of history. But one of the things that stuck in my mind about Machu Picchu was the realisation that the water in the Urubamba River, which runs past the ruins, eventually runs down the Amazon, past where I now live and into the Atlantic Ocean. Comprehending this elementary fact helped me to feel the relationship between the Andes and the Atlantic in a very personal way. Yet when I thought about the Pacific side of the Andes, I realised I knew nothing about that area. I had simply flown from Lima to Cuzco; I didn't have any on-the-spot observations linking the Andes to the Pacific. There was a blank space on the left side of my mental map of South America. I decided that doing a trip by surface transport from Lima across the Andes into my part of the Amazon would help to fill-in the blank.

Having worked on a German adventure cruise ship travelling up the Amazon, I signed off in Iquitos, Peru. Then I had one week of free time before boarding an American vessel that would take me down the river again. In this free week, I intended to fly from Iquitos to Lima on Peru's Pacific coast; catch a bus from Lima over the Andes to Pucallpa on the Rio Ucayali; and finally catch a boat down the Ucayali from Pucallpa back to Iquitos.

My enthusiasm for doing a trip over the Andes was fired by reading an account of the journey of Francisco de Orellana, the first European to make a major voyage on the Amazon River. Orellana, a Spaniard, accomplished his voyage somewhat by chance in 1542, after crossing the Andes on horseback and foot from the Ecuadorian coast in 1541. He was part of a large but disastrous expedition led by Gonzalo Pizarro, the brother of the conqueror of the Incas. The Spaniards' goal was to look for gold and spices east of Quito, Ecuador. Having crossed the Andes with great difficulty and ever-dwindling resources, the starving expedition reached a navigable headwater of the Amazon and split up. Orellana set off in a boat downstream to find food and soon discovered that because of the strong current he could not get back upstream. He kept going and successfully navigated the whole length of the Amazon to the sea. He even continued sailing around the coast as far as Venezuela. (Pizarro, furious at being abandoned, struggled ignominiously back to Quito.)

On his journey downstream, Orellana mentioned encountering ferocious female Indian warriors. Drawing parallels from Greek mythology, he called them "Amazons". The name, charged with sex and violence, stuck like glue, with the result that today the river on which he travelled is called the Amazon River. Nobody these days calls it the Rio Orellana.

It took Orellana nine months to cross the Andes from the Pacific coast to a navigable tributary of the Amazon. It then took him a further eight months to reach the Atlantic. In contrast, my trip over the Andes by bus from Lima to the river port of Pucallpa took just twenty hours. Next, by barge and cruise ship, I reached the Atlantic Ocean in three weeks.

My Andean adventure started one Saturday morning in April. I took my bags off the German vessel that had brought me up the Amazon to Iquitos and put most of them in storage. Taking just a light knapsack and my guitar, I flew immediately to Pucallpa to check the conditions of the road and the availability of river transport. I was in luck. The road to Lima, which frequently suffered landslides, was open and buses were making the journey in twenty to twenty-seven hours. Also, there was no shortage of boats back to Iquitos. At that time of year, water level in the Amazon was high and navigation was relatively easy; at least one boat sailed every day. The voyage downstrean to Iquitos typically took four days and three nights.

The following morning I flew to Lima and immediately took a cab to the bus station, where I found a bus leaving that evening to cross the Andes. The flight to Lima already gave me some idea of what I would see on the bus. The view through the aeroplane's window showed me that the Andes were an important climatic barrier. Lush vegetation and cascading rivers on the eastern slopes reflected the high rainfall in the Amazon basin. In contrast, the western slopes of the Andes were dry and barren with hardly a river to be seen. On the ground below me I could see palpable evidence of what my atlas had shown me in coloured maps: near the equator the general air movement was from east to west. The wet air from the east cooled as it rose to pass over the mountains, causing water vapour to condense into rain and snow. After crossing the Cordillera, the air warmed up as it descended, but it was dry. In fact the Pacific region of Peru included some of the driest places on earth. As we came in to land I saw that many poor people in Lima lived in houses with no roofs. Rainfall was so low there that protection against rain was not a high priority.

While waiting for the bus to depart I wandered around the area near the bus station. It was a poor district with lots of little hotels and small businesses, but one of the nearby squares contained an impressive monument to Manco Capac, the chief of the Incas at the time of the Spanish conquest. The Inca made me think of Pizarro; Pizarro made me think of Orellana; Orellana made me think about crossing the Andes; and that made me think it was time to get back to the bus.

As the sun set, I boarded the Leon de Huanaco, the bus that would take me across the mountains. The vehicle, a sturdy, no-frills 35-seater, was weather-tight but not air-conditioned. The upholstered seats were partially reclinable. It was full. Lots of people were travelling that weekend. The country was about to hold its presidential elections and voting was obligatory: everybody had to get to the place where they were registered voters, or face a fine – and there were no facilities for voting by post or by proxy.

The bus rumbled out onto a packed highway that ran north up the coast before heading inland. It was rush hour and progress was very slow in the heavy traffic. Horns blared. Vehicle fumes added to the evening haze. To keep the spirits of his passengers up, the driver put a selection of pounding discotheque music on the bus sound system. I later noticed that he was very thoughtful in his choice of musical styles. On the coast, where European culture predominated, he played discotheque and rock. When we got into the high mountains he played Inca music. In the transition zone he put on a popular cultural hybrid called *Tecno-Cumbia*. Towards the end of the trip, near the Amazonian lowlands, he played *merengues* and *llaneros*.

It was already completely dark when we eventually left the city and its seven million inhabitants behind. But there was still plenty of traffic. The road over the Andes was so important that vehicles were head to tail in a long winding snake of coloured lights. The serpent, red if you looked forwards and white if you looked behind, could only go as fast as the slowest vehicle in the line. There were lots of mines in the mountains and many of the vehicles were heavy trucks for carrying ore. There were few opportunities to overtake and drivers accepted that they would have to select a crawler gear and simply follow the slow-moving vehicle in front. However, the line of vehicles lights helped me to visualise the relief of the huge mountains in the dark. The line was seldom straight. More often it curved or zigzagged above us or across a valley. Only for rare, short periods did it ever lead downwards.

In the zone where our driver was playing Tecno-Cumbia music, I could tell that we were winding up the sides of huge valleys, with rock walls on one side and open views on the other. The stars too helped me to orient myself. In April, from the viewpoint of the bus at about latitude 12° S, the Southern Cross was high in the southern sky and the Great Bear low on the northern horizon. The clear, dry mountain air and the absence of streetlights made the stars very bright and the constellations easy to spot. On some hairpin bends, the Cross and the Bear actually seemed to change places, as the bus turned though 180°.

I must have eventually dozed off, but at about 2.00 AM a passenger woke me to tell me that we were making a refreshment stop and that we had reached the highest point of our trip. Through the bus windows I saw a modest restaurant set on a barren plateau. It was apparently the only building in the area and the only source of electric light. By the way people huddled in their anoraks, I could tell that it was windswept and cold. When I got up to leave the bus and refresh myself I forgot that we were at an altitude of over 4000 metres and I almost fainted through lack of oxygen. Just getting to the toilets and back seemed a major physical effort for my body, which in Manaus was used to being almost at sea level. I was glad to get back to the warmth of the bus and the reclining position of my seat.

By the time dawn came we had reached the town of Tingo Maria, which, although high in the mountains, was obviously situated in the Amazon watershed; the verdant vegetation of trees and ornamental plants indicated an abundant amount of rainfall. The town nestled between snow-capped peaks, but this time I did not feel any symptoms of altitude sickness. Motor-tricycle taxis (also seen in Pucallpa and Iquitos) circulated in the streets, adding a typically Peruvian touch to the scene. The passengers breakfasted at a restaurant near the entrance to the main street and then we continued on our way again. From now on until reaching the Amazon (Rio Ucayali) it would be downhill all the way.

One of the consequences of the high rainfall on the Amazon side of the Andes, in comparison to the dry Pacific side, was that the road was more subject to landslides. The heavy rain on the steep mountain slopes caused substantial erosion (the source of the mud in the Amazon). Earth and rocks could tumble down and block the road, or the road itself might fall away. For this reason there were road repair stations situated at regular intervals along the highway. They varied from units equipped with bulldozers and tractors to community groups armed only with picks, shovels and wheelbarrows. Everybody who lived along the road seemed to realise how important it was to keep the thoroughfare open.

As soon as there was a problem such as fallen rocks, potholes or whatever, work gangs went out to try to keep the traffic flowing. The road was largely unpaved on the Amazonian side of the Andes, but it was nevertheless an important and heavily used artery.

Various people I spoke to explained to me that the road was vital for welding Peru's different geographical regions into a cohesive nation. It was very difficult for Peru's government in Lima to develop the Amazon region; the Andes were a huge barrier. Before the existence of a road, any cargo from Lima bound for the Peruvian Amazon had to be put on an ocean-going ship in Callao. The vessel would then navigate along the coasts of Ecuador and Colombia, through the Panama Canal, past Venezuela and the Guyanas, then up two thousand miles of Brazilian Amazon, to reach Peru again at Iquitos. Here the cargo would be transhipped into riverboats, which would carry it to its final destination. This procedure was prohibitively expensive and time-consuming. With the building of the road, cargoes could go over the Andes by truck and be distributed by riverboat from Pucallpa. The prediction was that eventually Pucallpa would become a more important commercial centre than Iquitos. Nevertheless, Iquitos would continue to handle large cargoes that could only be transported by ship. Material for the oil industry in the Peruvian Amazon fell into this category.

The combination of mountains and abundant water produced delightful vistas from the bus. Much of the time the road ran along the valleys of rapid rivers with raging cataracts. As we got further down the hills, the forest started to give way to farms and we frequently passed trucks carrying timber to Lima. There would have been more farms in the area if the land had not been so steep; the soil was fertile. One of the refreshment stalls at which we stopped – by now the bus driver was playing *merengues* on his sound system – had a superb selection of locally produced fruit.

At midday the temperature became hot, the air clammy and the road more or less flat. We had reached the Amazon lowlands. In another couple of hours we arrived at Pucallpa on the Rio Ucayali, the major tributary of the upper Amazon. Here the bus journey ended and my river trip began.

I checked into a small hotel and went to look for boats heading downstream to Iquitos. In spite of Pucallpa's strategic location as an interface between road and river traffic, there was a total lack of port facilities. Boats moored as best they could at the river's edge and lorries tried to reach them by driving down the muddy beach. As it was rainy season many vehicles got bogged down, which of course stopped others from moving. It seemed that any able bodied man in Pucallpa could get a job on the beach: either carrying goods between vehicles and boats, or digging vehicles out of the mud. *Pucallpa* is Quechua for "red earth" and the place lived up to its name. Although at the water's edge the mud was dark brown, most of the mud above the high water mark consisted of bright red, iron-rich laterite.

I found a large, square motor barge that was sailing at nightfall the following day. When I booked a passage the skipper told me that I would need to bring a hammock (which I had) and that I would also need a plate, mug and spoon. I bought the latter items in the market and then spent the remaining time getting to know Pucallpa.

The town was obviously thriving and people I spoke to said that it was expanding rapidly. Some of the traders had moved from Iquitos, to take advantage of the road traffic. I saw one thing that particularly perturbed me: the overt commercialisation of wild animal skins. Two shops on the main square and others in back streets had lots of hides of jaguar, giant anteater, deer and other wild animals for sale. The business was apparently legal, because many of the skins were spread out in the sun to dry in front of the shops, with no attempt to hide them from officials. Although wild mammals in general are more abundant near the Andes than they are in the central Amazon, I was saddened to be reminded of how many creatures had lost their lives to the skin trade.

The motor barge on which I travelled sailed at about the appointed hour, but not without a demonstration of local ways of doing things. The marine authorities came to check the vessel at nightfall and gave it permission to sail. Once the officials had left, the captain took on more passengers and goods, so that by the time the vessel really cast off, it was overloaded. It seemed to be standard practice. None of my fellow passengers raised an eyebrow.

The vessel was built in a very utilitarian manner with parallel, straight lines. It was basically a flatbed metal barge. An open deck occupyied the forward two thirds of its length. Behind the deck was the raised wheelhouse, followed by a barn-like passenger compartment built over the engines to the full width of the vessel. Peruvians called this kind of vessel a *motorchata* (literally "motorised flat boat"). It carried about two hundred tons of cargo, most of which was stored under tarpaulins on the deck. Nevertheless, several hundred cooking gas cylinders were being transported in the sparsely illuminated passenger accommodation. There were forty or so passengers. They were expected to have dined before embarking, as the vessel provided no food on the first night. Once we had set out into the darkness, I followed the example of my fellow passengers, settled into my hammock and slept soundly.

I awoke to the voice of the young man from the neighbouring hammock informing me that breakfast was being served and that I should join the line for getting my food. I got up and grabbed my bowl, mug and spoon. The menu was the same on all three mornings: vanilla-flavoured sweet banana porridge, bread and coffee. Wholesome and cheap were the guiding principles in the chef's choice. After all, the whole trip including transport, three breakfasts, three lunches and two evening meals cost less than US$30.

The landscape was typical of the upper Amazon: low-lying flat muddy islands, some covered with arrowcane and other grasses, some covered with pioneer tree species such as *Cecropia* and False Kapok. It looked very much like the area around Iquitos, or even around Manaus. I had hoped that near Pucallpa I would be able to see the mountains of the Andes rising up behind the river, but this was not possible. The bus ride had shown me that Pucallpa was over a hundred kilometers from the first foothills of the Andes, too far for them to be visible.

Only once during the three-day voyage from Pucallpa to Iquitos did the view include a mountain that might be considered a forerunner of the Andes. About twenty hours out from Pucallpa, by the rich light of the setting sun we approached and sailed around a large isolated mountainous bluff. Otherwise, very little of the land rose more than fifty metres above the river.

We stopped at many small towns along the way. On the boat (just as there had been on the bus) were lots of people travelling to their respective voting centres in preparation for the elections. There was a constant flux of passengers leaving and joining the vessel. Sometimes there was plenty of space for our hammocks; sometimes we were uncomfortably crowded. In general people accepted the overcrowding with good humour.

At about 2 AM on the second night, our barge hit a sandbank. It didn't get stuck; it simply shuddered, listed violently as it grazed the bank, then resumed its normal trim and continued navigating. The effect on the passengers was dramatic. Most had been asleep when the incident happened. Now some screamed; some prayed; some hysterically shouted that there was no need to panic; some comforted the faint-hearted with complicated analyses of how stable the ship was; some compared the water level with that of previous years and tried to predict whether we would hit anymore obstacles; some told horrific stories of far worse incidents they knew of. The public was suddenly wide-awake and it was clear that it would be difficult to get back to sleep in the near future.

Amongst the passengers was a group of Peruvian Baptists on their way to a religious meeting. Their reaction to the nautical shudder was to start singing hymns. I lay huddled in my hammock, awake, but trying not to get involved. (After all, nothing had really happened.) One of the Baptists, who had seen my guitar, came over and asked if I would accompany their hymns. I would have preferred to sleep, but I knew that that would be impossible for a while. By coincidence I also knew the Baptist repertoire, because my parents were Baptists and my mother had been a church organist. So, in spite of currently having no religious inclination, I agreed to play.

It was, to say the least, bizarre. There we were, at past two in the morning, motoring noisily down the Ucayali River to the tunes of "Rock of Ages", "Will Your Anchor Hold in the Storms of Life?" "Breathe on me Breath of Life" and all the other protestant hymns of my childhood. Of course I didn't know the Spanish words, but the melodies had been ingrained in me at infancy. Somehow the hymns simultaneously brought me closer to the Peruvians and yet transported me back to England. After about an hour, the excitement died down and people started to get back to sleep.

The religious music session turned out to be a social icebreaker. The following day, after the Baptists had disembarked at a riverside town, some passengers came to ask me if we could sing together. Naturally I agreed. They sang a variety of ballads and folksongs in the vein of *"Cuando el Condor Pasa"*. (It was impossible to travel anywhere in Peru without hearing that song.) I sang a few numbers in Spanish, including *"La Bamba"*, which was well received. But, of course, when people discovered that my hometown was situated not far from Liverpool, they wanted to hear something by the Beatles, a request I was happy to fulfil.

I found it particularly touching that at the end of the song session, a young

Peruvian, who said he was learning to play the guitar, came and asked me if I could teach him "*La Bamba*". I felt my musical carrier had gone full circle. I remembered myself as a young man learning to play the guitar and looking for the words and chords to the very same song.

On the evening of the fourth day, a little less than 72 hours after setting out from Pucallpa, we pulled into the Port of Iquitos. It was Friday and the cruise ship I was due to join the next day had already arrived and was moored at the floating dock. Our barge tied up next to it. I could see through the ship's steamy windows that the passengers inside were dressed in their finery and having cocktails in preparation for the Captain's Farewell Dinner. Should I go on board immediately or should I stay in town and board the following day? I decided to ask. Soon, to my amazement, down the gangway, wearing his full dress uniform and with a glass of champagne for me in his hand, came the Captain—my good friend Uli Demel. We toasted my successful journey over the Andes, but he discretely suggested, in view of my dishevelled appearance and the fact that I had no immediate duties on board, that I should stay in town for the night. In fact, he said, I could stay two nights in town, because the incoming group of passengers had been delayed by problems with the airlines.

Perfect! To have completed the trip over the Andes was fine. To drink genuine champagne two thousand miles up the Amazon with a Ship's Captain in gala uniform was fine too. (I felt like a character out of a film about the rubber boom.) But to stay an extra night in Iquitos was perfect. The extra night appealed to me because Eric, a friend I had made on the river barge, had invited me to his house to make and consume the Indians' hallucinogenic drink *ayahuasca*. I was interested, but preparing *ayahuasca* required a lot of time, which, on seeing the ship already in port, I feared I would not have. After talking to the Captain, I was happy to be able to accept Eric's invitation.

As soon as the Captain went up the gangway to rejoin his cocktail party, Eric, who had been hovering in the background, came forward and we made plans. The following morning, he said, he would go to the market in the Belén district of Iquitos and buy the ingredients to make the drink. In the afternoon we would brew it; and in the evening we would sample the results. In spite of *ayahuasca*'s hallucinogenic properties, he assured me that it was quite legal and non-addictive. We could, he said, buy it ready-made in the market, but he liked to brew his own. In the meantime I could sleep at his place, a simple middle class house in the suburbs, which he rented with three other young men who, like himself, were students.

Ayahuasca interested me because in Manaus drinking it had become the basis of a popular religious cult which two young lady anthropologist friends of mine had studied. On separate occasions, each of them tried the drink. For one, a cheerful extrovert, it was a very positive agreeable adventure, during which she imagined herself soaring effortlessly over the forest like an eagle. However, the other, who had a nervous introverted disposition, found it a terrifying, morbid experience, which she certainly did not want to repeat. Classifying myself among the optimists, I felt that in my case the reaction would be positive. I was curious to see if I would be right.

Various native peoples all over the Western Amazon knew about the hallucinogenic drink. Often shamans used it to foresee the future or to communicate with the deceased. There were many different names for it. *Ayahausca* was the name in Quechua and meant "Holy Vine". Other tribes called it *caapi* or *yagé*. In Manaus non-Indians usually called it o *Santo Daime* (the Holy Gift) or simply o *Chá* (the Tea).

I slept in my hammock on the veranda of Eric's house and the following morning we took a motor-tricycle taxi to the Belén market in search of ingredients for the drink. What a fascinating place the market was! It extended over several blocks. It sold all sorts of natural products, both wild and cultivated – and it was packed. We left the taxi and headed into the throng on foot. Eric led the way and I followed close behind. I quickly noticed many differences between this Peruvian market and the Brazilian markets I was used to. The first thing that struck me was the sale of wild forest animals and meat from them. There were live turtles and tortoises for sale along with the salted or raw meat of agouti, *capivara*, deer and caimans. Such products were illegal in Brazil. Next I saw that there were far more varieties of potatoes than in Brazil. (Botanists consider Peru to be the "home" of cultivated potatoes.) The sale of fresh hearts-of-palm surprised me too; Brazilians usually purchased hearts-of-palm preserved in cans or jars. And when we passed the section of the market that housed lots of small restaurants, many of them sold *cebiche*, a famous Peruvian dish made by marinating raw fish in lime juice; Brazilians never ate raw fish.

Eric headed for the herbal-medicine section of the market. This turned out to be a long pedestrianised street with stalls on both sides. We walked down it between stacks of bark, leaves, resins, fruits and seeds – all harvested wild from the forest. The animal products on sale included the fat of manatis, turtles and anacondas. As we walked, the stallholders shouted out the miraculous properties of their wares, which seemed to be able to cure anything from rheumatism to impotence. Some stalls had bottles of strange infusions. A fiery tonic called *Las Siete Raizes* (the seven roots) was especially popular. It contained seven different herbal ingredients steeped in Pisco brandy. At one of the stalls Eric showed me a bottle containing a muddy, khaki-coloured liquid. This, he told me, was *ayahuasca*. However, he reminded me, we were going to brew our own.

A little further down the same street, Eric found what he was looking for, a pile of brown stems obviously cut from a woody forest vine. The stems ranged in diameter from the thickness of a finger to the thickness of an arm. Technically they were pieces of a Melastomataceous liana called *Banisteriopsis caapi* (or another closely related species, such as *Banisteriopsis inebrians*). In Spanish Eric called them *ayahuasca*, like the drink. He bought about 20 Kg, which he stuffed into a large rucksack. Then he purchased about 2 Kg of green leaves (which later research suggested were probably from *Psychotria viridis*, a plant in the coffee family). Adding the leaves to the brew of stems, Eric said, would add brightness to the visions we saw. Later, my anthropologist friends confirmed this. They told me that in Manaus some religious groups sang a canticle as they prepared "theTea". This canticle said that the vine gave the power [to see visions] and the leaves gave the light [to make them brighter].

We took another motor-tricycle taxi back to Eric's house and after lunch we were ready to prepare the hallucinogenic drink. Eight people were going to drink the brew: Eric and his three housemates, plus three girls who arrived during lunch, and myself. Apart from me, all the participants had drunk *ayahuasca* on previous occasions. They insisted that everyone who drank had to take part in the preparation. So, collectively we set to. While some cut wood and prepared a fire in the back yard of the house, others, like me, took turns pounding the *ayahuasca* stems between two heavy blocks of wood in the way a smith hammers iron on an anvil. One of the girls took care of cleaning the three vessels we would need, namely a big earthenware cauldron and two aluminium pots.

Once all the stems had been crushed, Eric put a layer of them in the bottom of the earthenware cauldron, followed by a layer of the green leaves, then another layer of stems, followed by another layer of leaves, until all the material had been accommodated. Finally he put enough water in to cover the plant material. By now the cauldron was heavy and it required a concerted effort by the men to position it on the fire.

Thus began a cooking party that lasted for about four hours. We had a lot of spare time while the brew boiled, so we sat around telling jokes and singing to the guitar, even dancing at one point. We did not drink alcohol, since most people who took *ayahuasca* thought that alcohol had a negative effect on the *ayahuasca* experience. The earthenware cauldron spent most of its time on the fire. One of the aluminium pots contained fresh water and stood near the earthenware cauldron, warming up. The other aluminium pot was used to collect the liquid decanted from the cauldron.

Eric led the proceedings, helped by the rest of us as necessary. To extract the active ingredients from the plant material, we basically boiled the roots in water three times. A chemical engineer would have described our antics as three hot aqueous extractions – I thought of it more like making tea three times with the same tealeaves. In practice it went as follows. After the cauldron containing the plants and water had boiled for an hour, Eric decanted the liquid into the collecting pot and topped-up the cauldron (which still contained the plants) with hot water. After the cauldron had boiled for a second hour he did the same decantation and refilling. After the cauldron had boiled for the third hour he again decanted the liquid, but did not add new water. By now, all the psychoactive substances had been dissolved out of the plants and were in the liquid in the collecting pot. We were ready to start the concentration process. Eric emptied the cauldron and filled it with the contents of the collecting pot. Setting the cauldron back on the fire, we waited for most of the water to boil off, concentrating the "tea" to about 10% of its original volume.

We stopped the concentration process when about 5 litres of liquid remained in the cauldron; we simply took the cauldron off the fire. Eric poured the contents of the cauldron into glass bottles to cool down ready for use. The "tea" was clear and amber in colour when hot, but became an opaque milky-coffee colour as it cooled. While it cooled, we set about making ourselves comfortable for drinking. I already knew that imbibing *ayahuasca* might cause vomiting and diarrhoea, so I checked my route to the facilities in case I should need them in a hurry.

We moved away from the fireside to the veranda, where some (including myself) rigged hammocks and others spread out carpets and cushions on which to lounge. Eric put a CD of gentle music on the player. It was about nine in the evening and we were finally ready to take our trip.

Eric put some glasses on the table and asked each of us how much we wanted. For himself he poured about 250 ml, but for me he poured about 150 ml. He said that since it was the first time that I had taken *ayahuasca*, I should drink less than he did. That way, if I had a bad experience, I could not accuse him of having given me an overdose. He dimmed the light and wished us all a good trip.

I lay in my hammock and drank my ration, putting the glass down carefully before any effect could be felt. Suddenly I felt very drowsy and the music seemed very distant. When I closed my eyes, I started seeing things. When I opened my eyes, the visions stopped, but then the drowsiness returned and I had to close my eyes again. After a bit of experimentation I discovered that to some extent I could censure what I saw. If something was frightening, I could eliminate it by repeatedly opening my eyes until a more agreeable vision appeared. Mostly what I saw were fantastic creatures and weird trees like those depicted on the covers of "heavy metal" music records. The pictures were stretched vertically and the left side was a mirror image of the right side. In general watching the visions was a pleasant and exciting experience, like travelling in some mysterious fairytale landscape.

After about an hour-and-a-half, the group spread out to the bedrooms and other areas where they could sleep more conveniently when the psychedelic trip turned into normal sleep. I moved my hammock further down the veranda and took the opportunity to go to the bathroom. (One quick bout of loose bowels, but no vomiting or serious diarrhoea – thank the Lord.) In my hammock's new location I was lying near the outlet of the air-conditioning unit of one of the bedrooms. Under the lingering influence of the *ayahuasca* the droning air conditioner began to fascinate me. I could hear (I thought) every single cog of its mechanism and it seemed to be a harmoniously tuned machine, like a beautiful giant clock. I felt as if I were listening to the movement of the whole solar system. While I was enjoying the clarity of my inner vision of air conditioners as cosmic symbols, a huge silver star came down a gaudy rainbow and exploded in my head with a loud "ping" and a bright white flash.

That was the end of the hallucinations. The next thing I remember, it was daylight and Eric was waking me to tell me it was time to get up, get my things together and join the ship. I had slept soundly, as he said I would, and there was, as he correctly predicted, no hangover. I felt wonderfully relaxed and ready for the voyage down the Amazon.

On the way to the ship I reflected on the events of the past week. I had seen something of the Andes, the Pacific watershed and the Upper Amazon – and there were no cogs in the air conditioner, but I did hear them.

Chapter 15

Fig 15. Old Waterfront, Manaus

WK

The Floating House

I bought my floating house the day my town house flooded. I didn't live in an area prone to flooding, but on that day, building work by my neighbours caused rainwater to accumulate against my backyard wall in a way it hadn't done before. During a torrential, early-morning downpour the wall couldn't stand the pressure of the water and fell down, releasing a muddy flood into my garden and house. The wave, which was mercifully short lived, swamped the floors in every room. I was in bed at the time the disaster struck. In my drowsiness, with lots of thunder around, I didn't hear the wall fall down. When it was finally time to get up, I looked down at the bedroom floor from the high vantage point of my mezzanine sleeping platform and was dismayed to find a slurry of mud lapping around record sleeves, picture books, maps and other objects on the bottom shelves of my book cases. I also sadly noticed that my collection of nature slides, still unpacked from a recent trip and located in a bag on the floor, had suffered drastically. To this day, some of the slides I managed to salvage bear strange marks that remind me of the flood and vividly illustrate the power of Amazonian rain.

In reality, the flood and buying the floating house were not directly related. It was pure coincidence. It would be more accurate to say my town house happened to get flooded on the day I paid for the floating house I had already agreed to buy. Nevertheless, at the time, it did seem a good idea to have a form of habitation that could never be swamped.

Many of my English-speaking friends referred to my new acquisition as a houseboat, but I never used that term myself. The floating house looked nothing like a boat. It was a massive log raft, so heavy that you would not want to move it around unnecessarily. Local people called such floating structures *flutuantes* and there were many of them in the central Amazon. Mine was basically a simple, zinc-roofed, wooden shack built on a platform that spanned four floating tree trunks. It measured 12m x 4½m. The roof leaked; the floor needed one or two new planks; and the walls needed a coat of paint. But at less than a thousand dollars, it was an affordable second home and a good base for getting out onto the water.

I bought the floating house because maintaining my riverboat had become too much work for the amount of free time I had. I was travelling professionally on other people's boats and had little time to enjoy my own. Having a floating house brought me close to the water at little expense and without the drudgery of having to do lots of upkeep. Moreover, in comparison to a riverboat, the floating house had more space, comfort and stability. My friend Adam lived on a *flutuante* and he encouraged me to buy mine, saying that I could moor it along side his. He would look after it for me when I was travelling. His suggestion was attractive and I took it up.

Adam kept his floating house in Cacau Pirêra, a bay in the flooded forest on the south side of the Rio Negro opposite Manaus. A fleet of ferries run by the government transported vehicles across the Rio Negro to a roadhead in the area. One of the ferry terminals was in the São Raimundo district of Manaus and the other was in Cacau Pirêra. The frequency of the ferry service varied with the time of day, and increased at the weekend, but except for late at night, there was usually at least one departure per hour in each direction. The crossing took about forty minutes. People without cars could either cross the river on the car ferry, which was free to them, or use a number of private launches, which provided a faster, fare-paying service. Because of these transport links, Cacau Pirêra was a convenient place to have a floating house.

Adam liked the easy access to Manaus. However, he disliked the litter and noise produced by the sometimes intense movement of people through the ferry terminal. Consequently, of the many floating houses in Cacau Pirêra Bay, his was the furthest away from the land and the nearest to the open river. Nevertheless, he could paddle his kayak to the terminal in about fifteen minutes and be across the river on the ferry within an hour.

When I bought my floating house, it was moored in crowded conditions (practically a floating slum) very close to the ferryboat terminal. It had electric light from the grid, via a precarious and probably illegal hook-up. Since I intended to use the place for aquatic leisure activities, I decided to forego mains electricity and tow the house out into the quieter and cleaner water near Adam's place. In spite of the huge weight of my new acquisition, Adam and I were able to tow it with a 25-HP outboard motor boat. The wide bay of the Rio Negro near Manaus had very little current and side arms like Cacau Pirera had none at all. Wind and other boats were potential hazards while towing, but we chose a moment shortly after noon on a calm day. The car ferry had just left and most of the other boats had stopped for lunch. The house moved slowly along at about half a knot. With no wind we were able to manoeuvre it easily into a berth alongside Adam's.

What a wonderful liberty, to simply tie your floating house up to a tree and live on it. Of course there were rules, but the rules came from coastal marine authorities with little regard to the realities of the Amazon. My house, like everybody else's in the area, had neither papers nor permits. In principle all floating structures had to be registered with the Port Authorities and conform to norms. But in practice, carpenters with no experience in naval architecture and no taste for bureaucracy built *flutuantes* at any convenient point on the waterfront where materials were available.

To make a *flutuante*, one collected a number of floating trunks, hewn from the sandbox tree species. Then one fixed the trunks together with massive crossbeams and gigantic iron nails to make a floating platform, on which one erected a more or less conventional wooden house. Floating houses were built in the water and usually never left it – they could break under their own weight if they became stranded unevenly on a beach when the river level dropped.

The amount and type of superstructure that owners built onto their basic rafts was a matter of individual choice. Adam owned three *flutuantes*, each of a different style. One was a floating hotel of four rooms, which he let out to visitors at the weekend. The second was a bar. It had a roof, but was open on all sides. The third contained his living quarters and a kitchen. Most of the space on my floating house was occupied by a roomy cabin, which was divided into a lounge, bedroom, kitchen, bathroom and toilet facilities. There were decks outside my front and back doors, but not along the sides.

Although with time I improved my comfort, including mending the leaky roof, I was able to live in the floating house as soon as I bought it. It immediately became my second home. Living in a floating house focussed my attention on the riverside in a way that moving around on boats had not. For instance, because I now saw the same trees for long periods, I was able to watch their flowering and fruiting and thereby identify them much more easily than was possible in a fleeting glimpse from a boat. (On a boat trip, one simply hadn't the time to watch a plant's life-cycle). I also became much more aware of the seasonal change in water level in the local rivers. The whole rhythm of life in our floating community was determined by river level.

The change in water level was dramatic – the whole bay of Cacau Pirêra usually dried out at some point between September and February, causing the ferry boat terminal to relocate to a spit of land a couple of miles away, where there was deep water all year round. As the ferry terminal moved, so did all the commerce of Cacau Pirêra. Merchants closed their shops in the bay and built temporary shops at the new terminal, called, romantically *Ponta do Amor* (Love Point).

During the low-water season Ponta do Amor was a remarkable phenomenon, a huge temporary shantytown of shops, bars and restaurants, with neither piped water nor drains. Fortunately the Rio Negro, flowing gently around rocky outcrops in the area kept the shore fairly clean. At weekends hundreds of poor people flocked out of Manaus to enjoy beaches nearby. Since the car ferry was free to pedestrians, a day at Ponta do Amor was an inexpensive leisure option.

One or two huge *flutuantes* functioning as discotheques also moved from their habitual moorings in Cacau Pirêra to Ponta do Amor to take continuing advantage of the clientele brought by the ferryboat. These floating dance halls were exceedingly loud and very basic. But they were always full on Sunday afternoons. Their clients danced in bathing suits to a rhythm called *brega* (a musical lament in bolero style with a rather techno accompaniment). By mid afternoon, many people were drunk, but even so, the atmosphere usually remained festive, although occasionally jealous fighting broke out – or somebody drowned though playing drunken games in the water.

Once the ferryboat had moved to Ponta do Amor, life in Cacau Pirêra became difficult. For some time the small passenger launches could still get into the bay, even though the car transporter could not. These launches brought a few customers to the rare shops and bars that remained open. But as the number of launches dwindled, so did the bus service on the landward side, thereby compounding our abandonment.

The lack of water in the bay was a serious problem for the owners of floating houses. Some of our community, knowing the exact underwater shape of their rafts and the contours of the riverbed underneath, let their houses rest on the bank as the river receded. One or two went to Ponta do Amor, but it was a dangerously exposed mooring if the wind came from the West. The majority moved their houses away from the abandoned ferry terminal towards occasional deeper ponds that did not dry out. There, at least, they were sheltered from tropical storms. Nevertheless, during the dry period, coming-and-going between Manaus and one's floating house meant longer commuting times and a mixture of canoeing and plodding through mud.

Fortunately, I was usually working on some ship or riverboat during the critical part of the low-water period, so that by the time I returned, Adam had got our floating houses back to their habitual moorings, which were much more fun.

Life in Cacau Pirêra during the high-water season was extremely pleasant. Most of the riverside vegetation in the area consisted of forest growing on land that was under water when the Rio Negro was high, an ecosystem technically known as *igapó*. In the months from May to August one could take a small boat and a machete, point the boat toward one's destination, and cut a way through the flooded trees to get where one wanted. Logically, there were some routes that were easier to bushwhack than others, but one could easily reach the Amazon by boat without having to go back onto the Rio Negro.

Once, I happened to be doing this type of bushwhacking trip through the flooded forest between Cacau Pirêra and the Amazon when the Soccer World Cup Final was taking place. (The World Cup, played in the northern Summer, always coincided with high water in the Amazon.) It was a match between Brazil and Germany, and I was leading a group of German tourists on a day trip in a motor-canoe. Because of the importance of the game, we had taken a small radio with us and listened in as we made our way through the gorgeous flooded forest. In spite of the noise of our motor and the radio, we spotted sloths, squirrel monkeys, morpho butterflies and all those things that one should see on an Amazonian safari. As we reached the Amazon River, Brazil won the football match and suddenly firecrackers and rockets exploded all around us. The Germans did not have time to be sad at loosing the very close match; they gazed in awe at the amazing spectacle of fireworks coming out of the forest. Without the fireworks, you would have thought that there was nobody living in the area, but in fact the banks of the Amazon are much more populated than the banks of the Rio Negro. And like all Brazilians, the riverside people love their soccer.

That particular river trip started off with a demonstration of Brazil's passion for football. It ended on the same theme too. After the voyage I was on my way to relax at my girlfriend's house, when I met a female acquaintance crawling up the street on all fours. "What on earth are you doing?" I asked. "Paying my promise," she said, explaining to me that she had made a deal with her favourite saint that if Brazil won the World Cup she would crawl from one end of the street to the other. Brazil had won and she was publicly doing what she had promised.

My neighbours in Cacau Pirêra were an interesting but penniless bunch. There was no up-market artistic floating community such as one might find in houseboats along the Seine in Paris or on the waterfronts of Amsterdam. My nearest neighbour was Minervinho. He was an old asthmatic *caboclo*, always wheezing when he talked to you, but still getting about between his floating house and the mainland in a minute canoe. His fragile craft always looked as if it were about to sink, but I never saw it do so. He lived with his wife and several of his offspring and grandchildren in a group of small, ramshackle and half-waterlogged *flutuantes* moored just across the creek from Adam and me. Minervinho made a little income looking after boats for weekend boaters who lived in Manaus. So there were always one or two pleasure boats moored near his house. He looked after Adam's and my *flutuantes* too, if we were both away at the same time. At night one would know he was there by the grey glimmer of his battery powered black-and-white television in the gloom. (He, like us, had no mains electricity supply.) Some nights, when he was particularly asthmatic, one would hear his terrible rattling cough.

Minervinho was one of the few people in Cacau Pirêra who liked the low water season. He liked it because it gave him the opportunity to plant manioc. As the river receded from the flooded forest, little islands of higher ground appeared. These bluffs constituted a no-man's land. Technically, like all land below the high water mark, they came under the control of the federal marine authorities. However, since the bluffs were small and hard to reach, the authorities didn't bother about them and let people like Minervinho use of them to plant seasonal crops. So, for part of the year, my neighbour was able to produce his own food. He cultivated an early-ripening form of manioc. It had to be fast growing, for the river would soon rise again and cover his garden.

Because Minervinho produced manioc, one of his group of floating structures was a manioc mill. This contained all the equipment necessary to process manioc tubers into flour. I have mentioned manioc flour in other parts of this book. (One can't talk about life in the Amazon without talking about manioc.) Nevertheless, Minervinho's manioc pan deserves particular mention, because such pans required a large fire and it was not easy to accommodate fire on a floating wooden structure. His solution to the problem was to build a thick-based clay fireplace on top of the deck boards. However, the clay was so heavy that the manioc *flutuante* lay low in the water. If a number of people gathered in one corner of it, they would get their feet wet as the boards dipped under the surface.

Another neighbour of note was a carpenter named Del. He was a remarkably dextrous man and if he had had better opportunities for education as a young man, he would probably have gone a long way. It was he who put the new roof on my floating house. More spectacularly he changed one of the log floats on Adam's *flutuante* without having to dismantle the whole structure. He dragged the old sodden float out with a hand operated ratchet winch and manoeuvred the new float into position with the same tool. When I needed a new oar for my rowing dinghy, he was able to carve one out of a solid piece of wood using only a handsaw and a spoke shave.

Del lived much nearer to the ferryboat terminal than we did. As a result of his location he was obliged to let his house settle onto the mud when the water receded in the dry season. By yearly practice he knew where the riverbed was reasonably flat. Consequently he could ensure that as his house beached, his floor wouldn't twist or have too much of a slope. Sewage disposal became a problem for him at that time of year. When the house was floating the river took care of effluent. When the house was on land, Del had to build a deep-hole latrine.

Like Minervinho, Del's wife took advantage of the low water period to plant crops on the mud. Although she also grew manioc, she much preferred growing black-eyed beans, which were the easiest type of bean to grow in the Amazon. Not surprisingly their name in Portuguese *(feijão de praia)* translated into English as "beach beans". (Rio's famous black beans don't grow in the Amazon.) Every time I visited Del's house, his wife would proudly present me with a kilo of her black-eyed beans, even though the family was so poor that it could hardly afford to give food away.

I will call my last noteworthy neighbour by the fictitious name of Cleideson. One weekend I happened to visit his floating house and found him and all his numerous children sitting on the open deck in front of their living quarters, compacting a grey powder into a lot of cup-sized cardboard cylinders. I had no idea what it was all about. The use of Coca Cola bottles as pestles and the obvious importance of the work added to my curiosity. "What on earth are you all doing?" I asked as neutrally as I could. "Making bombs to fish with," Cleideson replied cheerfully, as if everybody made bombs on a Sunday afternoon, and with the implication that I ought to be able to recognise gunpowder when I saw it.

Fishing with bombs was commonplace in Cacau Pirêra. It took place during the high-water period, at which time most fish lived in the flooded forest and could not easily be caught with nets. It was illegal (as in all Brazil). However, the local environmental protection service (IBAMA) turned a blind eye to it, presumably under the influence of local politicians whose electoral base included lots of fishermen needing an income and lots of housewives needing cheap fish. Adam hated the use of bombs and regularly denounced it to IBAMA, but nothing ever came of his complaints. Sometimes he would take the law into his own hands, put his shotgun into his kayak and confront the fishermen. Fortunately, when Adam was in this mood the fishermen always moved out of the immediate vicinity of our floating houses. But then later we would hear explosions ringing through the flooded forest as they struck somewhere else.

Fishing with bombs caused an environmental problem because the explosions were none selective. The bombs killed not only fish of the size and type appropriate for legitimate sale, but also all other fish in the area. There was an enormous overkill, in which lots of dead fish were never harvested because they were too small or the wrong species. Moreover it often happened that even valuable fish were inadvertently left to rot because the dead individuals had risen to the surface underneath floating vegetation or in thickets where no one could easily spot them. Later one knew the dead fish were there by the foul smell of their rotting, or by piranhas splashing as they devoured the corpses.

There was an interesting social hierarchy in the groups of people who went fishing with bombs. The leading players were the owners of the bombs, two to six men dispersed usually by pairs in one, two or three canoes. They would paddle slowly around the flooded forest together, looking for movements in the water that indicated the presence of a shoal of fish. If they detected a shoal they would throw a bomb and quickly harvest the majority of the dead fish with hand nets. Following the owners of the bombs came a group of hangers-on known as the *jacarés* (literally "caimans"). These would swoop in as soon as the bomb owners had taken their haul, or they would harvest areas affected by the bomb, but out of sight of the bomb-owners. Finally came canoes full of casual participants, including lots of children from the community of floating houses, The casual participants would watch the spectacle from a distance and scour the peripheral area in the hope of picking up a dead fish or two.

During the high-water season, fertile water flowed into the Cacau Pirêra area from the Amazon. This encouraged the growth of floating grass and water hyacinths, which were otherwise uncommon in the Rio Negro. The presence of the floating vegetation attracted numerous species of birds, including wattled jacanas, blue gallinules, oriole blackbirds, yellow-hooded blackbirds, diverse herons and egrets, snail kites, black-collared hawks, kingfishers and lots more. I particularly enjoyed watching the birds over breakfast, in the early morning, when it was still cool. Orange-fronted yellow-finches (known locally as *canários*) came and nested in my toolbox.

I also enjoyed the nights at high water. There was intense insect life in the floating vegetation. This meant that frogs were numerous and very vocal. There were lots of caimans too. A spotlight from the bedroom window would always reveal a number of beady red caiman eyes reflecting in the dark. Yet in spite of the caimans, piranhas and whatever else, one of my greatest pleasures was swimming from the floating house at night. I have the kind of skin that easily burns in the tropical sun, so that swimming at night was for me much more comfortable than swimming in the day. I loved to do what I called the "Archimedes Leap". This meant filling my lungs with air and jumping into the dark black water. Although it was easy to loose one's orientation in the plunge, Archimedes' Principle, which said that with air in my lungs I must float, gave me the confidence to know that I would eventually come to the surface. Once at the surface, I would swim on my back and watch the stars, which, because the house was far from the city lights, were usually spectacularly bright.

I performed the Archimedes Leap so many times and swam on my back under the starry sky so often that I gradually got to know the important equatorial constellations. I enjoyed recognising them as I swam, noticing some of the rules that astronomers have known for years, but that I had not really thought about before. For instance, the Southern Cross was visible practically all night in the month of April. In subsequent months it rose ever earlier, so that if I leapt in June, the Southern Cross would already be high in the sky at sunset and below the horizon after midnight. By September it was impossible to see the Southern Cross, because it rose and set at the same time as the sun. For the rest of the year one only saw the Cross shortly before sunrise. The Great Bear ("Big Dipper") did in the north what the Cross did in the south. If you could see one, you could see the other. By contrast, if Cassiopeia was in the sky, you could be sure that the Southern Cross was not. Orion, a constellation on the celestial equator, was a great reference point to help me locate many other constellations. Orion's belt pointed on one side to Sirius, the brightest of all stars. To the other side it pointed to Taurus and the Pleiades. I discovered that my own sign, Cancer, was relatively inexpressive. However, Scorpion was so large and bright that it soon became one of my favourite constellations. The two bright stars that pointed to the Southern Cross (often called "the Pointers") also attracted my attention. I learned that they were the brightest stars of the constellation of Centaurus and that Humboldt had frequently used them to ascertain his geographical position when he visited South America.

Only occasionally at the floating house were there problems with nocturnal animals. These were minor problems that occurred in the house itself, and had nothing to do with swimming. Sometimes bats managed to get into the house through gaps between the zinc roof and the wooden walls. They never interfered with me, but their erratic flight was spooky. I would open the doors and windows and try to shoo them out with a canoe paddle – a procedure that was frustratingly inefficient, but always amusing to onlookers. Another frustration came when a large bullfrog took up residence in the space between my floor and the wooden floats, an area very difficult for a person to reach to dislodge him. Just as I was about to go to sleep he would start croaking. If I stamped on the floor he would quieten down for a couple of minutes. But as soon as I stopped making noise, he started. In time I got used to the amphibian and accepted him as part of my amphibious life. Eventually he moved on and then I missed him when it was really quiet.

The quiet of the floating house at night was something very special. It was only possible because I had installed a solar electric system, which enabled my lights and fan to run off batteries without needing to run a generator. The solar panels were fantastic. They were expensive to buy, but needed no maintenance. Using a deep-cycle battery, I could run lights, fan, music system, water-pump and even power tools, though not all at once and not for long. Of course I had to monitor my energy use and have the discipline to switch things off before the battery drained too low. The most fragile part of the photovoltaic system was the battery. Adam, who had a similar system, once discharged his battery completely and it was impossible to repair it.

If I could use only one electrical device on the floating house, I chose to use the fan; I could get light from candles; I could pump water by hand; I could use a portable music system with its own batteries; I could use hand tools, but I could not substitute the fan. For me the fan, which blew on me all night long as I slept, made all the difference between being too hot and sweaty and being luxuriously comfortable. The fan was an economical 12-Volt model bought in a car accessory shop. It only needed 7 Watts of power.

After living for a few years at Cacau Pirêra, Adam, who worked as an electrician installing equipment on boats, decided that it would be easier for him to find work, if he lived on the Manaus side of the Rio Negro. New marinas were springing up on the west side of the city and lots of yachts were being built or needed maintenance. He suggested we move our floating houses to a creek behind the Hotel Tropical, where he had found a space on the beach right at the mouth of the Tarumã River. Though I would have preferred to stay in Cacau Pirêra, Adam had a sound argument. So, since he was a good neighbour, I decided to move with him.

There were advantages and disadvantages in our new location. On the positive side, one could drive from central Manaus to the water's edge quite close to the floating houses, without having to wait for the car ferry. We had a nice white sand beach behind us, and a superb view across the Tarumã River in front of us. On the negative side, we were on the edge of a large bay known as the Marina Daví. Lots of yachts and passenger launches used this bay, particularly at weekends. On Saturdays and Sundays the intense boat traffic near our flutuantes produced a lot of irritating noise and waves. However, during the week the new location was idyllic. It was hard to believe that we lived there free of charge, while not far away on the other side of the sand dune, people paid a small fortune to stay at the most expensive hotel in town.

Although most of the water in the Marina Daví was dirty, our houses at the beach caught the current of the main river and the water was fine. So I could continue to enjoy the Archimedes Leap to cool off at night before going to bed.

However, Archimedes unfortunately did not help everyone. One stormy Saturday night some young people in a heavily laden canoe with no lights set off from the Marina Daví to go to a party up the Rio Negro. When they left the bay and felt the waves of the open river, they turned round and asked for shelter at Adam's and my floating houses. We let them come aboard and they passed the time drinking and joking, while they waited for the storm to abate. Later they set out again, thinking that the storm had eased-off enough to travel. Shortly after they left, we heard their cries for help. Along with some neighbours we manned the available boats and went out into the night to try to find them. We found a group of people in the water clinging to the canoe, which was swamped but still floating. However one person was missing; the firemen dredged up his dead body the following day. Ironically the man who died was a good swimmer and had struck out for the shore, whereas a non-swimmer had survived by clinging to the canoe. The moral to the story was probably "less booze and more lifejackets" – in fresh water Archimedes only helps you if you can guarantee keeping your lungs full of air.

When my sixtieth birthday came around, I thought of many different ways I might celebrate it. Should I go back to England and see my relations and childhood friends? Should I climb some high mountain? Should I travel to somewhere outside Europe and South America? Finally I decided that I would celebrate here in Manaus with the friends who made up my day-to-day life. I would organise a musical birthday part on the beach.

The new location of Adam's and my floating houses was ideal for the celebrations I had in mind. Adam's deck was a perfect place to serve food comfortably. Then we could all ferry over to the beach to party by a bonfire. If I put a canoe-taxi at my guests' disposal, they could come and go to their cars whenever they liked. Arlete, my girlfriend from Belém, came to visit me and supervised the refreshments: Peacock Bass for the first course and birthday cake for dessert. Friends in a samba band agreed to come along and play acoustic music on the beach. Saint Peter, who looks after rain in Brazil, smiled on us and kept the full moon free from clouds.

The party turned out to be a superb evening. I was among friends: I chatted, joked, drank, sang, danced, swam and enjoyed my girlfriend's visit. What more could I want? Even the birthday bonfire turned out to be special. An old rubber inflatable boat that I owned was getting too old to repair and I wanted to get rid of it. So I decided to burn it on the fire. First I got the driftwood really blazing. Then, with all my friends looking on, I dragged the rubber wreck onto the flames. Fortunately, with the high temperature there was very little smoke and no acrid smell as the blaze consumed the boat. Many of us at the party had done trips in the vessel and as we watched it disappear, we laughed and joked about the good times it had given us. Far from provoking melancholy, the boat's cremation triggered happy memories of shared experiences.

At a certain moment, Arlete came into the campfire circle, carrying my birthday cake with the number 60 depicted on it in burning candles. The band stopped playing, so that everybody could sing the Brazilian version of "Happy Birthday to You", while I blew out the candles. Before the band could start again, English-speakers in the gathering took advantage of the moment and intoned the chorus of "Cacau Pirêra King", an English song my musical friends Paul Hardy and Martin Shead had written about me when the floating house was in Cacau Pirêra. Paul and Martin had recorded the song on a CD of their compositions that was played on local radio. Part of the words went as follows:

"In England he didn't want a house
So he BOAC'd it to Manaus
And folked his way around Brazil
Made his name at the top of the hill

He's the Cacau Pirêra King
Always doing his very own thing
He's the Cacau Pirêra King
Everybody comes to listen to him sing."

With lyrics like that, few people have had such a good time on their sixtieth birthday.

On the morning after the party, I cleaned the beach. As I raked the area where the fire had been, I found attractive, pear-shaped aluminium beads in the sand. The aluminium identification plate of the rubber boat had melted in the heat of the fire and drops of molten metal had run into the sand and solidified. I kept one of the beads and had it made into a pendant that aroused a lot of curiosity whenever I wore it. I told people that it symbolised having "burned my boats". One burns one's boats to force oneself forward. So, although I stop writing now, it is not the end.

Glossary of Portuguese Names of Plants and Animals

açaí	*Euterpe oleracea*
acariquara	*Minquartia guianensis*
amarelinho	*Plathymenia reticulata*
angelim rajado	*Pithecolobium racemosum*
aracu	*Schizodon fasciatum*
aruanã	*Osteoglossum bicirrhosum*
arumã	*Ischnosiphon spp.*
babaçu	*Orbignya speciosa*
balata	*Manilkara bidentat*
bodó	*Pterygoplichthys multiradiatus*
breu	*Protium spp.*
buriti	*Mauritia flexuosa*
buritirana	*Mauritia huebneri*
bussu	*Manicaria saccifera*
caferana	*Picrolemma pseudocoffea*
caiaué	*Elaesis melanococca*
candiru-açu	*Cetopsis caecutiens*
caparari	*Pseudoplatystoma tigrinum*
capivara	*Hydrochaeris hydrochaeris*
cará	*Astronotus ocellatus*
cedro	*Cedrela odorata*
coloral	*Bixa orellana*
cumaru	*Dipteryx odorata*
cupuaçu	*Theobroma grandiflorum*
curimatã	*Prochilodus nigricans*
dourado	*Brachyplatystoma flavicans*
itauba	*Mezilaurus itauba*
jacareuba	*Calophyllum brasiliensis*
jambú	*Spilanthes olercea*
jará	*Leopoldinia pulchra*
jaraqui	*Semaprochilodus insignis*

jauari	*Astrocaryum jauari*
louro	*Nectandra rubra*
malva	*Malva sylvestris*
mata pasto	*Cassia reticulata.*
matrinxã	*Bryncon hilarii*
maxixe	*Cucumis anguria*
paca	*Agouti paca*
pacu	*Myloplus asterias*
palha branca	*Attalea attaleoides*
paracuuba	*Lecointea amazonica*
patauá	*Oenocarpus bataua.*
paxiuba	*Socratea exorrhiza*
pescada	*Pachypops fourcroi*
piabinha	*Hyphessobryncon gracilis*
piaçaba	*Leopoldinia piassaba*
piraiba	*Brachyplatystoma filamentosum*
piranha	*Serrasalmus spp.*
pirapitinga	*Colossoma bidens*
pirarara	*Phractocephalus hemeliopterus*
pirarucu	*Arapaima gigas*
pitomba	*Talisia esculenta*
saboarana	*Swartzia laevicarpa*
sardinha	*Triportheus spp.*
sucupira	*Andira parviflora*
surubim	*Pseudoplatystoma fasciatus*
tamuatã	*Callichthys callichthys*
tambaqui	*Colossoma macropomum*
timbó	*Lonchocarpus nicou*
tucumã	*Astrocaryum aculeatum*
tucunaré	*Cichla ocellaris*
umari	*Poraqueiba servicea*
urucum	*Bixa orellana*
violeta	*Peltogyne catingae*

Glossary of English Names of Plants and Animals

agouti	*Dasyprocta punctata*
Amazon tree boa	*Corallus enydris*
annatto dye tree	*Bixa orellana*
arowana	*Osteoglossum bicirrhosum*
arrowcane	*Gynerium sagittatum*
bull's eye vine	*Mucuna sloanei*
emerald boa	*Corallus caninus*
false kapok	*Pseudobombax munguba*
giant Amazon water lily	*Victoria amazonica*
hogplum	*Spondias mombim*
Indian almond	*Terminalia catappa*
Jacob's ladder vine	*Bauhinia splendens*
jute	*Corchorus capsularis*
kapok	*Ceiba pentandra*
Malay rose apple	*Eugenia malaccensis*
lipstick tree	*Bixa orellana*
manioc	*Manihot esculenta*
peach palm	*Bactris gasipaes*
peacock bass	*Cichla ocellaris*
pot-bellied rubber tree	*Hevea spruceana*
sandbox tree	*Hura crepitans*
soursop	*Annona muricata*
sweetsop	*Annona squamosa*
tonka bean	*Dipteryx odorata*
toro-rat	*Echimys spp.*
water arrowhead	*Montrichardia arborescens*